THE MAGIC of MEMOIR

INSPIRATION for the WRITING JOURNEY

EDITED by LINDA JOY MYERS, PhD
and BROOKE WARNER

SHE WRITES PRESS

Published 2016
Printed in the United States of America
ISBN: 978-1-63152-147-8
E-ISBN: 978-1-63152-148-5
Library of Congress Control Number: 2016953560

Cover illustration by Sarah Lazarovic
Interior design by Tabitha Lahr

For information, address:
She Writes Press
1569 Solano Ave #546
Berkeley, CA 94707

She Writes Press is a division of SparkPoint Studio, LLC.

CONTENTS

INTRODUCTION

Therein Lies the Magic

Over the many years we've been teaching memoir writing—during which Linda Joy has written two of her own memoirs and Brooke has edited and published upward of three hundred memoirs—we've encountered three *s*'s that waylay writers on the way to writing their truths: secrets, silence, and shame. We know and have witnessed how important it is for writers to encircle and defeat this triumvirate if they are to free themselves to write what must be written, if they are to act as witnesses to and historians of the lives they have lived and the insights they want to share.

Why would anyone willingly go through this? It's a question we encounter often, and one most memoirists ask themselves. The great Mary Karr, in an interview with Brooke in September 2015, stated with complete conviction in response to the question of whether she would advise her own students to pursue memoir, "I say if you don't really have to do this, if you can live a happy life . . ."

The audience laughed, but Mary was serious, and many writers of memoir understand her assertion. They would not be writing their stories if they did not feel called to, if they felt they could possibly avoid it, if they didn't absolutely have to. Because we've taught and coached so many students over the years, we know how deep this need, this compulsion, this drive really is.

For Linda Joy, who's been teaching memoir for nearly twenty years and has written five books, two memoirs and three how-to books, the siren song of the three *s*'s has forced her to encounter them again and again, pushing her to grow beyond these dark forces. As a therapist, she knows how secrets and shame create silence, and she respects how hard it is for people to reveal their hidden stories.

Brooke, who's been working with memoirists since 2004 as a coach, editor, and publisher, has witnessed firsthand how insidious the three *s*'s can be. Exposing one's full self is an exercise in extreme vulnerability, and even writers who come to the page with a take-no-prisoners attitude, who feel ready to risk everything for the truth and their art, encounter shame. In fact, there's not a single memoirist Brooke has encountered—including high-profile and acclaimed authors—who hasn't brushed up against some fear when it comes to sharing and revealing things about themselves, their family members, their past, their desires and longings, their shortcomings and insecurities.

We live in a shame-bound culture, a culture that tries to paint a happy face over the many soul-stirring struggles that are a part of our lived experience. We may have stories that our friends and relatives don't know—or don't want to know—about dysfunctional families, abuse, addictions, loss, and the kind of suffering that ensues as a result of what we've lived through. Some of us have been told to keep secrets to protect others and ourselves. This level of conditioning not to tell vibrates at a cellular level, and therefore it's no small feat to interrupt a frequency we've been attuned to our entire lives.

Of course, not all stories contain dysfunction and darkness. Your particular struggle may reflect a more subtle shame. Perhaps you worry about exposing someone you love for the less-than-perfect human being they actually are or were. Perhaps, in order to be authentic in your memoir, you're being called to share the truth of your own striving and failure to be perfect. Maybe you have been a flawed parent, or an unfaithful spouse, or mean-spirited toward others in their times of need. None of these behaviors is uncommon, or even something we'd condemn in others, but exposing ourselves on the page for who we truly are means coming to terms with the unseemly sides of our human experience.

Those memoirists who refuse to delve into the darkness, or who insist that their story is nothing but a fairytale existence that anyone would envy, tend to uncover the family myths that perpetuated the fantasy in the first place once they begin to write. We all struggle; we're all less than perfect. We can be kind to ourselves as we expose our own underbellies, but memoir is not memoir if we are unwilling to gaze well beyond our navels. True memoir emerges like a beast from the gut and the heart, and it's the writer's job to tame it, to get to know it, to dance with it—until it becomes a more palpable and ultimately beautiful creature that we feel prepared, if not totally ready, to share with the world.

It's this experience of taming and shaping our own stories, of working through our shame and exploring the depths of our human experience, that brings us to another topic: transformation. As a therapist, Linda Joy has observed the magic moments when suddenly she has seen a light turn on in someone's mind, when the "click" they experience because of a new insight has been nearly audible. For Brooke, those moments have been equally palpable when writers have had a shift in perception, when they have realized how to convey emotion in a way that's universally resonant or why it matters that they synthesize their experience for the reader. These "click" moments are as powerful for writers as they will be for those authors' future readers.

Memoir is a journey of the soul as much as a window into it. The writing of our personal stories is both an opportunity and a gift, and while writing itself may be solitary, many, if not most, new memoirists are drawn to write both for themselves and to share with others. The stories may belong to the writer, but the destiny of the memoir, by design, is to be released into the world. At that point, it ceases to be ours and instead belongs to our readers, existing for them to make sense of, to relate to, and to know they're not alone.

Research has shown that writing helps to heal and reveal new layers of our consciousness. As this happens—as we allow our writing to lead us down the pathways our stories take—something amazing happens. We find ourselves writing words and sentences we had no intention of writing. We uncover things that we didn't know were there. We may come face-to-face with an inner critic who tells us our writing isn't good enough, but we also have moments of falling in love with our words. Through the storytelling, we relive the past, make new associations, and discover new ways of seeing ourselves. As our books progress, we continue to be in discovery mode, searching for more and deeper truths. Through this process, we reveal to ourselves surprising new aspects of our lives and illuminate our journeys, continuing to hold those things that will be universally resonant to our readers. We offer takeaways that keep the reader engaged, all the while delving more and more deeply into lessons and insights we didn't know about before we started to write.

Poet and philosopher Mark Nepo has said that writing is the trail of our own inquiry and that he writes to learn what he does not know. For memoirists, this trail of inquiry is a dive into a deeper level of self-understanding. The journey of memoir affords us an opportunity to learn things about ourselves, to uncover tender truths that we perhaps didn't fully own or understand before.

Writing a memoir is full of challenges, and looking for support and inspiration where you can find it is crucial. We hope you will discover both in these pages, and that the words of the writers included in this collection will help you to know that you're not alone. Through their words, we hope you'll discover connections that are ripe and ready for you to pluck and use and integrate into your own process. When we're writing memoir, everything around us is potential inspiration for the journey. And therein lies the magic!

—Linda Joy Myers and Brooke Warner, 2016

WRITING THE SILENCE AWAY

Jill Kandel

I moved to Zambia in 1982, a bride of six weeks married to a blue-eyed boy from the Netherlands. We stayed six years. Stayed in a village that took me two full days of travel to reach. It began with a ten-hour bus ride west across Zambia and through the Kafue National Game Park.

Imagine this.

Imagine a twenty-six-year-old North Dakota girl getting off that dusty bus and carrying her suitcase down to a small, sandy harbor and finding a banana boat with a thirty-five-horsepower engine. Imagine her crawling onboard and situating herself on a wooden plank. There are no life vests, canopies, or cushions.

She sits on that wooden plank, sits in the blazing sun and through the rain and out into the sun again, as she travels deep into Lozi country, past herds of long-horned cattle, past women on the riverbank bathing their children, past thatch-hut villages where people look up at the sound of the engine and wave.

Ten hours later, the canoe stops at a bend in the river and she gets out, sunburned, wobbly, and stiff. She has arrived in Kalabo Village, where five languages befuddle her ear: SiLozi, Luvale, Nyengo, Mbunda, and Nkoya. She cannot tell one from the other.

This girl will spend her days boiling the germs out of the drinking water, finding enough food to survive, and washing all the clothes by hand in a sink that only dribbles cold water. She will live here for the next six years, give birth to two children in the village, and bury her best friend.

Imagine her becoming quieter and quieter. Imagine her losing more than her voice; she is losing her way. She arrives in Zambia a newlywed and leaves six years later as the mother of two children. After all those years, she is mostly sand and grit. She barely remembers who she was.

I am that girl. I know what it is like to be lost. I know what it is like to cover up and hide my own story. I know the hopelessness of trying to forget.

When we left Zambia, we spent a year in England and then three in Indonesia. After living abroad for ten years, we moved to North Dakota and closed the door on our expatriate life.

I expected to pick things up where I'd left off. But the girl that I had been no longer existed. I had left Zambia, but Zambia had not left me. Each night when I closed my eyes, my thoughts returned to Kalabo Village. And the nightmares began.

I joined a writers' club with no specific intentions other than possibly writing some children's books. We were a strange group of five, each one of us writing in a different genre, including fiction, nonfiction, Christian devotional, poetry, and horror. One night, the horror writer asked if I'd write something about my years in Africa. He thought it would be interesting. I didn't. But the question bugged me.

I vacillated between wanting to please the group and not wanting to open up the memories. In the end, I wrote a very short story about a snake, and the club loved it.

I was forty years old and realized I had a story to tell, but I didn't know how. I applied to the Northwoods Writers Conference, at the University of Bemidji, and was accepted.

That conference opened my eyes to a whole new world. I'd never heard of a literary journal, didn't know what creative nonfiction was, and had no idea how to move forward. My teacher gave me a list of journals to read, online publications to explore, and books to learn from. I went home after that five-day conference and spent the next two years reading every single item on the list. As I read, I wrote. And as I wrote, my writing improved.

Every year, I'd choose one writing conference, workshop, or convention to attend. My writing shaped itself into essays, and I began to learn about submitting: how, when, where, what. I amassed rejection letters like candy, accumulating just shy of one hundred, before I got my first acceptance letter from a literary journal. Oh, happy day!

Publication brought new challenges. My husband is still alive. We are still married. I like him. I found myself navigating the emotionally vulnerable place of needing to write and publish stories that he didn't want friends knowing about, let alone strangers.

I wrote about the difficulties of cross-cultural marriage.

I wrote about the horrors of civil war, starvation, malnutrition, and traveling to remote villages that lacked water and food and seed.

I wrote about giving birth to my first daughter in Kalabo Village.

I wanted to be accurate, so I began to read through the hundreds of letters I'd written home, watched family movies, listened to cassette tapes. I heard, felt, saw, and smelled Zambia all over again.

And when I fell into bed each evening, I dreamed, Zambia fresh on my mind. A Zambian woman named Pity came to me every night for twenty years.

I close my eyes and Pity walks into my dream, wearing a threadbare *chitengi*, holding her newborn son. Her red-haired three-year-old stands beside her, clinging to her leg. His skin is patchy and white. His large belly seems out of place, but the lack of protein has weakened his abdominal muscles and they cannot hold his organs in. He's slowly starving to death.

Pity's firstborn daughter sits in the sand nearby. She is perhaps six or seven years old. Her eyes are milk-colored and staring. She tilts her head in the way blind children often do and stares into the void.

I look at them, this little family, and turn my eyes toward Pity.

She stands before me, barefoot and bone-weary.

We are the same height. Near the same age. Every night we look into each other's eyes and I watch as the flies settle on her baby's face. As the sores on her child's legs weep.

My husband teaches farmers nearby. He stands tall and blond under the shadow of the mango tree, busy and talking, while I lock eyes with Pity.

I cannot look away. There is nothing I can say.

When I wake, my body sweating and hot, my arms flailing, brushing at the flies in the corners of my eyes, I am crying.

I am always crying when I dream.

And when I wake, I write.

My husband doesn't understand the need to write. He loved Africa—his dream job. And my memories clearly baffle him.

"Your Africa was very different from my Africa," he says one day. "If I wrote a book, it would be very different."

Yes, it would be. His work significantly increased the rice production in Kalabo District. His work brought food and hand-irrigation equipment and seed and knowledge. His work brought hope and money to mothers so they could send their children to school. His work grew from a Dutch Volunteers position to a half-a-million-dollar Dutch embassy program.

His work.

I came home bitter from his work and long, long hours and all that blatant fortitude. I came home sick in body—bilharzia, hepatitis, giardia, dysentery—and sick in spirit. And words became my surgery—the cleaning out, the stripping away, and, later, the healing balm applied over the sutures.

Words rescued me.

They also upset me deeply.

Imagine this.

Imagine that you are in the passenger seat of a truck with your eighteen-month-old daughter playing finger games beside you. Your husband's driving. Imagine slowing down to twenty miles per hour and pulling over to the opposite side of the road to pass the bus parked alongside. Imagine tall elephant grass, yellow and dry, taller than your vehicle. Imagine your truck shuddering, coming to a sudden stop, a girl lying in the road.

I had to write it. My husband said I couldn't.

I wrote it anyway. He yelled. I cried. We stood, two hurting human beings, wounding each other again. And again.

She was twelve years old. We drove her to the hospital, her breathing awful and sporadic as she lay gasping for breath, held in the grandfather's arms. We drove for thirty miles to the nearest hospital; the doctor wasn't in.

She was twelve years old. I was six months pregnant with our second child. The doctor came, the police, the family. I played with my daughter. The hours passed. The day dragged on. The day a fog.

She lived twelve hours.

We still had a two-day journey to get home to Kalabo Village: one day on the black tarmac road across Western Province, and one more day to cross the floodplain, board the leaking pontoon, cross the Zambezi River, and drive on through the sand. Two days to drive, and not a word was spoken.

Writing is not for the faint of heart. I cannot tell you the courage it took to open that particular Pandora's box.

I can tell you the words we flung at each other when I was done.

You can't!

I have to!

Why don't you just leave it alone?

How we wounded each other once again.

But this is what writing memoir did: it opened up long-closed silences between my husband and me. I'd write, he'd read, and a week or so later, we'd talk. We would talk about the Zambia that I had experienced and never known how to be honest about. We would talk about it and then repair to our own corners, licking our wounds. Then come back again and talk some more.

One day he said, "I didn't know."

And the truth is, he didn't. I'd never really said.

Writing gave me this gift; I stopped hiding.

But even more than that, I started telling.

After fourteen years of writing and nine literary-journal publications, I completed the first draft of my book: a collection of essays nobody wanted to publish. Everyone in the writing world advised me to turn it into memoir. So I tore the essays apart and glued them together and created a bad memoir, with gaps and redundancies.

I tore it apart again, adding an emotional arc that bridged the book and gave it consistency, but it still seemed flat. Or missing something. A colleague and editor suggested I add another voice: the voice of experience. I'd written the whole book from the point of view of the young woman I had been, twenty-six years old, married six weeks to a man from the Netherlands. A journalistic-style book: I did this, then that, and—oh, yes—then we did this! It was both dramatic and boring.

Adding in the voice of experience changed the tone of the book. I added in the voice of myself now, looking back. *Who was that young girl? What was she doing in Zambia? Why did she go? Did she accomplish anything?*

Adding the reflective, older voice brought depth and contemplation. To do that, I had to go back to Zambia emotionally: back to the sand and the heat and the flies and the stench. Back to the desperate loneliness and an isolation that now seems incomprehensible to me. *Letters took six weeks. There were no phones. How did I survive?*

After I'd written most of the difficult memories out, something happened that surprised me completely. I remembered the color of the weaverbird nests. I remembered the blue-tongued lizard and the baby geckos falling in my bathtub with their cute, froglike, padded hands. I remembered my daughter carrying a newborn puppy tied to her back, like any other African mama. I remember her first, teeny blond pigtail tied up with a pink satin ribbon.

When I'd stuffed and hidden all my negative memories, I'd hidden the beautiful ones, too. You can't stuff selectively. Writing brought Africa back to me in a new way: it brought back the beauty.

And then, after I'd written out so much pain and so much joy, all of it falling onto the page three or four or five hours a day, I got up one morning and sat down to write, and my hands sat still on the keyboard. I didn't have a thing to say.

I'd written it all out.

And you'd think that would be magic enough, and it was, but it wasn't all.

That night when I went to bed, I didn't have a nightmare. I couldn't believe the relief. Pity stayed in her grave. I have never dreamed of Africa since that day.

The memoir is written, the nightmares stopped. What a powerful thing creation is. And you think this is enough. And it is. But, again, it is not all.

I spent the next year looking for an agent, a publisher, entering contests, shopping my manuscript around. I became a grandmother. And the night after my first grandson was born, I come home at midnight to an e-mail.

"Call me. I have some information that might interest you." It's from Michel Simms at Autumn House Press, and I am sure he does not want me to call him at midnight.

Imagine this.

Imagine a woman sitting with a cell phone in her hand, listening to it ring. She's dazzled over the birth of her first grandbaby, still feels the gentle weight of him in her arms, still smells his baby skin and the feel of his silky hair across her lips. The cell phone shakes slightly in her hand, and a deep voice tells her, "We want to publish your manuscript. It won first place."

Imagine this woman's sharp inhale and how she has to ask him to repeat himself, twice.

Imagine her, a woman who has lived on four of this earth's seven continents, sitting in a 1960s rambler in a small town in Minnesota. She can't stop smiling. She won't be able to sleep for the next forty-eight hours.

Writing changed my life. Writing brought understanding to ten years of silence. Writing gave me power, and I want to pass on that power. For three years, I've been teaching journal writing to female inmates at a local county jail. We talk about losing our voices as women, about filling in our own silences. We talk about the things we are afraid to remember.

One of the women said to me, "If you could do Africa, I can do jail."

If you could.

I can.

How is it that the words I wrote reached out and touched a woman in jail, a woman thirty years younger than I am? How can a story written about a small village in the middle of the African continent seep into another woman's heart? How can those tiny black scribbles on a piece of paper give another woman courage?

I do not know the answer to this question. But I do know that words are the most powerful thing in my life. I will never let them go.

And then there is this: one more thing. One more perfectly magical moment, when the world and the muse and time collide like a kiss.

I am sitting at AWP, the largest writing conference in America, with twelve thousand writers and teachers streaming, browsing, talking, and jostling around me. I am sitting beside a table with my newly published book on it.

I have worked on this book for sixteen years. And I find myself at AWP, doing a book signing. I want to tell everyone, *I am sixty years old. Today is my birthday!*

But the real magic is not that it's a specific day or event or location. The real magic is this: I feel like I'm twenty. I feel like my life has just begun. I feel like this is just the beginning.

✳ ✳ ✳ ✳ ✳

This essay, "Writing the Silence Away," won second place among all the essays submitted for consideration in The Magic of Memoir.

JILL KANDEL grew up in North Dakota, riding her Appaloosa bareback across the prairie. She married a man from the Netherlands and worked overseas for ten years in Zambia, Indonesia, England, and in the Netherlands. Her first book, *So Many Africas: Six Years in a Zambian Village,* won the Autumn House Nonfiction Prize and the Sarton Women's Literary Award. Her work has been anthologized in *Best Spiritual Writing 2012* (Penguin Books) and in *Becoming: What Makes a Woman* (University of Nebraska Press). Her essays have been published in *The Missouri Review, Gettysburg Review, River Teeth, Pinch, Image, Under the Sun,* and *Brevity.* Kandel is working on a second memoir set in the Netherlands. She currently lives in Minnesota near the North Dakota state line and the city of Fargo. She blogs about a writing life and living between cultures on her website: www.jillkandel.com.

MY OWN STORY

Eanlai Cronin

I was twelve years old when I wrote my first book. The Sisters of Mercy assigned my boarding-school class the summer homework of writing the story of our childhood. We were instructed to fashion our words in the fictional style of a famous Irish children's book, *Jimín Mháire Thaidhg*.

Copy that mold, we were told, *chapter for chapter, and see what ye produce. Ye can have real things in there about yerselves, but make up the most of it.*

I often wondered after that if they thought that we simply wouldn't have enough to say, that a dozen years of existence wouldn't qualify us for substance. Little did they know that thirty years later, I'd still be writing about those first twelve. But back then, I did what I was told, intuiting from their directions the flimsy stuff of a short life, viewed alone. Still, I'd pad it out, I thought, because the world and its mother already knew I could spin a yarn like no one's business.

My first job was to procure a new copy for a shilling at the local shop. Then I cut a Flahavan's porridge bag along its seams, turned it inside out, and covered my book in the pristine white inside paper. Then came the naming of the manuscript, which I whittled down from a short list of three, all with the words *me*, *my*, and *myself* in one form or another in each title, and landed on the one that made my heart skip a beat each time I saw it. Despite the fictional strictures of the project, I chose to call my book *My Own Story*, even before I'd composed a single line.

The first time I wrote those three words in colored pink marker on the white porridge paper, such a feeling of peace washed over me that I vowed from that day forward to be a writer.

The very sight of the title *My Own Story* delivered the perfect antidote to the shame and silence that saturated not only the small Irish village of my birth but my very bones. As I sat at the kitchen table before the turf range, pen and fresh copybook in hand, I did not know that this would be the beginning of a story that would take years to unfold, the story of eight years of sexual abuse I had already endured at the beck and call of a neighboring farmer, and the stories yet to come of a complicit community and culture engulfed in their own displacement and denial.

But that summer I was twelve, I knew nothing of the journey ahead, nothing but the joy of the blank page and the permission to put myself on it.

My father, ever the headmaster, peered in over my shoulder the whole time I penned, in tiny block letters, the hesitant first drafts of fiction blended with fact. Already, at twelve, I was experimenting with a key component of memoir writing: the re-creation of truth with license to embellish for the sake of crafting a compelling narrative. At the time, given my silence and the seeming denial of a family and village who thought better of ignoring certain gaping realities, it proved vital, indeed lifesaving, to me to see how much truth I could tell before permission was withdrawn or withheld. With the appearance of each fact, no matter how benign, on paper—brothers and their nail biting and smelly socks, sisters and their swiping tongues and soft spots—I grew in confidence and courage. Things could *actually* be written down, and if they could, what might I now be able to say?

Oddly, very little.

Such authority to speak was very new to me, so new that the push of buried truths felt more like an impulse that couldn't be identified, let alone satisfied. The truths were there and not there, all at the same time. This was my next naive taste of memoir's burden, that such permission to speak, which seemed at first a liberating cure-all, was merely the popping open of a substratum lode. Truth, once woken, does not easily take its place among the harmless facts of family meals and Sunday Mass times. Instead, there are things nudging against the skin of the storyteller, begging to be told, that may not announce themselves in the first draft, or even the second or third or fourth.

Truth, when given consent to emerge, requires time to take shape, especially when you, too, have to emerge from the many years of ferreting memories into corners of the brain that refuse to let you back in. Oftentimes, and with good reason, you have placed many versions of your small selves in separate vaults, their limited understanding back then translating abuse and familial dysfunction into blame placed squarely on them. To open such rusty doors is to feel once more the deadly shame that split your innocence back then. But even before you get to the metal frames, you must shed the many years of collective delusion and rearranged history, of *it wasn't all that bad* or *your father wasn't that sick* or *don't mind that one—she makes things up.* Oftentimes you remember only what you're allowed to remember, till you drop the many masks, filters, and disguises that conceal the real story even and especially from yourself. That is, until you're ready.

At twelve, I was far from ready. Still, despite the innocuous content of those first facts I wrote—Mamma's maiden name, Dadda's teaching post, my first-communion date—the impact of recording my own story in any form was exhilarating.

I felt alive. I felt important. I felt powerful.

The kitchen table became my new outpost. Everyone around me, sensing something wonderful, nodded their heads in approval. Fiction, it seemed, was their comfort, too, for as long as any small fact about them was perceived as being in service to "story," then the very permission to speak that had set me alight sparked something alive in them, too.

Here again was another lesson: that truth, if concealed in stage costume, can find its place in the world without offending others. Not that I didn't later write the full truth of events, but I changed names and identifying features to allow others their privacy. It seems, though it may not always hold true, that if you bestow upon others the courtesy of boundaries and fair treatment, then your truth, no matter how raw, may not come across as an indictment. This, along with your declaration of your story as *your* reconstructed version of events and not anyone else's, makes it easier for others to find their distance, even complete anonymity.

But that summer I was twelve, I was only forming the ideas of such things and reveled in my new identity as writer.

I sat long hours at the kitchen table, Dadda behind me. There was something of him peering over my shoulder that unnerved me. It wasn't just the appearance of his goose eggs around my grammar. It was the thing of which Stephen King later wrote, that everyone should close the door on their first draft. It was true. It was very hard to coax the harmless facts of an imagined adventure from the shadowed corners of creativity, let alone skittish creatures from the recesses of memory.

Still, as I was now something of a celebrity in my kitchen, such infamy brought its own compensation for the unknown loss of first-draft privacy. Dadda and his bad heart delighted in my enthusiasm for the written word. In his eyes, I now had the makings of the next Irish rebel leader penning proclamations of independence. Parker pen in hand, he corrected sentence structure, making suggestions for embellishment here and there to add to a sometimes flat story. Attached as I was to my blossoming yarns, I didn't yet fully understand the essential ingredients of crisis, conflict, climax, and resolution as the cornerstones of good storytelling. Nor did I consider that my poor reader wouldn't find an adventure interesting simply because I had lived it or made it up, that the feeling of aliveness that came over me in the re-creation of myself for story might not translate to holding another's thrall. Being me wasn't going to be nearly enough for a reader, no matter how revelatory the experience of seeing myself on the page.

This was news to me—disappointing news, at that.

The pull of a problem, Dadda said, was in a good story. You had to have the guts of a battle and the heat of a victory, and a lad or a lassie had to want something, even if it was only a new frock. And then, he said with a wink, they had to go about getting the frock—more likely the lassie, but you never fully knew. That right there was the beauty of story.

I couldn't tell which I loved more, the notion of a lad hankering after a dress or the sight of Dadda giggling like a schoolboy at his own humor.

Over the following days and weeks, under Dadda's watchful eye, I began to discern a plain old yarn from a compelling story. I learned grudgingly not to succumb to theatrics to augment an obvious anecdote into sinus rhythm. More important, I learned that I could, even if I made it all up, be the wounded hero of my own story over and over.

That was something you could take to the bank. That had eating and drinking in it.

That first summer of writing was the best thing that had happened up to that point in my childhood. Despite its many drawbacks—the push toward fiction, the fragile permission, the constant editing and correction, the exciting, albeit Herculean task of turning up on the page in whatever form my psychology at that time allowed me—that July and August laid the groundwork for a journey that would resume twenty years later.

By that time, I was thirty-two and had forgotten, or maybe had not yet put together the valuable lessons of, my first attempt, at twelve. Some deem anyone under thirty-five too young for an authentic memoir of reasonable distance and perspective. I am inclined to agree, because till then, I had only the accumulated mill wheel of life unrolling before me, compounding in me a sense of inevitability and predetermined outcome.

Why don't you just get married, have children, and be miserable like the rest of us? Mamma once said to me when she caught my eye following a visiting and very attractive young woman down the street.

At that point, Mamma and I were living together again. Having had some very covert lesbian relationships in college, all of which had ended in terrified disaster, I had graduated at nineteen with an honors degree. This feat baffled me, given that I had spent the bulk of my time pursuing my new passion in life: drinking. Dadda died two months after I was given a teaching job in my home village, as though handing me the mantel of schoolmaster and Gaelic preservationist. I felt instantly trapped.

I was now a certified closet lesbian in a village where being an openly gay woman was unheard of. It still is. But in the '90s, it earned you the moniker of pervert or, worse, pedophile. More than the social outcasting at even the slightest hint of being "abnormal," all primary schools, run by the Catholic Diocese, could fire you in an instant were you proven homosexual.

Many mornings, I walked the length of the single street to the primary school, the man who repeatedly raped me in childhood often cycling past me on his bike, chuckling or smirking. His sense of certainty about my silence was not arbitrary. I was surrounded by a blanket of delusion among people committed to denial as a way of life.

Don't throw stones at my house and I won't throw stones at yours was the collective agreement. It was all about appearance.

This was the thickest of veneers, one that made it seem as though everything I thought or felt or wished to bring to mind was unreal. This barnacled facade, I would come to understand, is one that every writer, especially the memoirist, encounters. A chisel is a vital mental tool for those coming to the memoir page—a chisel and the tenacity to use it over and over.

Those first years back in the village, I had no chisel, nor did I know I had permission to use one. Everywhere I looked, reminders of things I couldn't name inflamed my nervous system into a state of complete agitation: every shed, abandoned house, field or meadow, even, and especially the church that loomed large at the heart of this tiny hamlet—all places I had been violated and discarded, all places that had no voice yet to speak their buried shame. All I felt was self-hatred and blame.

You're dirty. You're filthy. You're a liar. You make things up. You're not right in the head. You're a disgrace to your family for even thinking to share things that no one would believe.

All the voices of indoctrination, both external and internal, that needed, over the years, to shut me down and shut me up in order to survive returned in a flood.

This very experience would echo in the years ahead when I finally picked up my pen again. This is what it is to begin the process of memoir. It revives the cacophony of buried voices designed to keep a lid on things that you, at one time, could not understand or that your family refused to address, in deference to saving face. These voices return to assault you in waves of dissent, disbelief, and disdain. They call your name with such conviction that you are left to wonder if maybe you are mad after all—mad, worthless, not to be trusted.

This is the eye of the storm for memoir writers. When you are at your most despairing, when it feels hardest, nearly impossible, to proceed with your search for truth and, more important, meaning, it is then that you are closest to the marrow of your story.

I say, build yourself a singular place in your heart that says, *This is your haven when all else is chaos.* This singular place, one that some call Divine Consciousness or Higher Self or Sky View, holds the entire scope of your existence and its evolving patterns. This is the place of unfailing reason and perspective, even if it takes many rounds of the chisel to get there. This place exists inside everyone.

When I began my second memoir, I knew very little of this place. All I knew was that my life had fallen asunder.

Severely ill with chronic fatigue syndrome, I came out as a lesbian to my family as a way to stem the pretense that I was certain was making me ill. Overnight, with those three words *I'm a lesbian*, I lost everything—job, family, home, community, good name—and found myself in America, with a lover.

A funny thing happens when you leave the viper pit of your poisoned existence: things don't just magically become better. This was the next lesson of memoir for me, that living a life of hardship, surviving a tragedy, discovering some secret, whatever turns your life on a penny, is not the story you eventually tell. The real story is the meaning you claw from the ashes of your misery.

When I first returned to the page, I had not yet even begun the unspooling of memory, let alone found meaning. Much like the nuns who planted the first seed, my lover at the time was the one who planted the next.

Write, she said.

I had just been discharged from a hospital in Massachusetts with a second diagnosis of chronic fatigue syndrome. Scolded by one nurse to "just eat," or else I "would die," I was seventy-eight pounds, five foot three, and could understand her somewhat hysterical indignation at my wasting frame but not her indictment of me as the sole source of my own suffering.

We lived in a small log cabin in the Berkshire mountains. I sat at a table beneath a skylight for three days. I cannot remember whether it was because of the sudden snowfall that winter afternoon, flakes falling so gently that their consideration hurt me, but something came over me and I wrote the first word that came to mind: *grief*.

It was as though I had written a tome, an entire testament to my existence. The memory of my exhilaration at twelve returned in an instant. Indeed, I consider it the spark that brought me back from the brink of giving up.

As before, writing was not an overnight cure-all. It took twelve years and two million practice words for that memoir, *Girl in Irish*, to emerge.

It taught me many things: that a word after a word after a word can save you; that shaping narrative from the ashes of a life asks two tasks of you: read voraciously and study craft; that crafting a compelling story from the chosen fragments of your entire existence requires a singular discipline: theme.

And how you give the reader hope comes down to that one gift that is your reward for perseverance: meaning. Who is telling the story, and why?

I heard some years ago that my first childhood book had been burned in a barrel fire. I'd given it to an elderly aunt for safekeeping. She died. All her belongings were subsequently burned, including mine.

I realized then how important it is not simply to write down our stories but to value them, not just the finished product, but every step it takes to claim our victory.

My name is Eanlai Cronin, and this is my own story.

* * * * *

EANLAI CRONIN is a teacher, memoirist, and certified facilitator in the Amherst Writers and Artists Method. As a sexual abuse survivor and silenced Irishwoman emerging from a culture of lies, silence, and denial, Eanlai was drawn to the ability of the AWA Method to empower the disempowered and give voice to the voiceless. A latecomer to claiming her own story, Eanlai designed a workshop series called Writing the Soul Awake based on three tenets: permission to break long silence, to claim lost voices, and to speak soul truths. She runs writing groups in the Bay Area for those in recovery from trauma, addiction, and codependency, and for anyone longing to return to the well of their own forgotten words and stories. A long-time contributor to the *Kerryman* newspaper in Ireland in the '90s, Eanlai's work has appeared in *Courage to Heal, Sinister Wisdom,* and *Sonoma Women's Voices.*

THE SHOWER AND THE FISH

Peter Gibb

Without the shower and the fish, I would never have known the joy of memoir.

My daughter had been after me for years. "Dad, you should write a memoir. You have so many interesting stories to tell."

Some writers, so I've heard, choose a cold shower to jolt them into the zone. I prefer to ease in. A warm shower opens my heart, helps the scenes flow, sets me on the path to possibility. I don't fully understand why, but I've learned to trust the shower.

Warm, soothing water cascaded down on me as I considered my daughter's suggestion. *Memoir? Not for me. I'm a novelist. Memoir is not that creative. Too dry and boring. All that begat stuff.* I was making a classic mistake: confusing autobiography with memoir. Autobiography—as I now see it—focuses on facts and dates and usually progresses chronologically. This happened, and then that, and then that.

A record, but often dry and episodic. Memoir, on the other hand, is theme focused. It can be structured in many ways, uses any literary devices that work, and relies on great story-telling. Memoir is about the luscious weave of the outer and inner life. Creative? You bet.

Something about the water that day. Something loosened inside me. *If I did write a memoir, what would I write about?* For the first time ever, I opened to the possibility. Water welcomed my muse to the party. Ideas cascaded out of me, memories I didn't even know I had, and by the time I stepped out of the shower, I had birthed an opening for a memoir. The scene flowed spontaneously, just like the shower water. Although I was equally unsure about the source of my idea and the true source of the shower water, I was clean and refreshed and I had framed the scene I wanted to write. I wasn't yet fully committed to writing a memoir, but I was ready to give it a test-drive.

Three years after that shower, I am proud to say that I have finished my memoir and am well into my second book, this one about the spirit, art, and craft of memoir writing. I teach a class on memoir and mindfulness. I have learned about the transformative power of memoir writing, and I have experienced the joy (and the struggles) of the genre.

Memoir writing, for me, is about discovery. I now understand my life in a way that I never did before. Sure, I knew the facts of my life, or at least the ones I could remember. But even though I'd had lots of therapy and thought of myself as an introspective, self-aware person, I had only a cursory understanding of my story. I knew the skeleton but relatively little about the blood, the tissue, and, most of all, the heart. Writing my memoir breathed life into my skeleton. It put skin on the bones and hair on the head. I discovered the meaning of my journey—in short, my story.

I approached writing what I thought might be the first scene of my memoir—a muddy foot race that took place at my first school, in Scotland, when I was five—with a mixture of excitement and trepidation. I knew there was something very important that had happened during that race, but it was fuzzy, an out-of-focus photo in my mind. How could I write about it when I remembered so few of the details? I sat down to write and realized I needed to check e-mail, make more coffee, clear my desk, and put in the laundry. I sat down to write again. I got up again, washed the dog bowl, checked e-mail once more (still nothing exciting), made a couple of calls, and folded the laundry. I sat down again. I typed a title: "Scotland—the Race." Maybe I should call my sister and ask her if she remembered anything about the race.

When I had finally exhausted every possible opportunity for procrastination, I opened a new Word document and began to type. At first it was awkward and slow. I closed my eyes and tried to re-create the scene. What did I see? An image of the big stone school, the thin box of ten tin soldiers that was my prize for winning, parents huddled under black umbrellas. It was a start, but I knew there was more. I stared at the screen. My words dribbled to a halt.

I stumbled upstairs into the kitchen, where our fish dinner lay waiting on a plate, ready to be cooked. The fish smell tossed me back across the decades and thousands of miles to Campusdoon School, where the smell of fresh fish from the market mixed with the salt air that blew in from the Firth of Clyde. Instantly I regressed to five years old again, the only Yank in the school, lined up in the mud to race against twenty-three hardy Scottish lads, I with my shorts drooping and my knobby knees clanking like a rusty locomotive.

I rushed downstairs to my computer and typed as fast as I could. I was shaking. I remembered more and more: not just what it looked like but how it felt, racing in the mud and the night after I won the race, at home, my parents so proud, while I was overcome by shame and wanting to hide. And why was that? I stared into the meaning of that scene, six decades after it happened, and I realized that a tiny seed planted at that race, so early in life, had sprouted and grown and spread and been joined by other seeds, and that those seeds had been the start of a briar patch that strangled me, well into adulthood. It was then, too, that I first realized that the deepest memories are stored in the heart, not in the brain. And I knew beyond doubt that this was a story I had to tell.

So I have a shower and a fish to thank for my memoir, *King of Doubt,* and for the joy—and, if I dare say so (and I do), the wisdom—that I've gained from writing it. Not that the initial attempt was perfect. Later, I refined and revised that muddy race scene at least fifty times. I replaced it several times with other scenes, but I always returned to it, like going back to an old girlfriend whom you just can't leave. And that muddy race scene is now the opening chapter of my memoir, *Walking Straight, Down a Krooked Path.*

You'd think that, having lived it, I'd have had a good handle on my life. Not so. Living life is one thing; turning it into story is another. Shaping a story from life is high, creative adventure. I learned that the magic of memoir rests on a three-legged stool. The legs are spirit, art, and craft. I knew about craft from my experience as a novelist but had only a hint of the other two vis-à-vis memoir. I dove in, never imagining the world of surprises that awaited me, from right inside my own heart.

Socrates famously said, "The unexamined life is not worth living." In support of this belief, he chose death over exile. Writing a memoir is not an issue of life or death today. The issue, rather, is how much I am willing to see and understand about my own life. How deep will I go to face up to my own prouds and sorries? Will I confront my cultural, family, and personal norms? How clear can I be in articulating my own truth? Am I willing to walk naked in the sunlight?

When I reflect on the shower and the fish, I see how this incident holds some basic principles of memoir that guided me in writing my memoir and that I hope will help other memoirists.

1. Write from the heart. I dreamed about being a writer for years, but I was lying in the wrong bed. I wrote from my head, rather than my heart. After that fateful shower, something shifted. I cut back on questions like "What will they think of me?" and "How should I present my mother?" and "What if I can't remember?" and "Why is my writing so superficial and dumb?" The brain sponsors such questions, defending its territory, protecting the ego. Monkey brain. Worry brain. Fear-full brain. Doubting brain. The brain has its role to play, don't get me wrong, but it is not the primary source of memoir. When I tuned in to my heart, I uncovered a waiting treasure trove of memoirabilia. You will forget what someone said, you may even forget what they did, but you won't forget how they made you feel. The deepest memories are stored in the heart. The heart is the source. Search there to find your memoir in the raw.

When I went to my heart, I began to write from a desire to discover and explore my life, rather than to justify and explain it. I shifted from writing for others, trying to impress or at least not to alienate, into writing to and for myself. And I realized, to my amazement and delight, that others often found commonality and solace in my writing. I shifted from doubt to wonder, and oh, what a difference it has made, both to the writing and to the living. This is the joy of memoir.

2. Respect and cultivate your most sacred writing tool: your voice. For a long time, I heard about the importance of voice in memoir. I didn't really know what the word *voice* meant. I just wished that I had one. My voice (whatever the word means) was mundane and flat, and I had no idea what to do about it. My many attempts to develop my voice produced prose that was affected and inauthentic. Then came the shower. And the fish. When I began to follow the wisdom of the heart, my words flowed from a different source. I no longer had to effort them. They magically began to sparkle. They were fresh and humorous, uniquely mine, alive with discovery and authenticity. More experimental, less staid, less forced. I liked them more, and I enjoyed writing them immensely more.

I still don't know exactly what "voice" is, but I use mine all the time.

One last tip: shower. Hot or cold, your choice.

PETER GIBB is author of the multiple award–winning memoir *King of Doubt.* He writes, teaches, and coaches memoirists from his home in Ashland, Oregon, where he lives with his wife, Wendy. Read a chapter from his memoir and find him online at www.petergibb.org.

FROM THE PROJECTS TO PROSPERITY: WHY ME?

Lynette Charity

I n August 2014, I traveled to Kuala Lumpur, Malaysia, to compete in the Toastmasters World Championship of Public Speaking. For two years in a row, I won first place in District 9's International Speech Contest, telling stories of my childhood experiences living in the segregated South of the 1950s and '60s. The overall conclusion was the same from those who heard the many speeches I gave before winning: "Lynette, you need to write a book and share these stories with others!"

My Toastmasters friends' motivation pushed me in the direction to write my memoir. As an anesthesiologist, I had authored medical papers and lectures, but never something as personal as this.

One person asked, "Lynette, how did you go from being the 'little colored girl' in the projects to being Dr. Charity?"

I pondered the question, but the answer wasn't forthcoming at the time. I knew the "how," but not the "why."

I'd won a third-place trophy in Kuala Lumpur, my third recognition for my speaking, with a seven-minute speech titled "I'm Going," in which I told of my experience as one of the first colored students at a previously all-white high school. The year was 1967, thirteen years after *Oliver Brown, et al. v. Board of Education of Topeka, et al.* The state of Virginia was mandated to comply with the decision, which occurred using a "freedom of choice" approach. I chose to attend the white school but needed to walk there the first few weeks because no bus service was in place. I used Dorothy from *The Wizard of Oz* and her quest to reach the Emerald City as an analogy to describe my walk from my neighborhood through the white neighborhood to my new school.

My quest to reach this high school stemmed from a desire to prove my worth in the world at a time when Negroes/Coloreds were deemed less intelligent than their White counterparts. Dorothy was my "inner voice" supporting me down the yellow brick road and through the Haunted Forest to my Emerald City.

After my win, I was overwhelmed by the number of non-Americans, without the knowledge of segregation and the civil rights movement of the 1960's, who wanted to know more.

"I guess I need to write a book," I said.

"Yes, please, write a book!" a young woman from China squealed. She then gave me a big hug.

I returned to my home in Richland, Washington, excited to begin my book-writing journey. I joined a women's-only writing group. One evening I shared a passage that I wrote about a very traumatic event in my life. I shared a night when my father hit my mother so hard that he knocked her unconscious and I truly thought she was dead. I was inexperienced in the art of dialogue versus narration and "showing" versus "telling," but I described what I saw in vivid narrative detail.

The ensuing critique of my passage was as brutal as the event itself.

First, one attendee said, "That didn't really happen, did it, Lynette? You were nine years old, right? I think your imagination as a child made you see it that way, but I just can't imagine something like that could be true."

Another person chimed in, "Yes, I can't imagine anyone being that cruel. Your description seems over the top. I think readers won't believe it."

I felt skinned alive! I sat naked in a room where everyone else was fully clothed. I had shared a deep-seated, intimate trauma and now felt even more traumatized by the group's opinion that I had "made it all up." I wanted to slink out the door, but I stayed and listened to others read and discuss the other "volunteers'" works.

At the end, I thanked the hostess, who said, "Lynette, thank you for joining us. We look forward to hearing more as you continue writing your book." She awkwardly gave me a hug, and out the door I went.

I sat in my car for a moment, thinking, *What the hell did I just get myself into? Is this what writing groups do?* I never returned, and I stopped working on my book. I continued to enjoy writing my five- to seven-minute speeches for Toastmasters, but I felt stifled, wondering, *How do I truly tell my story in six hundred words or fewer?* I knew I wanted to write again.

I shared this epiphany with a "friend," and he said, "Lynette, why the hell do you want to write a memoir? You want to be famous? It won't sell, because your life is pretty good. Look at you—you're a doctor, you have two condos, you travel all over the world. Waste of time, in my opinion!"

Well, I guess he told me!

I tabled my writing until October 2015. While attending a local writing conference, I learned of NaNoWriMo, National Novel Writing Month. I loved the challenge of writing fifty thousand words in the thirty days of November. I created a novel online, titled *From the Projects to Prosperity*, and began writing it on November 1. I earned badges for personal achievements; I was inspired by other authors in my group; I absorbed all the free advice and resources available to me. It was *fun*!

On November 30, 2015, I finished NaNoWriMo with more than sixty-two thousand words. It was a great accomplishment for me, but then it was over. *Now what?* I thought.

NaNoWriMo forced me to write words, but word count doth not a book make! I was again lost. I called a writing friend after sending her some of my "words," and she suggested Writer's Digest University. I enrolled in Memoir Writing 101, and it changed my outlook on writing. I learned about scenes, character arcs, protagonists, antagonists, and dialogue. I took long narratives and turned them into scenes with dialogue, putting the reader there with me. It was fantastic! But it was still not enough.

On one of the resource pages, I was directed to an organization called the National Association of Memoir Writers (NAMW). On the website's home page, I "met" Linda Joy Myers, PhD, and Brooke Warner for the first time. I watched their video and joined immediately. I also watched Brooke Warner interview Mary Karr and decided that in order to be a good memoirist, I needed to read Karr's books; I needed to read more than *Clinical Anesthesia* and *Ultrasound-Guided Regional Blocks*.

I became a voracious reader of memoirs, not necessarily as much for the plot as for how the story was organized and the authors' use of words, imagery, and dialogue. I returned to these books for inspiration when I got stuck. My words were finally becoming a memoir in the making.

Becoming a member of NAMW was the best investment in my future I have made as a writer to date. During one of the monthly members-only telephone sessions, I met my writing buddy, Cora Ruff.

I called in for the session and listened intently for signs of life on the other end. I thought I heard something.

"Hello, is anyone there? This is Lynette Charity from Richland, Washington."

There was silence for a moment, and then this sweet, calming voice replied, "Hello, this is Cora, Cora Ruff. Hi, Lynette."

We began chatting about our books, but Linda Joy needed to get the show on the road, so we tabled our conversation. With our permission, Linda Joy exchanged our contact information and we began regular, long-distance, Saturday-morning critiques. It was during one of those critiques that I changed the direction of my memoir. My original idea was the story of how a "little colored girl" growing up in the segregated South of the 1950s and '60s managed to overcome life in a dysfunctional family, school integration, and the negativity of some members of her community, who wanted to see her not succeed in her quest to become a medical doctor. I wrote about all of this in my now one hundred thousand words. I found, however, it was not the story I needed to tell—yet. There was another story fighting to be heard, and Cora squeezed it out of me. She heard my angst regarding writing this memoir and brought clarity and purpose to the process.

The following is an excerpt of what I wrote after a "come to Jesus" meeting with Cora.

Recently, I sat at the dining room table enjoying the company of a wonderful friend and her husband, who invited me over to celebrate my sixty-fourth birthday. The two of us met through a mutual friend over fifteen years ago and enjoyed our periodic get-togethers to go hiking, skiing, or wine tasting. She shared a story about one of her sisters, who wrote a book and was speaking on the subject of her book, on environmental changes.

I listened politely, but inside felt so envious. She has two wonderful sisters and I have none! I thought. She can share her struggles and triumphs with them and get hugs and kisses from them and can call each of them Sis! I miss Beverly!

I drove home in my Cadillac CTS and pondered a question that had plagued me from the day my then-two-year-old sister, Beverly, died to the present. Why her and not me? Why was I alive? Beverly was the "precious, precocious one" and deserved life. As for me, no big fanfare occurred when I was born on May 2, 1952, and I was never "Daddy's little girl." That was Beverly's title, and she retained it even in death. After she died, I became the tormented older sister, the one who lived. I struggled to make sense of it all.

In the privacy of my three-bedroom, two-bathroom condominium facing the Columbia River in Richland, Washington, I picked up a framed black-and-white picture of the two of us sitting on our granny's couch. The year was 1956. We lived in the

Roberts Park Housing Projects in Norfolk, Virginia, with Granny, our two older brothers, and Mama. Daddy was not living with us but was "around." I was four years old, and Beverly was eight months old. I held her tightly on that couch as she sat propped against my chest. I smiled toward the photographer. Beverly's attention was in the same direction, but her look was not a smile. It was more of an "I'm not sure what you want me to do," inquisitive stare.

"I miss you so much, Beverly," I said out loud as I kissed the acrylic frame over her face. I stared at that picture as tears engulfed my vision. I then cried myself to sleep.

My younger sister, Beverly, was struck by a car and killed five months shy of her third birthday. I was six and witnessed the event and have since wondered, *Why her and not me?* My inner critic stopped me from writing this story because, after fifty-seven years, I thought, *Are my memories accurate? Will there be someone reading the book who thinks I made it all up? Do I dare share secrets that might change people's opinion of me?*

I tried to interview my two older brothers about that day. One brother refused, saying, "It's still too painful." The other brother stated, "I don't remember." They were sixty-seven and sixty-eight, respectively. My mother was not present, but, at age eighty-seven, she filled in a lot of details of the events that occurred before and after Beverly's death. This was a tremendous help in "validating" my memories. In fact, my mother gave me the green light to write this memoir, since she is a very important person in it. The story about my father hitting her so hard that she was knocked unconscious was difficult to write, but it was even more difficult to share with my mom. I read some of it to her, and she said, "That's about right. Yeah, it happened. Can't change it. What's done is done." As we've continued to share memories, it's brought us closer together.

What was so wonderful about this epiphany was the realization that the *Projects to Prosperity* story can still be told, through the eyes of a child traumatized by the death of her younger sister and full of drive to find her purpose, as the one left behind. Originally, I started the book when my character was nine years old, with the scene between my father and mother where I thought he killed her. I was originally told that my timeline—age six to twenty-two—was too long for a memoir. It was "suggested" that I truncate the number of years, so I "eliminated" my brief life with Beverly.

But when I pulled out the "Beverly pages" that I wrote during NaNoWriMo and reread them, knowing all that I had learned since November, these pages translated into vivid moments that, while I'm sure I will struggle to write them, will aid me in the painful process of healing and will keep my *good* memories of Beverly alive and well in my heart.

I used Linda Joy's Timeline Exercise to find the "bullet points" in my life. As I now revisit significant events and turning points, I try to make sure they have a common theme. The theme for me now, I think, is how Beverly's death defined my future, how it shaped my present persona. For the longest time after her death, she was my imaginary friend. We "spoke" every day, and she was the one who got me through that walk through the white neighborhood.

This is my first foray into memoir writing, and after leading the analytical life of a physician, I welcome the chance to challenge my brain to do something completely outside my comfort zone. I have grown so much in the past two years and continue to evolve. I will call my one hundred thousand words a first draft but by no means a complete memoir. With the continued guidance of my new family at NAMW, I will continue to write and rewrite my story and visit and revisit this life of mine. I'm excited!

* * * * *

DR. LYNETTE CHARITY is a board-certified anesthesiologist with over thirty-five years of experience. In 1970, she received a full, four-year academic scholarship to attend Chatham College for Women in Pittsburgh, Pennsylvania, after graduating with honors from a previously all-white high school in Portsmouth, Virginia. She received her MD degree in 1978 from Tufts University School of Medicine. Although she has written numerous medical articles and lectures in her career, this is her first memoir. When she isn't writing and rewriting her book, she continues to practice anesthesiology and performs at an occasional open-mic night for comic relief.

✱ MARY KARR ✱

Author of *The Liars' Club*

BROOKE WARNER: You've said in other interviews that you feel you need to defend memoir. Why does memoir need defending?

MARY KARR: When I was in graduate school in the late '70s, memoir was the province of weirdos and film stars and Winston Churchill and people like that. I heard Geoffrey Wolff once describe memoir as inscribing the Lord's Prayer on a grain of rice. It's been something that nobody really wanted to do or be caught doing. Obviously, that has changed in recent years. The genre has a huge readership. But still, it's a trashy, kind of ghetto-esque, primitive form. It's not an exalted form. Anybody who's lived can write a memoir. For that reason, I want to have a conversation about it. Nobody elected me the boss of memoir, but I did want to create something with my new book, *The Art of Memoir*, that would do for memoir what some of the major works about fiction— like John Gardner's *The Art of Fiction*, or E. M. Forster's *Aspects of the Novel*—do for the novel.

BROOKE WARNER: People have said that you have an amazing memory. You are somewhat critical of these details about your memory, yet you acknowledge that you probably have a better-than-average memory. Do you think that traumatic memory is part of that? That's it's more acute?

MARY KARR: Doctors have suggested to me that my cortisol levels are as high as if I've always just run a marathon—super-super high. I have symptoms even now of some traumatic stress. I have night terrors, but nothing like what I used to get. I've been meditating for twenty-five years, and I do a lot to try to make things better for myself. I also think I'm a super-physical sort of person. I'm a carnal person. I don't mean that necessarily in a sexual way, but I'm somebody who's in my body a lot, and my memory comes with a lot of physical sensation. Maybe you've had this experience—like, I went to my high school reunion and it was full of old people, instead of adolescents. And this girl comes up to me and says, "I'm Janna White," and I'm thinking, *I'm so sorry I can't place you,* and she says, "I sat next to you in Miss Picket's English class." The minute she said that, I could see her thirteen-year-old face. I could see her hair and remember this denim dress she had. She played the clarinet, she had braces, her dad was a dentist. I remembered the boy I had a crush on sat at the back of the row and she sat right next to me. And Miss Picket sang to me, "The principal is your pal," as a way of telling me how to spell it. I remember after that class that I walked out the door and then I went right to Miss Burns's speech class and my locker was just beyond it and then I came back. So it was as if the minute she said, "I sat next to you in Miss Picket's English class," clowns came out of a car unbidden. I was just flooded with all these sensory memories. Who knows how that happens? I don't know where my car is. I don't know what city I'm in. But I remember those kinds of details with such acuity.

BROOKE WARNER: In *The Art of Memoir*, you write that self-awareness is critical for memoir writers. Is that something you can cultivate? What do you do with memoir students who aren't self-aware?

MARY KARR: None of us is fully self-aware. All of us deceive ourselves about our pasts. There's a not-very-funny joke in my family that the trouble starts when you hit me back. If you'd just let me hit you and take it like a woman, then we'd be fine. So I've never written anything that I didn't wind up changing my mind about. And I'm somebody who's in therapy, who is supposedly trying to live an examined life, and has been forced by certain traumas to look at my past more than the average person, just to keep from being a nut-burger on the subway every day. When I'm working with students, there'll be some really sweet girl who's writing these very slutty poems, and then this girl who's really traumatized by her romantic travails who doesn't want to write love poems, because they're too corny, so she tries to write in this sort of cool, "I couldn't give a rat's ass," kind of disaffected voice. So I think on the page we all believe that we have autonomy, that we can just invent the selves we are and take it to an audience. But that can take you only so far. For me, writing is a deflating process.

✳

BROOKE WARNER: You have said that memoir writing is brutal.

MARY KARR: I say it's like knocking yourself out with your own fist. I always feel like the main sergeant on *Platoon*— you know, the Tom Berenger guy who's standing over some screaming soldier, going, "Take the pain."

✳

BROOKE WARNER: Do you think you have to experience that to write a good memoir?

MARY KARR: I don't know anybody who's ever written one who didn't have something like a nervous breakthrough in the middle of it. Frank Conroy, who wrote *Stop-Time*, used to get drunk about every three weeks, and he'd stay drunk for a month when he'd finish a chapter. Carolyn See described that the minute she finished *Dreaming*, she had meningitis. When I finished *Cherry*, my editor was in my house in Syracuse. When we turned the last page, I could feel the fever crawl up my face. I had a fever of 104 and I had pneumonia, which I'd never had. It just grinds you down in a way.

BROOKE WARNER: You're a big champion of memoir writers, and you know that it's very difficult to get published in the current publishing climate. What do you tell your students or people you are mentoring about their own projects?

MARY KARR: I have a little test in *The Art of Memoir* to see if you are psychologically ready to climb into your own skull, with what's up there. The people I know who've written a memoir and have done it well really have a burning need to figure out what's true. If I hadn't had to do it, maybe I would've eventually written *The Liars' Club*, but I think it would've been a long time coming.

BROOKE WARNER: What is the magic of memoir for you?

MARY KARR: The magic of memoir is that we all survived—so far, at least. Also that we'll all die and these stories will serve as our legacy, whether we like that or not.

*   *   *   *   *

This interview was adapted from a September 2015 live interview hosted by Berkeley Arts & Letters.

MARY KARR is an American poet, essayist, and memoirist. She rose to fame in 1995 with the publication of her best-selling memoir *The Liars' Club* and followed that success with two other memoirs, *Cherry* and *Lit*. She is also the author of *The Art of Memoir*. She is the Jesse Truesdell Peck Professor of English Literature at Syracuse University.

I TOLD HER TO SHUT UP

Donna Barnes

I write in my study with the door closed. No one is allowed to enter without knocking. I respond, "Come in," unless I am in the middle of a great idea or perfecting a sentence, or just staring at the computer screen, waiting for such. My husband, the only other person in the house, respects, accepts, and adheres to my request that borders on a demand.

This arrangement was not without a struggle. I commandeered the spare bedroom against my husband's objections.

"But where will our guests sleep?" he asked.

"On the couch," I said.

"Well, at least keep the double bed in the room," he said.

"No, it goes out," I said.

I felt like the head of an army of one, refusing to back down. His insistence on keeping the bed petered out as I called 1-800-GOT-JUNK. Two men came the same day and hauled it away.

I had clearly won the battle for the right to have a private space to work in. However, this was not the only battle I faced. It wasn't long before I had uninvited company who didn't knock or observe my privacy policy. She infiltrated, or maybe I was born with her. She was my inner critic. Her frequent insults were *Who do you think you are? You probably won't ever get a publisher. Who's going to read it, anyway?*

I told her to shut up.

This was out of character for me, as I was raised in a household that considered "shut up" bad manners, characteristic of someone with a poor upbringing. But I didn't have time to entertain her negative thoughts, as I had plenty of doubts of my own.

One of my biggest struggles was wrestling with secrets. Where was the drill manual from the US Department of Writers containing instructions on how to determine what to disclose? What about my life would I include in my memoir? My abortions? *Shame on you*, my inner critic whispered. My husband's alcoholism? *It's your fault for keeping liquor in the house!* she bellowed. My being his second or third priority? *What did you expect? You married a minister, for God's sake.* It appeared to me that my husband put the congregation's needs first and his recovery from alcoholism second, which seemed reasonable. But that left me third—unless somebody died; that trumped everything—and I was on my own emotionally.

If I were to be authentic, I had to decide what was going to become public, on my terms. Whom would it hurt? How would my husband, my siblings, and church members respond to my secrets? *Don't expect any praise from them*, my critic said.

My family knew I was writing personal essays. But to protect myself, I gave my work only to other writers, my daughter, and my writing coach. They gave me critical feedback and posed questions, as well as offering encouragement and praise. If family members were in an essay, my practice was that they could read it prior to publication and I would hear their comments. Still, as the author, I would have the final decision. I did not intend for my family to have the option to change what was my story to tell.

During the writing process, there were touchy times. When I needed to verify facts about my parents, or events or dates, I would ask my siblings. I was the third daughter, often too young to have understood certain family dynamics. One sister was disagreeable about my writing and the questions I asked about Mom and Dad. She said, "Why are you digging up our past?" Her attitude, though unspoken, was *Who do you think you are?* The critic shows up in many forms.

My other sister was completely supportive and proud of me. My brother, younger by five years, was bemused and confused about why I was working in retirement, which was how I thought about my writing, instead of playing cards, watching television, or taking up a hobby.

Closer to home, my husband was likewise confused. His questions were perplexing, like the time he picked me up at the airport after I'd attended my first Association of Writers & Writing Programs conference, in February 2011. He said, "Did you learn to write better?"

More routinely, he asked, "How's your writing?"

"Fine," I always answered. I preferred not to talk about it with him.

In the fall of 2011, I was driving home along the coast of California from Tomales Bay after a four-day workshop with Dorothy Allison. I decided to pull off the road. I walked to a point overlooking the ocean where my only company was a seagull sitting on a bluff. I was thinking about how

I had been challenged, and even bruised somewhat, about my writing. Then I thought about the two women in my group who wrote with such honesty that they'd left me impressed with their courage. In our private conversations, I had learned that they commanded what they needed from their life partners.

Standing there, overlooking the ocean, I attempted to reflect upon and integrate my experience. One of Dorothy Allison's commands was to be authentic. As she put it, "Be naked on the page."

I asked myself, *How can I be naked on the page if I can't be honest with my husband about my writing?*

When I got home that night, my husband said, "How was it?"

"I need time to assimilate my experience before I can talk about it," I said, feeling no compulsion to say more.

He offered to get a pizza for dinner. I was grateful. I stayed up late that night and watched *Saturday Night Fever* alone.

The next morning, I took a walk and afterward sat at my desk to write. By the afternoon, I had managed to clarify three things I wanted to tell my husband. I emerged from my study and asked him to sit down with me at the kitchen table for a talk.

"You have said that I am selfish for spending time on my writing," I began. "I agree. I am selfish."

"Yes, you are. I didn't think you were aware of that," he said, with a Cheshire-cat grin.

In the moment, I chose not to respond to his self-satisfaction. Instead, I moved on.

"And since writing is a solo practice," I said, "I need to be with other writers who understand that. We might talk about our writing practice and our frustrations. One friend with young children talks to me about her husband's lack of support. But primarily we know not to ask questions about our writing, unless we request them."

"Really," he said.

For a long moment, I stared at him without speaking.

Then, carefully, I said, "I don't share my writing with you. I know that you might feel left out. I know you've said at times that you learn about my writing only when we are out to dinner with our friends."

"Yes, I know that," he said, his voice edgy.

"I know you want me to share more with you," I said. Then I laid out my boundaries. "When you're in an essay, prior to publication, I will offer to have you read it, but not before."

"Well, that's up to you," he said, looking away.

"One other thing: you don't need to ask about my writing. Honey, the truth is, your questions are not helpful to me."

At that, his shoulders relaxed. Was he relieved, I wondered, or was he hurt?

"So I'm requesting that you not ask me questions about my work."

After a few moments, he said, "Well, okay, if that's what you want. I don't exactly understand, but I can do that."

I felt pleased and proud that I had shared what I needed to have happen in our relationship in order to feel supported and respected in my writing. But part of me wondered if I had been too hard on him. So the next morning I asked him, "Was what I said yesterday hurtful to you?"

"No. It was clear," he said with a smile.

He did stop inquiring about my work. I appreciated that. But I was startled by his comment one morning about two years into my retirement and full-time writing career.

I was leaving the kitchen to go downstairs to my study, coffee in hand. "I'm off to work," I said—my usual departure announcement.

"You say you're going to work, but you're just writing," he said.

In my study that morning, I could muster only a weak "shut up" to my inner critic's *you are so naive* when she inevitably showed up. Sometimes it's those who love us the most who stoke the flames our inner critic uses to burn us.

When I first started "just writing," it was personal essays to submit to literary journals. The more I wrote, the more I considered working with a writing coach. I had originally believed that I had a possible book of essays in me. When I later hired a coach, she helped me to realize that I had a memoir.

Before I began creative writing full-time, I was in academia. In the early 1990s, as a sociologist, I was invited to author an academic paper based on videotapes that mothers with HIV had made for their children. These mothers believed they had a death sentence. My two coauthors had assisted them in making their tapes in Rochester, New York, and Washington, DC. I viewed and analyzed them and wrote the paper as first author. We were proud of these women for their courage in telling and preserving their stories.

My first attempt at creative writing was an essay about a woman, one among eighty whom I had interviewed for my research. Her pseudonym was Meria. She and her husband were in their twenties. Both had HIV/AIDS in 1993 when I met them at their home. I began working part-time on Meria's story while teaching and doing research.

Dreaming big, I submitted an application to Hedgebrook, a women writers' residency, in 1995. As an example of my writing, I included the academic paper about the mothers making videotapes, since the only essay I had was Meria's unfinished manuscript. To my enormous surprise, I was accepted.

The first person I called was my daughter, who was not surprised. "Mom," she said, "you are an artist. And Hedge-brook is an acknowledgment of that. It is so well deserved."

My husband's response was, "How much will it cost us?"

Shut up, I thought, but I was too elated to bother answering him.

During my three weeks at Hedgebrook, I thought I would prepare an essay about Meria and her family for public media, perhaps a magazine. Instead, I developed the structure and drafts of several chapters of Meria's story, with the goal of publishing a book.

Hedgebrook gave me the opportunity to write full-time without any responsibilities, except to be the best writer I could be and to come to dinner on time at the farmhouse. Through the generosity of Nancy Nordhoff, the founder, I had the space and privacy to learn about my natural rhythms for writing, thinking, reflecting, exercising, and sleeping. Without being accountable to job, family, and church, I could write from sunrise to midnight and, if I wanted to, sleep until noon.

I was struggling with a craft for which I had no training. I was so ill equipped that I was still figuring out the first person versus the third person. My inner critic was quick to point this out. *This is high school English, stupid*, she hissed. This was before I'd learned to tell her to shut up. I faced my fears with tears, and in the process I wrote. Most important, I developed a writer's practice.

One night as the writers in residence gathered after dinner, I read from one of my essays. The feedback was supportive; however, all agreed that, as one writer put it, "Meria is naked, and the narrator is fully clothed. I want to know more about the narrator."

The essay, "Meria, May You Rest in Peace," was published in 2005. It did include me, the narrator, partially naked. However, I eventually discarded the idea of a book. The most prominent reason was Meria's brother's refusal to let me interview their mother. And then there was the Hospice nurse, who was Meria's case manager and with Meria and her family when Meria died. The nurse had been supportive of my writing and had met with me several times, even offering to go with me as translator at the interview with Meria's mother, before her son refused. But then the nurse became concerned that I would portray Meria in a less-than-favorable light. Given these restrictions, I had no compelling reason to continue once there were potential constraints and possible lawsuits. I felt I had already told Meria's story as best I could.

I was conflicted about abandoning the project. Personally, I found it unsettling to have put eighteen years into it and to have produced only one published essay. Had I wasted my time? I was also realizing that the public's interest in a woman's story of HIV had probably passed. Later, in the 2011 workshop, when Dorothy Allison told me, "That train has left," she effectively put the nail in that coffin.

It was my artist daughter who said, "Mom, nothing is wasted. Those eighteen years have prepared you for writing your memoir." As always, her insight was profound and supportive. She gave me comfort.

From 1990 to 2009, through my academic writing, I gave invited talks on my research about women with HIV/AIDS at national and international conferences. I continued my research interviewing women with HIV/AIDS in Oakland, California, Chicago, Illinois, and Rochester, New York. Clearly, I was far more comfortable with and educationally trained for analyzing and presenting other women's stories.

When I retired, I settled into the full-time writer's life that I had begun to cultivate among the supportive community at

Hedgebrook. I had also attained a level of confidence from recognition for my published academic work, and that served me in my transition. Still, I considered myself more of a novice writer, but after two more writers' residencies, I began to overcome these insecurities.

Today, I can see that I inched toward being a writer for a long time. I had been shy about exposing myself and scared of revealing secrets and being vulnerable to potential fallout from certain family members. It was a relief to accept that I was in control of what I revealed and that I had no control over others' responses. I knew my inner critic would continue to show up, but I was becoming stronger in telling her to shut up.

Writing my memoir was therapeutic in helping me deal with my anger toward my husband about his lack of support and respect for my work. Now, I don't hesitate to confront his bullshit comments. It has also become clearer that most of my anger was toward myself for not demanding more from him emotionally, for complying with the role expected of a minister's wife for twenty years, and for denying my ambitions. Returning to graduate school and developing a career with federal funding for my research was a turning point. My satisfaction propelled me into a radically different lifestyle.

The inner critic has always been with me, as with any writer. While I write my memoir, she seems stronger but has less power. She is stronger because of the personal nature of memoir writing. She has less power because I am more comfortable with myself. For example, as I am walking up the path to meet with my coach, my inner critic inevitably says, *Your writing is shit.* And yet I come away from our sessions feeling elated, supported, and challenged. My inner critic loses her intensity compared with the feedback and support I receive from my communities of writers and my daughter.

✳

In 2008, when I retired, I had no doubt that I would be disciplined in writing the essays that became the first draft of my memoir. I've developed a morning writing practice where I am at my desk around 8:00 or 9:00 A.M. five days a week. While working, I attempt to avoid looking at e-mail and schedule all appointments for after 4:00 P.M. My days vary as I listen to myself, and when I need a day off, I take it. My job is to write.

In time, I began to grasp that my experiences of listening to and examining other women's stories helped make my story clearer and urged me to write it. Now, I have gained more confidence in my writing, my marriage, and myself. Despite what I was taught as a child, I have cultivated a way to deal with my inner critic without experiencing any doubts about my own character. And it's actually quite satisfying to tell her to shut up.

✳ ✳ ✳ ✳ ✳

DONNA BRAZZI BARNES's nonfiction has been published in *Newsweek*, "My Turn," and *Great River Review*. She has been awarded residencies at Hedgebrook, The Anderson Center, and Ragdale. In her mid-forties, Barnes entered graduate school at the University of California, San Francisco, earning a PhD in sociology. She taught women's studies and conducted research about women with HIV/AIDS, presenting her work nationally and internationally. Her research has been anthologized in three books, including *Women, Motherhood and Living with HIV/AIDS,* and in various scholarly journals. Barnes lives with her husband in Kensington, California. She is currently in the process of finishing her memoir, *Too Big for My Britches,* about creating her life while confronting cultural assumptions about women in work, marriage, and motherhood.

OF KIDS AND RABBITS

Roseann M. Bozzone

Ever watch a magician? He pulls all kinds of things out of that hat of his: rabbits, kerchiefs, and even an occasional duck. Memoir is like that. The trick is to keep tugging on the memories until you have what you need. A word of caution, though: What you think you need, you might not get. Your windfall might come to fruition in a story you didn't expect. And that's the point.

Once a week, I help second-graders with their writing exercises. They pen haiku, acrostics, and fanciful stories. Their lessons are filled with various topics. Who is the tooth fairy? If you were a comic-book hero, what superpowers would you have? What would your dream house look like? They also tell stories about their lives. They call them personal narratives. At seven and eight years old, they haven't collected many memories, but the ones they write about are honest and true.

My pint-size friends ramble. They struggle with grammar and punctuation. But they write. So should we. I realized long ago that I could learn a few things about memoir from them, including the fact that letting the words flow without restriction is key. People and events may be a jumble initially. Write everything down. Forget about being perfect. Nothing ever is. Once you look at what you've written, sift through it. Fish around in that magic hat of ideas, and you will discover what you need—a character, a place, a truth that you had forgotten or were too afraid to face.

I'm an amateur. I've written two memoirs, published none. Fear of upsetting Aunt Tillie and being sued by offended friends and enemies has prevented me from getting my books out there. But I keep writing. Why? Because it has been an incredible journey of self-discovery and an opportunity to sort out my feelings, realize my mistakes, and forgive others for theirs.

I haven't overcome my fear of publishing. Maybe somebody else can help me with that. But I have learned a few things on my three-year writing journey and my stint with kid writing:

- **Write down your thoughts.** The kids make webs that look like spiders: an oval in the middle, and spikes that look like legs. They put an idea in the body and add supporting facts.
- **Journal.** If it's in a book, you can refer to it. The kids use black-and-white notebooks, and that works just fine.
- **Keep your notes everywhere.** My resourceful school companions tend to keep their notes on Post-its on huge sheets of chart-pad paper around the classroom. You can, too. Post those notes all

over your house, in your car, in your gym bag. Make notes on your tablet, your smartphone, your laptop. Jot down your thoughts. A word. A phrase. A sentence. You'll be surprised how useful those few words you thought of when you were sweating on the elliptical can be later on.

- **Find a focal point, a theme.** This isn't easy for kids. They tend to meander all over the place. Sometimes it isn't painless for grown-ups, either. But try. They do. I began writing about my relationship with my mother and wound up talking about artichokes. I learned a lot about the two of us while inspecting my childhood memories of cooking that prickly veggie in the kitchen with her.

- **Begin with a title.** Children love titles. They look for them in the books they read and like to give their work an important name. I found that helpful, too. Heading my topic gave me an opening and an ending to strive for. The metaphors derived their power from my focal point.

- **Organize your thoughts.** Kids are messy. They write that way, too. Deciding on a beginning, a middle, and an end helps them to sort out their ideas. It does that for our disheveled, rough-around-the-edges thoughts, too. Rearrange your real and metaphorical Post-its until they make sense to you and fit your purpose. Then flesh out each idea, moving the story forward with dialogue and characters who interact as they did in your memories. I didn't worry about historical details until later. Only after I blurted out my recollections did I make sure of my facts.

- **Take the time to check out "the times."** This is the hardest part for the kids. They often have to get their parents to write out a timeline for them. Many of us don't have the luxury of consulting our folks to verify some of the facts, but looking into historical years on the Internet and checking out family photos and random letters from relatives can provide invaluable information. Researching specific eras adds authenticity and credibility that are necessary not only in order for your reader to take you seriously but also so you can solidify to yourself that you are writing as true a version of your take on things as possible.

- **Fix your grammar and spelling, but later, with the help of spell check and a competent and encouraging circle of writing friends who help you to nitpick the mistakes.** This is the last step for the kids. After they consult their teacher and me, they have a checkup chart for CPUM: capitalization, punctuation, usage, meaning. Not a bad idea for us to do the same.

Once you've gotten your story written:

- **Read it out loud.** It helps. You can pick up additional errors that you might have made or things you thought you said but didn't. The kids love this part. Sharing makes it real. It does the same thing for me and helps me to clarify my thoughts.

- **Edit, edit, and edit again.** Edit for better words that say what you mean. Get rid of sentences that sound great but do nothing for the story except confuse the reader. Root out the chapters that don't enhance the story. Save them for another book.

- **Enjoy the process.** The kids do. "Can I write another story about my grandma? Did you know she told me there are no squares in Guatemala?"
- **Be a kid again.** Be fearless. Continue to write, and the rabbits and the ducks and maybe even a frog will appear from your pen like magic.

✳ ✳ ✳ ✳ ✳

Kids teach! That's what **ROSEANN BOZZONE** believes. An educator and lifelong student of language arts, Brooklyn-born Roseann began her love affair with the written word teaching English and Reading to seventh and eighth graders in New York. Mother to two rambunctious boys and four ferrets, Roseann spent several years as a full-time mom before going back to the classroom to help first- and second-grade storytellers pen their imaginations. Retired after thirty years of teaching, Roseann is working on two memoirs and a children's book with the help of a diverse group of writing buddies. She loves to travel with her husband to places like Alaska, Ireland, and Germany.

WHAT IS IT ABOUT MEMOIR?

Carol E. Anderson

WHY

The toughest thing about writing a memoir is that you risk not only falling on your face but also falling on your heart. You are not telling a story about why you think weather patterns in the Arctic will lead to climate change—an opinion based on scientific fact. You are telling a story about something, usually painful, that has shaped your life in an unalterable way—a fact that only you can verify, but one about which many may argue. When you write memoir, you open yourself to people challenging the veracity of your life, rather than the validity of your ideas. Not that both concepts aren't painful, but the levels of vulnerability involved in each are seismically different.

My desire to write a memoir about growing up gay in the 1960s as a child of evangelical parents was to offer hope to young people today who are struggling with their sexual identity—to encourage them to believe in their fundamental goodness and to trust worthy friends with the truth about themselves. Having lived through decades of religious and societal angst about the prospect of gay people existing, let alone having rights, I have learned how to be happy and successful, in spite of warnings that I'm dangerous to society. I have also learned, in spite of my fear, that my mother's love was more powerful than the religious dogma to which she subscribed.

Because of the era in which I was raised, when being gay was not only against religious doctrine but also against the law, I have been trained to be fearful of the consequences of sharing that information. Today, there remains great rancor about gay rights from many fundamentalist groups, so those fears also remain in me at various levels on different days. This makes it even more important to tell a positive story in which love and difference can live together with respect.

What has kept me going is the belief that my story can help young people of this generation who struggle with the complex, invisible dynamics that still arise for gays—taught values of honesty and authenticity by society but forced to violate these values daily in order to survive. And because gay youth today are at greater risk for suicide than any other group, it is important that I move beyond my comfort zone and take the risk that more good will come to others as a result of this work than harm will come to me.

So I write in spite of my fear, because I believe that personal stories are powerful vehicles for social change and that my voice can contribute to that change in a positive way. When I am tempted to stop, I remember a favorite quote by Audre Lorde: "When I dare to be powerful, to use my strength in service of my vision, it becomes less and less important whether I am afraid."

TRUTH

Recognizing that there are many truths in every situation, and that each one is emotionally complex and virtuous in the eyes of the person whose truth it is, I see memoir as a way to tell *my* truth, trusting it can rest alongside other truths without either claiming preeminence or offering apology. I accept that I am a unique blend of historical context, family system, and personality type, with particular sensitivities, preferences, and perspectives, and that my memoir will reflect my experience as seen through these multifiltered lenses. My job in sharing these facts through my story is to be honest with those that are knowable, and discerning about the truth that I shape. The art of truth for me is to tell my story without blame or judgment—to give readers a glimpse into my personal world and help them understand how I made sense of it and how it had a lasting impact on me.

It is not only rigor in truth that matters, but the tone through which the truth is expressed. Because many memoirs deal with big issues—fairness, justice, ethics, morality—they evoke potent feelings of anger, disappointment, betrayal, outrage. This terrain is fertile ground for ranting, but while screaming on paper provides a momentary relief for pent-up stress, it does not evoke a caring response from readers who are seeking understanding through measured constraint. They count on you to tell a difficult story in a way that engenders compassion on their part, rather than irritation, and to express your passion without the attendant rage that the content may justify. This kind of truth telling requires a certain distance from the evocative events that inspired you to write a memoir, combined with deep reflection that brings insight and transformative power to the work.

My hope in telling *my* truth is to help people see *why* what happened to me would have meaning in their life—how the struggle to be authentic while keeping a secret would be relevant to them, even though they might not be gay. Finding and telling this level of truth humbles, reveals, and strengthens your heart, regardless of the outcome.

ASTONISHMENT

The raw, volcanic emotions that hijacked me each time I wrote a scene from my past were my biggest surprise. I was sure, after the $50,000 I had spent on therapy throughout my life, that I had worked through all of my feelings about being gay, about keeping a secret, about the fear of rejection, and that now I was merely telling the story of what had happened. I was wrong! Upon completing a chapter about my first real love of a woman, I realized I had never grieved the loss of her in my life. There was never a formal breakup, because there was never a formal beginning or acknowledgment of the meaning of our relationship.

For a week, I hacked away at the overgrown shrubs in my yard with a machete, while watering the garden with my tears, screaming along to Chely Wright's song "It Was," proclaiming that the love we had "was real, it was magic… it did all the things love does, that's how I knew it was."

I fell asleep singing those lyrics in my head and woke up hearing them again, as though I were asserting to myself and to the world that the love I'd had was real and that it mattered—something I had never admitted then, even to her. It was a Mount Vesuvius of the soul that went on for days, purging me of the sorrow that I had stored within me for forty-eight years. I had no idea it was there, but all those tears were cleansing and gave me back a part of myself I hadn't known was stolen.

INNER CRITIC

The major job of my inner critic is to undermine my belief that writing my memoir matters at all. She shows up randomly, usually after I've written a piece that I like, to remind me that no one really cares about my life and that this book probably won't get published anyway. She has a snarky voice and speaks in a persistent whisper, like a low-grade toothache you know will turn into an abscess if you don't take care of it. Sometimes she can take me out for a whole morning, her gloomy predictions whining in my ear.

For me, the most effective antidote to her bullish ways is a method developed by Lucia Capacchione in her book *The Power of the Other Hand*, in which she describes a technique for combating my powerful left-brain, analytical self—home of my inner critic—with my equally skillful and clever right brain, where my fledgling author resides. Through her book, I have learned how to have a written dialogue with each side of my brain using my dominant and nondominant hands.

I start by using my right hand (connecting to my left brain) and write down whatever discouraging thing my inner critic wants to say. Then I place the pen in my left hand (connecting to my right brain) and let my creative self respond. It happens that my right brain is also home to my sassy inner child, and she always has plenty to say to the big-bully analytical side. In fact, she loves to get on a soapbox and tell off her tormentor with relish and gusto.

What streams out uncensored from my creative champion often moves me to tears. She believes in me. She cheers me on and invigorates my courage. There is power and beauty in the words that flow when I let her speak, and I feel inspired to go on with renewed confidence and purpose.

According to Capacchione, using your nondominant hand allows you to bypass the analytical side of your brain and tap into hidden feelings and deeper wisdom that the voracious analytical part often devours. I have found this process to be an extraordinary way to take down the critic and redirect my energy, as well as to remind myself that I am the only one who can write this particular story with my unique history, sensibilities, and passion.

SUPPORT

I have been working on this memoir for fifteen years, writing it in my head while driving down I-94 or preening my two acres of lawn with my Toro SS5000. I have written scraps in journals, scribbled on napkins in boutique cafés, and hammered away on my keyboard at writing workshops from North Carolina to Montana. But my sincere, not-getting-out-of-the-seat-till-it's-finished effort began in 2013, when I took the online class Kickstart Your Memoir. One of the first assignments was to make a timeline of events and outline the whole book, starting with the end in mind. While this exercise felt grueling at the time, it enabled me to set direction and to write with intention. Prior to that exercise, I wrote randomly about experiences in my life that had no order and no arc.

Finding the end allowed me to find the beginning and the middle. Though all of those have changed in the editing process over the last three years, I could never have gotten a manuscript completed without that initial step. I also found that, while writing is a solitary activity, becoming a better writer requires help from skilled mentors who offer, in equal doses, an honest critique of your work and encouragement for what you are doing well.

My positive experience with Kickstart led me to enroll in a two-year MFA program in creative nonfiction at Goucher College. It was there I discovered that I didn't really know what my story was about, until I finished a first draft and got feedback from my mentor. In my tale of growing up gay in an evangelical household, my primary focus had been on the challenge of living a lifestyle in opposition to my religious upbringing, but that was only a symptomatic thread in a much larger weaving of my life. The real story was about how to live an authentic life while keeping a secret. This framing provided a much richer exploration of how I engaged with family, friends, colleagues, and society at large over the fifteen-year period before I came out. Seeing how keeping the secret of being gay had shaped every interaction I had with people was a revelation. Being so close to the work and dealing with the emotional impact of reliving scenes while writing had made it impossible for me to see the larger story, but as soon as my mentor offered this new perspective, I knew it was the key to the whole book.

The Kickstart program gave me a great foundation upon which to build and enabled me to further develop my manuscript with the support of other writers and teachers. The MFA program helped me stay on track and see it through to completion. While others may not need the level of structure that helped me to develop and then to finish my manuscript, I think the skillful and timely use of a coach, mentor, or writing program can significantly accelerate your progress and keep you committed.

I've also needed those outside the writing circle, though in a certain way. While your friends are often eager to help, they are not always reliable judges of good writing, unless they also happen to be editors. Their job is to keep you moving, to honor your process, to encourage your heart. You can't do without them. Just make sure you rely on them for emotional sustenance more than for confirmation that you are a great writer.

PAYOFF

There have been many benefits in sticking with my book: the pleasure of watching people's eyes light up when I mention I am writing a memoir, the feeling of accomplishment in completing one of my deathbed goals, requests by my book club to read a section, and, of course, the student discount I've received at conferences the last two years. But the most precious and unexpected payoff has been the way the struggle to find my voice through this book has magnified my respect and compassion for myself in the last three years.

Writing about my life from a historical perspective allowed me to see more clearly the courage it took to choose the path that was true for me, regardless of the religious and social conventions of the day. I saw how being gay built my character and gave me compassion for the "other," whoever that may be. It required me to trust my own voice and believe in my own value, regardless of what the outside world had to say.

Rereading the 150 letters my mother wrote to me in college also changed my relationship with her, even though she has been dead for twenty-three years. At the age of sixty-eight, I was able to hear the repeated messages of love and care in each letter that, in my twenties, had been overshadowed by religious references that made me fearful. The further discovery of love letters she wrote to my father before they were married offered a glimpse into my mother's hopes and dreams as a young woman. It is hard for a child to imagine that her parents were ever children themselves, and that their life events also shaped them into the adults they became. This discovery was the doorway to my greater benevolence and love for my parents as human beings. Writing my memoir brought me closer to them in spirit and has provided enduring comfort and appreciation for who they were.

Finally, spending three concerted years focused on this project, and completing five or six rewrites of each chapter, demanded a level of precision in speech that had never been asked of me before. Each word became important in my effort to express a deeper truth, and with utmost precision, rather than relying on surface clichés. Had I stopped writing, I would have missed out on the gift of self-acceptance, self-love, and self-respect I garnered by living through the tempest and finally committing to paper, to the absolute best of my ability, the story that was mine alone to tell.

* * * * *

CAROL E. ANDERSON is a Life Coach and former organizational change consultant with thirty-five years of experience in large and small corporations supporting people to live more authentic lives in and outside of work. Her love of travel took her to many countries, engendering a deep respect for "other" and the resilience of women around the world. Carol is the coauthor of the essay, "How Women are Transforming the Practice of Leadership," published in *Enlightened Power* (Jossey Bass, 2005), and the author of a book of inspirational stories, *When You Add Up Life* (2003).

Carol holds a Master's in organizational development and a doctorate in spiritual studies, and recently completed her MFA in creative nonfiction. Carol lives with her spouse, Archer Christian, and their sassy, energetic pup, Saxon, in a nature sanctuary outside Ann Arbor, Michigan.

WRITING NAKED: THE BENEFITS OF EXPOSING YOURSELF THROUGH MEMOIR

Bella Mahaya Carter

I used to believe that if I wrote what I wanted to write, I'd be arrested, my parents would disinherit me, my husband would leave me, and I'd end up living in the streets. Thoughts about self-exposure can be irrational—and scary. It's hard enough to do the work of mining memories and turning the chaos of life into literature. If I ruminated over possible responses to my work before it was written, I'd never get anything done. The Muse shrivels under a microscope.

An award-winning author once said that the best way to get through writing a memoir is to be in denial that anyone will ever read what you're writing. I get this. In the writing classes I teach, Write Where You Are: The Art of Being Present on the Page, lesson one is about getting out of your own way so that what wants to come *through* you is free to do so. I tell my students no one will read their work (for now). I encourage them to give themselves permission to say anything—without judgment—and to release their shame.

Inevitably, my students let it all hang out, and their ugly, beautiful, naked selves shimmer and shine as they shed inhibitions and reveal secrets. This is possible in a space that feels safe, in an environment where acceptance trumps judgment every time, and when you know that nobody "out there"— especially the people you're writing about—will know what you're saying, until or unless you are ready to share.

And more often than not with my students, that day arrives. They *want* to share. They may be scared. They may be insecure. They may worry what people will think, but once a story wraps its delicate tendrils around a writer's heart and mind, the writer *needs* to address the complex task of unraveling it. This process sometimes leads to the creation of a manuscript. My students write because they have something to say and something that needs to be *received* in order for their work to feel complete.

Veteran writers realize what they write is larger than they are. They understand that people buy and read books not because readers care about the writer, per se, but because readers long to see themselves reflected in the pages of the books they read. They are looking for clues to help them navigate their own lives.

By the time my students are well into book projects, they've matured as writers, at which point denying that anyone will read what they've written stands at cross-purposes with their goals. After all, they've *chosen* to write a book. If they're doing things right, they're already cultivating a readership across multiple platforms, through blog posts, social media, readings, conferences, and more. They *want* people to read their book.

This is an auspicious moment in which, if you're open to it, a shift occurs. You realize that denial, as a coping mechanism, may compromise your creativity and self-expression and rob you of opportunities for healing and growth. Beneath this directive to be in denial that anyone will read your writing lurks the disempowering notion that it's not okay to speak your truth.

I slip into the numb illusion of safety that denial offers when I think—consciously or not—that by writing I'm doing something wrong, or when I worry that others might be hurt by my words or will disapprove of me or what I'm saying. I go into denial when I think I don't have a right to express myself, or that there's something wrong with me for saying the things I'm saying. In the past, I've taken these thoughts very seriously.

It was a relief when I learned that just because I have a thought doesn't mean it's true. I am not my thoughts; I *have* thoughts, but I am no longer constantly fused with them. Resisting the natural inclination to identify with my thoughts means that when I become aware of them—*I suck as a writer*; *I'm not good enough*; *no one will ever give a shit what I have to say*—I recognize that they are *just thoughts*. I can choose to believe them and invest time and energy in them, which will enlarge them—or not. This "or not" part is where life—and writing—gets juicy. It's where fun and magic happen. I've been experimenting with this lately, choosing to see limiting, hurtful thoughts for what they are: expressions of fear. And not just *any* fear, but destructive fear.

There's *productive* fear, and then there's *destructive* fear. Productive fear is a response to a real threat in our environment. It is present-moment-focused and keeps us safe. Destructive fear happens in our heads. It stems from our imagination, from scary or unpleasant stories we tell ourselves about something that happened in the past or that might (but probably won't) happen in the future.

Understanding this can lead us to ask ourselves, *What choice will I make? Am I going to listen to Destructive Fear, who has a reputation for being the world's biggest liar? Or am I going to honor my desire to write and express myself, which is a generative, creative, and Soul-affirming process? Which do you trust—Destructive Fear or your Eternal Soul—to guide you through your writing and your life?*

The insecurities I mentioned above, which catapulted me into denial as a coping mechanism for my writing in the past, were fueled entirely by my Destructive Fear. He called those shots. He had me running for cover and hiding underneath denial, a form of banishment.

My Soul doesn't believe in hiding. She is light and luminous and sees this glow in others. Through her eyes, humans, with all our foibles and flaws, are magnificent. She applauds my efforts to bear witness to my life experience, which is a sacred act—sacred because it's a labor of love, rooted in my desire for understanding. She prizes storytelling, inquiry, and authenticity.

When she hears, "It's not okay to speak your truth," she lets out a deep belly laugh and says, "Are you kidding? That's the most ridiculous thing I've ever heard!" My Soul knows that speaking my truth is essential. And she knows my intention is to express *my* truth, and that all truth is subjective.

I tell my students to go for the *emotional* truth of their stories. Sophisticated readers understand that a memoir is a construct, an act of *creative* writing and remembering. I'm less concerned with reporting things exactly as they happened—no one can do that—than I am with conveying the emotional center and integrity of a story, which requires tools of fiction, such as scene making and dialogue. One could argue that our *lives* are a fiction, since we make things up as we go, creating one event after another with our thoughts, emotions, and actions. We are creative beings on and off the page.

Let's face it: memoirs are subjective. The same family event narrated retrospectively by five family members will sound like five completely different stories. We each have our own lenses through which we view the world; there is not one clear, definitive truth. We remember what we want to remember. We bury painful memories. We edit the narratives of our lives every day, often without realizing it. This isn't a bad thing; it's a survival mechanism—and it's who we are as co-creative human beings.

Remembering this helps me realize the story I'm telling represents a sliver of life's gigantic pie. It's not absolute, nor am I attempting to tell anybody's story but my own. I may reference family and friends, but what I say about them reflects upon *me* more than it does them. It's *my perspective*. When the intention I hold in my heart is a loving one—meaning I'm speaking honestly about my experience from a place of empathy, rather than harboring a hidden agenda, such as trying to get back at someone who hurt me—the outcome is positive.

I have no control over how others will respond to my work or to me. "What others think of me is none of my business," the saying goes. Still, I'm a caring person and am mindful about protecting the privacy of people who show up in my memoir by changing names and other identifying characteristics. And if I have the slightest inkling that something I've written might hurt a loved one whose relationship I cherish, I get their permission before publishing it. I yanked a poem about my husband from my poetry book because he wasn't ready for that information to be shared. My husband means more to me than any poem.

It's helpful to remember, when you're working on something fresh, that *you* get to decide when and how you'll share it, and with whom. But these decisions come later—*after* you've got your story down on paper. Life circumstances change over the course of writing. Time eases sensitivity around many issues, and things you think will be a big deal to others often turn out to be nothing. So much depends upon how you, the writer, hold a particular subject. The people around you are mirrors: they reflect back to you ideas you carry but disown, ideas you'd rather not harbor and may not realize you do.

What makes memoir writing, and the exposure that comes along with it, so rich are the opportunities it presents for personal transformation and growth. The process asks us to cope with the feelings our writing draws out. It challenges us to practice acceptance and forgiveness, toward others and ourselves, which enhances the quality of our lives. It also challenges us to remember that there is nothing wrong with us, that what we do or say is honest and brave. It gives us permission to stand tall, to know that our anxiety and fears—our so-called imperfections—are fine. The lesson in all of this, which is a practice, involves saying yes to our dreams and to ourselves—repeatedly. It means granting ourselves permission to be who we are, and to share ourselves through our writing, and to know this is an act of generosity of spirit. Anything else is a lie.

Writers in general, and memoirists in particular, are called to show up in their writing and their lives wholly and unapologetically. Exposure is daunting only when a lack of self-acceptance lurks in the shadows, when egos swell, and when validation is sought from the outside, instead of within.

My work and life rise to a higher level when I refuse to buy into someone else's ideas about what is and is not possible or acceptable for me. It's sometimes hard to keep my center, to stay grounded in my own truth. This happens when I'm criticized, but also when I'm congratulated or praised. If I believe what I say or do is not okay or not good enough, or that I'm unworthy of a compliment, nothing anyone says will change my mind.

Few things in life are more unsettling than the thought of standing naked in front of a crowd. Even standing before a crowd fully clothed scares the daylights out of many people. I've heard this fear harkens back to caveman times, when, if you weren't part of the crowd, if you were left alone, you might end up as a wild animal's dinner.

"You're exposing yourself a lot," my editor said to me in response to a comment I made about feeling uncomfortable as I neared the finish line of my memoir.

I've struggled to bare my Soul in front of those I love and trust first, starting with myself. I try to make peace with my imperfections; forgive my bad choices, my tempers, my cruelties, my insensitivities; and learn from my mistakes. It's a practice. So is self-acceptance, which is my biggest challenge and perhaps the most important thing I teach in my writing classes. It's as important as the writing. I teach art and craft, and I teach my students about platform, publishing, and reading their work in public, but I also teach them how to stand in their truth, how to dust themselves off and shine—as the exquisite naked writers they are!

Recently I read *The Art of Possibility*, by psychologist Rosamund Stone Zander and her husband, Benjamin Zander, conductor of the Boston Philharmonic. They write about Michelangelo's famous description of how he worked. He believed that inside every block of stone or marble dwelled a beautiful statue. He removed the excess material to reveal the work of art within. Great teachers have the opportunity to chip away at whatever gets in the way of their students' self-expression. We writers can do this, too—for ourselves.

"Your eye is on the statue within the roughness of the uncut stone," Benjamin says about teaching. I couldn't agree more. Shame (which thrives on secrecy and denial) is excess material that needs to be chipped away. So are pride, fear, blame, resentment, jealousy, and self-doubt—all noisy distractions that prevent us from bringing into the world what longs to be expressed *through* us. In other words, we get in our own way.

The notion that you need to deny that anyone will read what you've written to get through your memoir certainly has its place but will take you only so far. Why swim in murky waters teeming with eels ready to bite you with shame and fear when you could rise, like a phoenix, out of ashes and flame, resurrected and transformed?

Publishing memoirs will be fraught as long as we continue to protect our shame, as long as we believe, on any level, that there's something wrong with what we're saying or doing—or that there's something wrong with us.

As memoirists, we are in a unique position to reinvent ourselves, which requires compassion, insight, forgiveness, and love. Maybe mastery and enlightenment aren't achievable goals, but questing for them lightens my load, lifts my Spirit, and illuminates my path.

Nakedness—in the sense of seeing and accepting myself *as I am*, and allowing others to see my authentic self—has been a recurring theme in my life. I have been blessed with the gift of transparency, though at times it has felt like a curse. In my writing and in my life, I tell it like I see it. I strip naked. Not because I'm an exhibitionist, but because I'm a healer.

And I cannot heal what I cannot see. I cannot clear what I'm unaware of. My negative habits and behavior patterns have their way with me—until I become conscious of them. Once I realize what's going on, they dissolve. It's like shining a light onto a shadow—the light of awareness makes the shadow disappear. So I keep trying to illuminate my foibles, scars, aches, and pains, keep trying to remain connected to my Soul, in order to know myself better and to live my life as fully as possible. As a writer, I do this in public—I speak *out loud*—hoping that people will see not me, but themselves, in my story.

✳ ✳ ✳ ✳ ✳

BELLA MAHAYA CARTER is a poet, author, writing teacher, and coach who believes in the power of writing to heal and transform lives. She's the author of *Secrets of My Sex*, a collection of narrative poems and the forthcoming memoir, *Raw: A Midlife Quest for Health & Happiness*. Her poetry, fiction, and creative nonfiction appear in *The Sun, Lilith, Calyx, Two Review, Onthebus, Pearl, Literary Mama, Quill & Parchment,* and elsewhere. Her work has been anthologized in *Grandmothers' Necklace, Writing Our Way Out of The Dark: An Anthology of Literary Acts of Bravery.* She's a featured columnist at Shewrites.com, and maintains her own blog, *Body, Mind, Spirit: Inspiration for Writers, Dreamers, and Seekers of Health & Happiness.* Visit her online at www.bellamahayacarter.com.

✳ ELIZABETH GILBERT ✳

Author of *Eat, Pray, Love*

BROOKE WARNER: What drew you to write a memoir in the first place?

ELIZABETH GILBERT: As somebody who has written in a lot of different forms, I would say that it's almost like you're in conversation with your work. I think you have to ask the work what the work wants to be. Whenever I have an idea, I always have to ask it, "Do you want to be a novel? Do you want to be journalistic nonfiction? Are you supposed to be a magazine article? Are you supposed to be a poem? What do you want to be?" You need to find the form that best suits the particular story that needs to be told. I could have written a thinly veiled autobiographical novel about a woman leaving her marriage and traveling, looking for clues to her new life, but it didn't feel like what that idea wanted to be. The great Joan Didion said, "I write in order to find out what I think about things." For me, a lot of the writing of *Eat, Pray, Love* was an assistance for myself, in that it helped me understand myself better. Writing it was very healing for me, and ultimately there was no other way to tell that story that seemed appropriate.

BROOKE WARNER: You write in *Big Magic* about ideas being up for grabs for whoever is ready for them. How is this concept—the magical idea—different for memoir writers, or is it?

ELIZABETH GILBERT: There's a level at which it's not any different for memoir. People ask me about how it feels different to write different things: magazine journalism, or a novel, or narrative nonfiction, or memoir. There's a level at which it's all the same process. The most important level at which it's all exactly the same process is your commitment to continue to show up and be present for that idea and to be in conversation with it and not be resentful of that idea, not get angry at the idea, but to try to continue your piece of a very strange relationship, which is a relationship between a person of labor and inspiration. That's how every creative process has been made. It's not easier or harder to do that writing a novel or writing a memoir, I find. You're not off the hook from inspiration's demands and rewards just because the story happens to be true, or just because it's about your life.

✶

BROOKE WARNER: This is the ten-year anniversary of *Eat, Pray, Love*. When you set out to write it, did you have any idea it would resonate with readers in the way that it has? What's been the most rewarding aspect of that?

ELIZABETH GILBERT: Unless you're some sort of ragingly delusional, grandiose freak, you would never say, "I'm going to write a book, and it's going to sell a million copies, and Julia Roberts is going to love it." *Eat, Pray, Love* was definitely a phenomenon, and the definition of a phenomenon is that it comes out of nowhere, and you don't know why it happened, and it doesn't happen again. I'm very comfortable with that book having been a phenomenon. For me, the most gratifying thing is to see how people, mostly women, took that story and then applied its questions to their own life and made changes in their own lives based on what they had read. Because, as outrageously insane as this may seem in 2016, there are enormous numbers of women out there in the world who still have not gotten the memo that their lives belong to them. Somehow that information, as much as we think that it's been disseminated, has not filtered down to them. What I hear when people come to me and tell me what *Eat, Pray, Love* meant to them, if it meant a lot to them, is that there came a moment in the book, and it's a different spot in the book for all different readers, when all of a sudden they realized about a situation in their own life, *Maybe it doesn't need to look like this anymore. Maybe I can change everything. Maybe I don't have to be in this toxic relationship anymore. Maybe I don't have to be suffocated by my own family. Maybe I'm not supposed to be a mother, and that's okay. Or maybe I can approach childbearing and child rearing in a different way than my mother and my grandmother did. Maybe I have agency.* To have *Eat, Pray, Love* be a delivery service that brought women to their own attention, in a way—so many women in so many different parts of the world—is the greatest experience of my life. Now I feel connected to some richer, deeper sisterhood than I ever had before, and it's fantastic.

BROOKE WARNER: Do you ever find yourself in the position of defending memoir, given the harsh climate/reaction to the genre out there among writers and media and social media?

ELIZABETH GILBERT: I'm not a confrontational person by nature, so I'm not comfortable, generally speaking, with defense, which is of course is just another kind of attack. I often think that when you're on the defensive, you've already lost. I don't think memoir needs to be defended. What I see, though, is a lot of fear in the attacks and the harshness that people have, particularly about women writing memoir. All I hear is fear and anxiety about these questions: Who is allowed to participate in a cultural conversation? What intimate details of a person's life are appropriate to share? Why does this make me so deeply uncomfortable? A woman is revealing emotional things about her life. But women's writing not going to stop, and it shouldn't, because for far too many centuries, no stories were allowed to be told about women's lives, particularly in their own voices. I've gotten pushback for being a writer who crosses genres, and certain people in the literary establishment are uncomfortable with that. They are uncomfortable with the idea that somebody can live in the world in multiple voices. That I can have a particular voice that I use when I'm talking about my own emotional experience and my own spiritual journey, and another kind of voice when I'm trying to make a certain kind of art, makes people in the high-class literary world highly uncomfortable. I'm amazed at how little patience or capacity people have to be able to imagine a world big enough for people to have different and sometimes contradictory creative voices. But I'm not doing my writing for those people, and that's very liberating. I wish more writers would give themselves the liberty to write in lots of different ways, and in lots of different voices, because the human imagination is literally limitless. There's no rule that says that you can't write a deeply emotional, spiritual, revealing, confessional memoir and then write a postmodern novel right after it, or a biography of Winston Churchill. You can do whatever you fucking want. It's your mind.

BROOKE WARNER: What is the magic of memoir for you?

ELIZABETH GILBERT: There are certain events, incidents, and experiences in my life that I cannot glean the merit from until I have written about them. So, as it's happening to me, I'm aware that something very interesting and important is going on, but it's not getting into my bones until I sit down and craft it into a story. By the time that story is finished being written, that experience is sewn into the embroidery of my life in a way that it never could have been any other way. For instance, when I was traveling for *Eat, Pray, Love*, I knew I was going to be writing a book about that trip, so I was writing and taking notes every day. I had these huge, life-changing, transformational experiences in that year. But often something amazing would happen at 2:00 P.M., but then it wouldn't be until 9:00 P.M., when I sat down to write about it, that it would become part of my own narrative. You're literally writing your own story in a memoir. For me, it's almost as if the writing is the place where you redeem the casino chips and turn them into a currency that's actually going to be valuable to you for the rest of your life. You're handed all these casino chips, and then you need to turn them into something real. Writing is the window you approach to do that. That's the particular magic of memoir writing for me.

✷ ✷ ✷ ✷ ✷

ELIZABETH GILBERT is best known for her 2006 memoir *Eat, Pray, Love,* which was made into a film starring Julia Roberts. The book became so popular that *TIME* magazine named Elizabeth one of the one hundred most influential people in the world. In 2010, Elizabeth published a follow-up to

Eat, Pray, Love, called *Committed,* a memoir that explored her ambivalent feelings about the institution of marriage. Her latest novel, *The Signature of All Things,* published in fall 2013, is a sprawling tale of nineteenth-century botanical exploration. *O, The Oprah Magazine* named it "the novel of a lifetime." The novel was named a Best Book of 2013 by the *New York Times, O, The Oprah Magazine,* the *Washington Post,* the *Chicago Tribune,* and the *New Yorker.* Gilbert lives in the small river town of Frenchtown, New Jersey, where she and her husband (more widely known as "that Brazilian guy from *Eat, Pray, Love*") run an imports store called Two Buttons.

TAKEAWAY:
THE HEART OF MEMOIR

Linda Joy Myers and
Brooke Warner

When writers hear the word *takeaway*, it evokes something specific. It speaks to what your reader gets from reading your work. What they walk away with. We originally started using the term *takeaway* in our memoir classes because of Brooke's background as an acquiring editor, where every single manuscript evaluated for acquisition had to pass a litmus test: Did the story have a takeaway? Was there something the reader could learn from the story?

As we developed curricula for the various memoir classes we teach together at WriteYourMemoirinSixMonths.com, we started to see something interesting. Many of the memoirs we were reading were heavily reflective. Reflection happens in memoir when the writer is making sense of their experiences, synthesizing it for the reader. But there was something more, something deeper and more nuanced, in the reflections we were seeing. Writers were offering wisdom, insight, and universal truths. So we appropriated an industry term for this all-important element of craft, and we've been teaching it to memoirists ever since.

REFLECTION VERSUS TAKEAWAY

Reflection happens between scenes, and sometimes after scenes. (While a whole scene can be composed of the author's reflective thoughts, we don't recommend doing this. Balance between action and non-action is needed.) Reflection is an internal moment when writers explicitly tell the reader how they feel about something, or what something meant to them, which is why it's best when it's supplemental to a scene.

Reflection can be analytical, but it's often emotional. Some critics of memoir believe that reflection is the navel-gazing part of memoir, and can be overly reflective. In an article called "Writing the Z-Axis," Sean Ironman refers to overly reflective writing as the "bar essay." This kind of writing, he says, "reads as if the writer is on the barstool next to you, rambling about their life over a Guinness." This can happen in chapters, too, if reflection is not offset by all the good elements of scene writing. That said, reflection is critical in memoir. Without it, you fall more easily into the trap of relaying just your experiences, the "what happened" part of your story. Without it, you do not connect on a deeper level with your reader. Because memoir readers have come to expect an intense level of intimacy and sharing, the modern memoirist needs to learn how to connect through reflection.

Takeaway appears within a reflection. Takeaway can be a reflection, but not all reflection is takeaway. Now, let's unpack that. This means that wherever there is reflection, there is an opportunity for a takeaway, but it doesn't necessarily mean that all reflections are going to be takeaways. In our teaching, we often describe the takeaway as the arrow that pierces the reader's heart. If you're a reader of memoir and you've experienced a really good takeaway, you'll recognize these moments as the ones when you experienced a chill, a deep level of connection, or when you needed to put the book down for a second to sink into the powerful truth the author just revealed.

To further distinguish between the two, reflection is a moment of inner musing—thoughts and feelings written for the express purpose of making sense of experience. The takeaway is something for the reader. It's a nugget where the writer offers the reader a moment of connection and in that connection mirrors a human experience—thus the arrow to the heart. These moments are not about the author; they're for the reader.

Here are two passages from *Wild*, by Cheryl Strayed, that showcase reflection and takeaway:

REFLECTION

I felt that perhaps being amidst the undesecrated beauty of the wilderness meant I too could be undesecrated, regardless of what I'd lost or what had been taken from me. . . . The wilderness had a clarity that included me.

TAKEAWAY

"The thing about hiking the Pacific Crest Trail, the thing that was so profound to me that summer and yet also, like most things, so very simple, was how few choices I had and how often I had to do the thing I least wanted to do. How there was no escape or denial. No numbing it down with a martini or covering it up with a roll in the hay."

HOW TO START WRITING TAKEAWAY

If you want to learn how to incorporate takeaway into your memoir, start by learning how to identify takeaway. See if you can find sentences and passages like these in the memoirs you love. Takeaways don't need to be full paragraphs, and they are never full scenes. They're moments within the narrative when you tap into something bigger than yourself. They're moments when you think about your reader and attempt to connect them to something bigger than your book.

Consider this profound takeaway from Dani Shapiro's memoir, *Devotion*:

"I didn't know that there was a third way of being. Life was unpredictable, yes. A speeding car, a slip on the ice, a ringing phone, and suddenly everything changes forever. To deny that is to deny life—but to be consumed by it is also to deny life. The third way—inaccessible to me as I slunk down the halls— had to do with holding this paradox lightly in one's own hands. To think: It is true, the speeding car, the slip on the ice, the ringing phone. It is true, and yet here I am listening to my boy sing as we walk down

the corridor. Here I am giving him a hug. Here we are—together in this, our only moment."

Shapiro is explaining the nature of paradox, how two seemingly opposing things are true at once. It's reflective, and it's a universal truth. This kind of paradox is something we all know, something we've all experienced, whether or not we've experienced it in exactly this way.

When attempting to write takeaway, think about your message. What do you want your readers to get from the scene or the chapter? What do you want them to know, to understand? How can you connect with them on a heart level? Takeaway is always more about the heart than about the head. You can explain something in a deeply intellectually satisfying way and change the way a person thinks about something, but there is nothing more resonant for a reader than experiencing a heart-connection moment. These connections and how an author articulates them are a tipping point that can elevate a memoir from being simply well received to being something that changes lives.

This essay was originally published by Writers Digest.

THE JOURNEY OF
THE TWO-HUNDRED-
THOUSAND-WORD MEMOIR

Krishan Bedi

M y memoir starts with a central question: What was it like for a young man fresh off the boat from a tiny village in India with big dreams of finding success in the world?

I bluffed my way through difficult college courses at the University of Tennessee, Knoxville, falling hard when I discovered that bluffing didn't work as well in America as it did in India. I had memorized the content of the course material but not its meaning, and consequently failed all my courses. Ultimately, I decided to work toward a bachelor's degree in mathematics at Knoxville College instead. (They didn't have an engineering degree, which was my original choice.) It was the 1960s, and when trying to fit in with the white students failed, I found myself trying to blend in with the black students, picking up their slang and gestures, hoping one day I could once again grace the prestigious halls of UT and eventually earn a degree in engineering. At my lowest point, it seemed this would never happen.

There is something special about writing down memories as they come to you. It amazed me how much I remembered, five decades later, in clear detail, about the early years of my life. Driving a bus in Chicago. Working as a cook in a hotel in New Jersey. Dating a Jewish girl. Then, even further down the road, meeting my wife for the first time. I had gone back to India to have an arranged marriage after living in America for nine years.

These are just a few of the many memories that shape my book. Not even my closest family members knew some of my experiences or emotions, many of which I had kept to myself because I'd gone through difficult times and it was always my way to put on a cheerful face, especially later, for the sake of my wife and my sons. But I set out to explore my truth in my memoir and achieved a few things I can be proud of as a result. My memoir takes readers through a life of hard work and perseverance. It elicits laughs at young and foolish days. It inspires by illustrating the power of hope in difficult circumstances.

I enjoy reading memoirs to discover what it's like to walk in another person's shoes. It is thrilling to see life from a perspective much different from my own, and in a place and time I will never get to know. It's my hope that my memoir adds one more rich color to the genre. Plato is credited with having said, "The unexamined life is not worth living." Perhaps that is one reason memoir writing has become so popular—it's a way for ordinary people to discover and share the extraordinary in their lives.

Writing my memoir has been a wild experience, a long journey that started approximately eight years ago when, after I regaled a colleague with tales from my student life in the 1960s in Tennessee, she exclaimed, "You should write a book!" She nearly died laughing at my stories, and her words planted a seed in the back of my mind that maybe one day I would write a memoir. A couple years later, my daughter-in-law listened with awe as I told her about some of my younger days as an Indian going to college in the States and trying to get a date to blend in with the other Americans. "Your experience—everything you went through back in the sixties—is very unique," she told me. "You should definitely write a book."

And so it began. In 2011, I started writing down my stories for the first time. While I began writing my memoir because of the many funny anecdotes I had to share, I knew I would encounter difficult memories. I knew in my heart I must tell the truth of what happened to me, even if it was painful or embarrassing. At times, tears came to my eyes as I delved into my recollections, especially about my youngest son and the medical issues he had to deal with from a young age.

Do you want the world to know how poorly you did in school? my inner critic asked me as I wrote. Up until then, no one in my family knew I had flunked out of my classes at the University of Tennessee or that I'd ended up going to a much less prestigious school, a community college. *Yes*, I said to myself. *I must include everything.*

While no one was against the idea of my writing a memoir, my wife and sons were quick to say I shouldn't include certain stories. My wife was hesitant for me to share information about the girls I had dated before I met her, and she didn't want me to go into too much detail about my son's medical conditions. I suspected she was a little embarrassed about the fact of our arranged marriage, even though that was typical in India at the time. "But this is my memoir," I told her, "and these stories are part of my life." In the end, she acquiesced, as long as I changed the names of the girls.

On the topic of my son, I had a difficult, emotional conversation with him and his wife about what I could include regarding his health. He is my son, and his medical concerns were a major part of my experience, a time I did not want to skip over. In the end, he agreed to let me write about him.

Once I got knee-deep into the memoir, with hundreds of pages written and a rough draft taking shape, I lost momentum. Was this a good idea after all? Was I in way over my head? But reviews from my friends and family, especially my daughter-in-law, kept me going. They wanted to know more. "You have to keep writing," they would say. My daughter-in-law told me one day, "I am rooting for this character." Feeling revitalized, I returned to the page, determined to finish the book.

Many times during the writing, I consulted friends, relatives, and especially my wife to make sure I remembered certain stories correctly, to glean as much truth and detail as I could. I didn't want one false word or one error in memory to sit on the pages of my book. I had to relay it all exactly as it happened, and sometimes that meant doing more research, or having discussions with and gaining perspective from others who had been with me at certain times in my life. At times, I found myself writing in the present tense in order to transport myself into a certain time so that I could relive it and bring to life the emotions of the moment.

In the end, my book was very long, more than two hundred thousand words. It had taken more than four years to write as I whittled down and edited three drafts, tightened the stories, decided what to keep and what to delete. The hardest part turned out to be getting rid of the stories I'd worked so hard to write, most of them very special to me, simply because the manuscript was too long. I wanted to keep everything! But I discovered that in order to structure the memoir as a compelling story of my life, I had to make crucial decisions about what stories I included or left out, and in which order.

Not everyone excels at typing, grammar, and editing, so here is where a ghostwriter became invaluable to me. She also provided an outsider's perspective, which my memoir greatly needed in order to become a practical length publishers would accept.

I am happy to announce that my memoir is done at ninety-five thousand words and I am currently seeking an agent. It is through my own experience that I say never to give up on what you really want to achieve in your life. Just as life has many ups and downs, so does memoir writing. You must find a way to overcome the obstacles that may arise. In the end, you will have a complete book of stories for people throughout the world to read, so that they can learn from your experiences and know what it is like to walk the path you traveled.

✳ ✳ ✳ ✳ ✳

KRISHAN BEDI left the tiny village of Punjab, India, in 1961 with only $300 in his pocket. His journey has been a bumpy one, and not without a host of failures and obstacles. He eventually earned a master's degree in industrial engineering from the University of Tennessee and developed a career as a health care executive, becoming successful and ultimately presenting papers at professional health care societies. He has since served as member of several health care–related professional organizations and is currently a member of the board of the Indo-American Society of Peoria.

THE TASTE OF HER MILK

Sarah Conover

I was dragooned into writing my memoir because a dear friend, a former newspaper writer and talk-show host known for her instincts to out a good story, said, "If you don't write your effing memoir, I'm going to." Her last name is Mack. Like the truck. She accomplishes what she sets out to do. Uncertain whether she was joking or truly serious, I conceded. It was time—in truth, decades past time.

She had good reason to be fierce with me. I roosted atop a dramatic and public story but sat in faith that my story and I might just live out our days, feathers unruffled, eyes closed, in our cozy nest. In January 1958, my family tragedy was featured in a *Sports Illustrated* story called "Nature Keeps a Grim Date at Sea." Readers of papers from the *New York Times* to the *Fresno Bee* followed its unfolding for weeks. In March of that same year, *Boats* magazine published a comprehensive investigative piece entitled "The Mystery of

Revonoc." The lede read: "For the first time in ocean sailing history, a superb new boat commanded by a first-class skipper is lost in a Florida storm."

Yet from my twenties onward—until pressed to write my memoir in my midfifties by my friend—I would blithely summarize the story in careless shorthand to others: my parents and grandparents all drowned during a freak storm in the Bermuda Triangle. As my grandfather was a renowned businessman and yachtsman, his disappearance initiated one of the largest marine searches in US history. My father, too, was a champion sailor. Wrapping up the story, I'd add: my childhood was embroiled in a vicious custody battle between my paternal and maternal families that left me adrift, an orphan without a place to feel at home.

People would look to me for some clue about how I felt but would find little in my affect to guide them. In the ensuing awkwardness, either they would blurt, "Oh . . . well, I love stories about the Bermuda Triangle!" or they'd find themselves speechless and we'd change the subject, both of us ignoring the brief, shocking squall that happened to blast through the room.

The thing about the past, say the Irish, is that it's not the past. Tragedy, I now know, lodges itself in the lives of the surviving family and the generations that follow in eerie repetition, convoluted and even compounded. I clearly saw the disaster surge outward in the lives of those immediately touched by the vanishing. I then saw it surge forward into the lives of the next generation. And the next. More drownings, maybe through alcohol, maybe through drugs, maybe through bunkered disassociation. Trauma's power to persist terrifies me yet.

Whatever the guise our particular tragedy took, through writing my memoir, I began to understand that each member of my family was its unique heir. The abrupt chaos triggered an achingly slow unraveling of the before: relationships and loyalties frayed and snapped, lives and fortunes divided. As if the whole chessboard of my Conover clan, the careful moves and placement of pieces over many generations, was tossed up to let rain down helter-skelter, all continuity and order lost.

But no one ever spoke of it. No one held a memorial for the lost. None of my parents' generation could hold this cataclysmic break in their lives. It was a permanent rupture of all they'd loved and believed in. And further reasons for silence: the accident occurred in the Eastern Seaboard's yachting culture, where cocktail hour was the daily vespers. In the fluid gold of a Manhattan, in the cheerful clinking of ice cubes, anguish could be smoothed over much the way a wave retreats to the ocean and leaves the sand momentarily flawless.

A baby boomer, I thought I'd done better than my elders. For starters, I didn't drink. Apparently, however, I had my own ways, even in the therapist's office, to shun the unbearable. "What doesn't come to awareness comes to us as fate," said C. G. Jung. What hadn't come fully to my awareness until I began my memoir was that our story had also written my life's trajectory page by page—its repeating signature etched into every single day since January 2, 1958.

And so it came to be that my brazen friend took me by the shoulders and turned me to face it. The story that wrote my life story. The story that wrote the story of my entire extended family for three generations and counting. The story I've come to call not so much the me-moir, but the we-moir. My friend, my badgering, caring bully, pushed me out of the nest into the sea where past, present, and future still churned. Sink or swim.

When I read the first page and a half of my memoir-to-be to my writing group, a peer, Julia, reached out and put her hand on my forearm. "Stop," she said. "Please. We must let this sink in." Mother of a child with cancer, Julia never lets emotional truths do a drive-by. She will stand in front until it screeches to a stop. She continued to weep.

I was ready to move on and talk craft, but no one spoke. They knew better. They held me unmoving in that space, in that roaring, swallowing sea of silence.

We listened together until I, too, began to cry.

Although I'd struggled with serious depression as an adult—like clockwork during the month of January, when my parents went missing—and although I'd been a therapy client, as well as an ardent student of healing and spirituality, for four decades, it was within these few moments of my memoir-writing group that I saw her. For a mercurial moment. For the first time. The trembling, fearful, tender child who had waited for me. She was an orphan twice abandoned. First by the sea's hand, and then, in not having braved my story, by my own.

Orphan is both noun and verb. Yes, I am an orphan, but I also inhabit the verb *to orphan*, my vigilant psyche practiced at orphaning others in order to bypass the original torment of separation. We orphans want what Keats describes: "The feel of not to feel it/ When there's none to heal it."

But now I knew. Now she knew. We'd seen each other, and I could no longer walk away.

What was her story? *Our* story? I didn't know. I was eighteen months old when my parents and grandparents disappeared. Sadly, I have no memory of them that is mine alone. All that I have gathered is what I have gleaned from interviews, photos, stories, magazines, newspapers, films, anecdotes—all thirdhand.

Whatever imprint is mine alone exists as the truthful tale of my genes: the color of my hair; my father's wide smile;

my squat, muscled body, which loves to dance a wild streak like—I'm told—my mother did.

And, too, whatever I experienced as an infant must also be within. The tethered gaze between my mother and me. Her voice, which I surely recognized straight from the womb. My father's touch as he stroked the tiny wings of my shoulder blades. The smell of my parents. The taste of her milk. My primal known world.

On a recent cross-country flight, I found myself transfixed by a twelve-week-old and his mother sitting next to me. I tried to be surreptitious, but I couldn't—or wouldn't—look away. Gaze fastened upon his mother's eyes, the boy glanced from her face only for the briefest moments of visual exploration elsewhere. Then, without fail, he homed right back in on the touchstone of *mother*. Clearly, in the boy's experience, there was just a single *us*, not two individuals. I stared, full of wonder.

For any human, it's the most exquisite feeling, being an *us*. I remember the experience when I nursed my son and daughter. A complete surrender to undefended presence and love: my body, my arms and breasts, my words and lullabies, my full attention, belonged to them more than to me.

Words are a pitiful fraction of an infant's expansive moment-by-moment experience. During the writing of my memoir, I've finally let myself visualize and feel *my* primal us— my mother, Lori, and me. My father, Larry, and me. I know that somewhere in my psyche, the imprints of remembrance echo. I will not abandon us, this poignant, surprising, and joyful reunion that entering the world of memoir brought about. When I imagine them with me, I feel something like I might if I waded into the world of Monet's water lilies—tranquil pastels tinged with both longing and fulfillment.

I've heard it said that all good writing must be a discovery for the writer and the reader. Perhaps memoir, at its very best, bears out this axiom. I gladly conjure these moments now—the before and after of my family's tragedy. Not just because my friend pushed me into these waters. I do it for all orphans, for myself, and for each person in my close and extended families. To say, *Look!* Really *look.* This *is what happened to us. This is why we still stumble.* I write our story to gather and braid together the threadbare but gleaming ribbons of continuity. I write in order that perhaps my tribe will, at last, no longer be afraid of our legacy but also unafraid of each other.

I write because, eventually, all are orphaned. All are born into a world that is fragile. A world in which everything cherished can vanish in an instant.

✳ ✳ ✳ ✳ ✳

SARAH CONOVER has a BA in religious studies from the University of Colorado and an MFA in poetry from Eastern Washington University, and has authored seven books on world wisdom traditions and the spiritual education of families. She teaches creative writing and Buddhist meditation in Spokane, Washington. A former high school teacher, she was the recipient of US State Department grants that initiated classroom collaborations between students worldwide. Previous to her role in education, she was a social worker for Catholic Family Services, and before that a senior producer at Internews, an international NGO committed to fostering open media. Writing a memoir has finally allowed her, at age sixty, to stop adding to the previous career list, slow down, and simply be amazed with the world. She is the mother of two remarkable progeny who seemed to have dodged the hard stuff of the family legacy.

✳ MARGO JEFFERSON ✳

Author of *Negroland*

BROOKE WARNER: When did you know you wanted to write this memoir, and what was the writing process like for you, in terms of both duration from idea to publication and the drawing-out of your memories to tell your story?

MARGO JEFFERSON: I suspect I knew in 2002. That was the year I wrote and performed a solo theater piece that had early versions of some *Negroland* material. Then I put it away and went back to my *Times* criticism. Writing the Michael Jackson book was a necessary transition, partly because it was my first book and it showed me the kind of sustained tenacity I'd need, and partly because I was writing about a figure—an artist; a series of cultural symbols; a screen for racial, sexual, and gender projections—who stirred complicated and mixed feelings in me. It prodded me to start thinking about how the personal and cultural connect—about what I came to call "cultural memoir." I started *officially* writing the book in 2008, but there were plenty of stops and starts, for reasons internal and external. And you have to find the method, the way of composing, that keeps you going. It took me a while to see that I had to write it in bits and pieces, to shape memory and experience through the disruptions of collage. I needed to violate and interrupt chronology.

BROOKE WARNER: Your title is provocative, putting race forward as the central issue of your memoir. Tell us why you called it *Negroland*, and also what your thoughts are on whether race and ethnicity serve as assets or burdens to authors of color in the current publishing climate.

MARGO JEFFERSON: *Negroland* was meant to evoke and identify a time and place. The time: the early to mid–twentieth century, when the word *Negro* was considered the proper and preferred term. The place: the world of the African American elite in those years, with its many rituals and rules, and the racially fraught, law- and convention-bound world in which all Negroes then lived. And in my Negroland, race was inextricably bound up with gender and class. Whether race, ethnicity, and gender are assets or burdens depends very much on your editor and your publishing house, and on the cultural and social politics of the time. Right now, there is real interest in these experiences and narratives because race and ethnicity and gender are pressing on the consciousness and conscience of the nation. But there can always be—there always have been, historically—retreats, periods in which these subjects seem to become fatiguing to the larger audiences publishers seek. We're still always at risk of falling out of fashion, so to speak.

BROOKE WARNER: You were admonished as a child, as I think many people of your generation were, not to "tell your secrets to strangers," as you write in the book. Did those voices carry through into your memoir writing? Did you hear echoes of the warning not to tell, and, if so, how did you overcome them?

MARGO JEFFERSON: These cautionary voices followed me as I wrote. I came to realize that they could be useful to the dramatic conflict and tension, both inside the narrative and also between my readers and me. That's why I began the book by summoning those voices from the deep. And I knew I'd be much more at their mercy if I didn't name them.

✳

BROOKE WARNER: What is it about your book, in your opinion, that has struck a chord with the media and with readers? To what do you attribute your success?

MARGO JEFFERSON: That's hard to answer. It may be the fact that I speak in more than one voice, adopt various masks and personae. Does that let readers with varied experiences enter the narrative where and when it most compels them? I think so. But the variations keep their curiosities on the move. I hope they can't settle into just one kind of response or identification. And think it matters a lot that class, gender, and race are constantly entwined.

✳

BROOKE WARNER: What is the magic of memoir for you?

MARGO JEFFERSON: The intricacy of a single life moving within yet also apart from culture and society.

✳ ✳ ✳ ✳ ✳

MARGO JEFFERSON is a former book, theater, and arts critic at the *New York Times* and a professor at Columbia University's School of the Arts. She received her BA from Brandeis University, from which she graduated *cum laude*, and her MS from the Columbia University Graduate School of Journalism. She became an associate editor at *Newsweek* in 1973 and stayed at the magazine until 1978. She then served as an assistant professor at the Department of Journalism and Mass Communication at New York University from 1979 to 1983 and from 1989 to 1991. She joined the *Times* in 1993, initially as a book reviewer, then went on to win the Pulitzer Prize for Criticism. She published *On Michael Jackson* in 2005. In 2016, *Negroland* won the National Book Critics Circle Award for Autobiography.

THE EMPTY SPACE

Leza Lowitz

I never thought I'd publish a memoir. Or be a mother. Or open a yoga studio in a foreign country—Japan. But I've done all three after years of trying. And failing. Or maybe because of that. The Japanese have a term: "the nobility of failure." It means holding your head up high when you've done your best, even if things don't quite work out. The yogis have a term for it, too: *surrender*. Writers must have an expression for it, but I don't know what it is. Samuel Beckett comes to mind: "Ever tried. Ever failed. No matter. Try Again. Fail again. Fail better."

I try a lot. I fail a lot. And sometimes I succeed. But it wasn't always like that. Moving to Japan forced me to see myself differently—as someone new, someone I could invent, or reinvent. Japan helped me enter the empty space of potential. A space where I could try and fail and grow. And fail better. My memoir came from that empty space, which the

Japanese also have a name for: *ma*. It's the way they describe the white around a scroll on an ink painting, or the blank space around a haiku on the page, or the air between ropes hung from two sacred rocks in the ocean, or the sound of silence. *Ma*. The universal name for *mother*. The emptiness I'm learning to embrace, even to love. I thank my memoir for that.

I always dreamed of being a writer. Writing was the healing balm that helped me feel less isolated as a teenager, when I often felt unheard or misunderstood. I wrote in little-girly locked diaries, then journals, then college notebooks. Later, I published poems and stories in small literary magazines. I wrote book reviews for newspapers. Eventually, I translated other people's writing and sent my own out into the world. Sometimes a piece was published here and there, but that brass ring—a published book of my own—eluded me.

Was a writer someone who wrote or someone who published? In order to make the dream real, I believed, it had to be shared. But what if the world wasn't all that interested in this "sharing"? Hundreds of rejection slips later, I let the dream slip away. I had to make a living. Writing took a backseat, and I moved to Japan.

There, it was possible to parlay an MA in creative writing into gainful employment. I met a Japanese man and fell in love. I studied yoga, which helped me break down the walls I'd built around myself. I discovered I was an expatriate in my very own skin. Yoga led me back into my body, which was like an unexplored world. Since I love to travel, I thought, *Here's my next trip*. My bags were packed. I wrote a book of yoga poems. It was published. Then another.

Yoga taught me how to change myself, to forgive myself and those who might have harmed me. Those lessons spread as I opened a yoga studio in Tokyo and created a home for others, though I myself was far from home. We offered community classes for charity, though I'd been warned they wouldn't fly in status-conscious Japan. I didn't listen. I offered partner yoga, although everyone said Japanese people would never touch strangers. Again, I didn't listen. And they did. And they laughed and smiled, and partner yoga became a *thing*. I knew that what had broken down the barriers for me and so many others was universal. If you're lonely, reach out to someone else. Our yoga teaches us to surrender to everything—even our long-cherished notions of being singular. Soon we had a *sangha*, and I had a new home.

Then, after a decade of trying to start a family, I understood that my child was not going to come from my womb—it was going to come from my heart. We applied to adopt, though Japan was notoriously difficult to adopt in and I was forty-four and my husband was forty-eight, ages that made us a low priority among the many waiting. I'd been hearing a child call to me for years, and the voice wouldn't go away. I understood that I'd have to fight for this child, as I'd fought for everything in my life.

I bore down. I was not a victim. I was a *yogini*—a warrior of surrender and acceptance. I told myself if I got to the end of the road and my child didn't come, I'd find other ways to be a mother. I'd embrace the quest as another practice of finding the balance between will and surrender. I'd embrace the *ma*.

From then on, when I went to my meditation cushion, instead of waiting for my child's voice to come to me, I spoke directly to him.

HOUSE OF DREAMS

The more I practiced yoga, the more the experience of quieting down and listening to the breath, the body, and the silences between breaths began to resonate in life off the mat, too. I stopped being so harsh toward myself and others. I learned to embrace uncertainty, or at least to stop struggling with it. I learned to practice gratitude, to see the many blessings I had in life. To see the open spaces, rather than the closed.

Except in one area: writing.

I didn't even realize it until a friend suggested I write a memoir about my long road to motherhood—how I adopted and adapted in Japan. *Good idea,* I thought. And then I couldn't. Because when I sat down to write, all the old demons I thought I'd slayed came back to party in my head.

Why would anyone else care? How dare you think you have anything to say!

And so on.

My mind was too crowded. Tokyo was too crowded. There was not enough space to think, to create, to *be*.

Then I looked outside the window and saw my mother-in-law's teahouse in our garden. Kyoko had spent her inheritance on serenity, built herself this small rush-mat refuge. She lived her best life as a mother and wife, savoring both the sweetness of the cake that melts in the throat and the bitterness of the tea that washes it down. The teahouse—now a museum of Celadon tea bowls, brown-flaked earthenware cups, iron pots red with rust—was her haven from husband, kitchen, and children. No one had used it in the decade since she had passed away. Not even me, though I'd inherited the place, which, like all good teahouses, had a name: the House of Dreams.

That's it! I thought. *It will be my writing room, a room of my own.* A century earlier, Thoreau—who lived in a hut in the woods—had written: "A man is rich in proportion to the number of things which he can afford to let alone." With a teahouse in Tokyo, I'd struck gold. There was much I wanted to "let alone."

I took a pillow, notebook, and pen—a computer seemed

sacrilege to such a place—and crouched down through the *nijiriguchi* (crawl-in entrance) to meditate and quell the demons. But the once-beautiful place had been neglected, had fallen into disrepair. The windows rattled; it smelled of mildew and earth. The clay walls were crumbling. Spiders had taken over. There was very little difference between outside and in.

I tried to focus. But without the ring of the telephone, the doorbell, and even electricity, the hut was too quiet. I couldn't write a word. So I did what I did in the "outside" world: procrastinated. I swept the tatami, dusted, lit incense, put flowers on my personal, improvised altar. I breathed life back into my mother-in-law's sacred space.

But still no memoir emerged.

I'd always blamed my inability to write on lack of time, space, and quiet. Now that I had all three, what was there to blame?

Days turned into weeks turned into years. I wrote nothing. And not a Zen nothing—*nothing*. Time after time, I went back to the blank page. But it remained empty. My mind, on the other hand, was crowded with the demons. The critics. The committee.

Why should you write a memoir? Who would care? What's your story, anyway?

If you've faced the blank page, you know all too well that writing reveals our inner critic, which is often our harshest voice. In the same way, I might once have come to my yoga mat with set ideas about who I was and what I can and cannot do. But by the end of a yoga practice, I'd have more compassion for my imperfect self, more gratitude and appreciation for all that I do have. Why couldn't I face the blank page with such compassion?

I considered my friend's suggestion—to write about how

a nice Jewish girl got to Japan, fell in love with the grandson of a yakuza, and created a rainbow family in a homogeneous country. Did I even know myself how this had happened? How had I come to adopt in Japan, my adopted country, and make a home for others through my yoga studio? How had I come to find a home in myself? Or had I?

Seasons changed. The clay walls let in moisture when it rained, baked when it was hot. I meditated on the flowers for each season—camellia, hydrangea, cherry blossom, a universe in their petals—just as my mother-in-law had done. The House of Dreams was my haven, too, but I didn't need to run away from my husband or our beloved child. Clearly, I was still running away from myself.

One day, I smelled the incense she used to burn, Kyoto jasmine. Like an animal covering itself with the smell of the dead to disguise itself from predators, she'd infused me with her wisdom, woman to woman. It floated out under tables, in cupboards, in wooden boxes and tea bowls, into the deep recesses of the tatami mats. It seeped into my skin. And in this way, she lived on.

I'd always resisted marriage and motherhood as too constricting. And now I was in one of the most constricting countries in the world, married to a Japanese man, carving out a little oasis of California calm in the center of the city. I'd uncovered my own impulse, late in midlife, to be a mother. I'd fought to adopt a child, to become a mother in a foreign country. Why? All because she had challenged me to marry her son as she lay dying. Because she was so certain that it was our destiny. That we loved each other and belonged together, so what was holding us back?

We took the plunge.

A decade later, I wanted to become a mother, to parent a child with the man I loved. We were blessed with a child.

She knew it all.

No one else had ever looked me in the eye and insisted that I stay a particular course. I still remember what she offered me: her own full gaze. And in that gaze, she saw me wholly. And I saw myself.

But I'd lost that vision.

I was still scared, afraid of being at home in my own skin. Afraid that my marriage would combust, as my parents' had. Afraid I'd never discover and be able to live my own dreams. But the truth was, none of that was reality. It was an illusion, past fears. None of it applied to my life anymore. It was time to let that imprint go.

One day, I hit upon an idea. I took my yoga mat into the teahouse and started to move. Could the blank page and the yoga mat be one?

I decided to tell Kyoko what had happened in the decade she'd been gone. To write a memoir for her. And while I went through my sun salutations with a notepad by my side, when I wrung out my fears in twists and flooded my heart with energy through backbends, I realized that the House of Dreams was a construct. Nature was here first, with its own cacophony and chaos. The original inhabitants of the garden had arranged their lives around this quaint obstruction. I'd battled them at first, but they were resilient. No human was going to win out over nature. I surrendered.

I told Kyoko of my yearnings, my desires, my failures, my hopes and dreams. I decided to tell the story without trying to prove anything, be anyone, or make a point. I wrote as an *offering*. A prayer. A thank-you note.

Make no mistake—what I wrote was a mess. It was full of holes and dirt and crooked lines that made no sense. It was drenched in *wabi-sabi*, full of imperfection and disrepair. And that was okay. I surrendered to all of it, breath by breath, line by line. Throwing words out into the empty space. Seeing what stuck, what was worth preserving. Being open, receptive. Surrendering. Considering the fact that maybe *failure* was the wrong word, the wrong perspective. Maybe a better way to look at it was *acceptance*. Even *grace*. Then crafting the memoir as I'd crafted my life—not leaving out the pain. Which I came to see as beauty in its own, very human, vulnerable way.

To be a yogi is to be in a constant state of becoming. To be a writer is to capture that "becoming" state in words. Yoga helps us to open our hearts and recover our emotional core and connection to the world through breath, movement, and awareness. Poetry, called the "original breath," seeks to do the same through words, images, and sound. Can all writing be poetry? Can the world be poetry? I wanted to say yes.

Humbled, I began to notice the different strains of the frog's song, the varying melodies of the cicada's cry, and the unique designs of each spider's web. I took a page from Issa, who'd observed the world in this small universe, which expanded his own:

Every creeping thing,
Listen!
The bell of impermanence.

I began to track the comings and goings of my tiny roommates. I got out of their way. And I discovered that what I'd mistaken for silence was in fact a symphony. In the rainy season, the frogs croaked. In the summer, the cicadas cried. On the humid days, mosquitoes feasted. And in winter, spiders spun their webs and hunted. We coinhabited this house, giving it a new life. It became an incubation room.

And then one day, my friend who'd encouraged me decided

to work on her own memoir. So I left the rarefied atmosphere of the House of Dreams and sat down in that most ordinary of community coffeehouses: Starbucks. We women writers met each other for timed writings, critique groups, kvetch sessions. I wrote for them. They wrote for me.

And I finished my memoir.

And the empty space became a fullness. A celebration. A place to listen and be heard.

✳ ✳ ✳ ✳ ✳

The Empty Space © Leza Lowitz 2016. "House of Dreams" appeared in different form in Wingspan, ANA's *in-flight magazine, in May 2013.*

LEZA LOWITZ (www.lezalowitz.com) is an award-winning author of more than twenty books in many genres. Five of her titles have been number-one Amazon best sellers. Her new memoir, *Here Comes the Sun: A Journey to Adoption in 8 Chakras*, about her journey to motherhood over two oceans, two decades, and two thousand yoga poses, was one of them. Her YA novel about Japan's March 11, 2011, earthquake and tsunami, *Up from the Sea*, was another. Her perennial best seller is *Yoga Poems: Lines to Unfold By*.

Lowitz's essays have appeared in the *New York Times Motherlode* blog, *Yoga Journal, Yoga Journal Japan, Yoga International, Elephant Journal, Shambhala Sun, The Best Buddhist Writing 2011*, the *Huffington Post, Wanderlust. com, Origin, Mantra*, the *Manifest-Station*, the *Japan Times, Art in America*, and many other publications. She lives with her Japanese husband, young son, and two wolf dogs in Tokyo, where she also runs a popular yoga studio.

I'M RUNNING CIRCLES AROUND YOU

Nadine Kenney Johnstone

It's September, and I'm at a Starbucks in Chicago with my friend Kate, who's talking about her MFA program. Between her girlie tone and her skinny limbs, she's so damn sweet and innocent that she's rarely seen as a threat, but there's a reason why grad schools competed over her.

We're sitting on high stools, and she's playing with the sleeve of her coffee cup.

"So, we got assigned a story last week," she says. "And right away, I go home and work on it and finish it."

"Of course," I tease, and push my straw out of its wrapper.

"Then, yesterday," she says, "I'm talking to this girl in my class, and she's like, 'I haven't even started my story yet.'" Kate bugs out her eyes in disbelief. "I smiled at her," she continues. "But in my head, I was like, *I'm running circles around you.*"

We laugh hard, and the lady next to us looks up from her laptop, annoyed. I take a sip of my drink and lower my voice. "So, I'm not the only competitive weirdo out there?"

Kate shakes her head, smiling. "Nope," she says. "I'm competing with everyone all the time. Sometimes they don't even know it."

That afternoon, while jogging, I think about what Kate said. And even though it sounds a bit, well, aggressive, all of us who want to progress in our passions share that competitive nature. Don't we? Even now, while running on the lake path, I set my sights on the ponytail a few yards ahead and switch my Pandora station to Jay-Z. Then I pick up my pace until I pass her.

I write at cafés in Ravenswood, like Lillstreet and A Perfect Cup, but the majority of my work happens at the window counter of my local Starbucks. Just as I can't run on a treadmill at a gym, I can't write alone in my apartment. In order to be creative, I need to be surrounded by noise, by action. People need to be cranking the espresso machine and flipping through the newspaper and discussing business over dark roasts.

I write two days a week and set up my laptop next to my friend Stef. She's a stay-at-home mom who writes every morning while her daughter is at preschool. That's four hours a day, plus revising on the weekends. When we start typing, I feel the pressure to be as productive as she is.

If I procrastinate by doing necessary but nonwriting things, like checking work e-mails and grading papers, she chips away at her novel and I think, *She's running circles around me.*

So I close Gmail and type until my pace matches hers. On the days when Starbucks preps to close and I'm still typing away, immersed in an essay, I slide an imaginary gold medal around my neck.

In any writing session or run, there are good days and bad. Some days I hit the lake path at Irving Park and the fall air is perfectly crisp and I have crazy energy and Pandora is playing fast rap and I make it to Belmont in a blink and I breathe in the air and I look at the boats and I feel so damn alive.

Some days I write at Lillstreet and they're baking quiche and pumpkin pie and I'm surrounded by handmade jewelry and pottery and I'm scrawling in my journal like a madwoman and Fleetwood Mac is singing songs in the same mood as the essay I'm writing and I'm in the Zone with a capital Z.

And then there are the other days.

Every step of my jog is lead. It's rainy. My breath labors. Everyone on the path—even the sixty-year-old guy in short shorts—is passing me. I can't appreciate the misty skyline because I'm staring at the puddles beneath my soggy shoes.

Those are the same days when I grumble over my $400 monthly MFA loan payments. My Word doc is blank. It's like I've never written a single sentence. The basics of a scene have escaped me. A million responsibilities are pressing in on the precious hour I've given myself to write. My agent forwards me yet another near-miss from an editor who loved my memoir but couldn't convince her team to buy it because there's "not a big enough market," which really means that I don't have enough Facebook followers.

Those days suck.

But here's the thing about running and writing that I take solace in: neither is a fad; neither is something I do only when inspired.

Some days I might pass everyone, and some days everyone might pass me. But I'm going to keep returning to the path, because there's always one ponytail to set my sights on—and it belongs to the me who wanted to sleep in and skip my run, the me who wanted to relax instead of revising.

No matter what, when my foot hits the pavement and my fingers strike the keyboard, I'm still running circles around her.

✳ ✳ ✳ ✳ ✳

The circle running paid off and **NADINE KENNEY JOHN-STONE**'s memoir, Of *This Much I'm Sure,* is forthcoming from She Writes Press in the spring of 2017. She teaches English at Loyola University and received her MFA from Columbia College in Chicago. Her work has been featured in *Chicago* magazine, *The Moth, PANK,* and various anthologies. Nadine is a writing coach and presents at conferences internationally. She lives near Chicago with her family. Visit her at nadinekenneyjohnstone.com.

NO MORE SECRETS AND SILENCE

Lynette Benton

Go to where the silence is and say something.
—Investigative journalist Amy Goodman

A ll memoir writers confront common challenges—excavating memories; researching and documenting names, dates, and places; separating vital information from chaff; and developing a narrative voice, thread, and arc—all to coax forth, record, and shape the soul of their personal stories.

But every memoir presents its own *particular* problems as well. It's a testament to the creativity and persistence of memoirists that we discover strategies for overcoming these unique challenges so we can tell our stories in ways that resonate with readers.

A unique challenge in writing my own memoir, *My Mother's Money*, was that two of my central characters were, for all practical purposes, mute. My mother, as a result of a stroke, was unable to speak; my brother was unwilling to speak.

My African American family had endured slavery and Jim Crow rule—eras when an ability to keep silent and keep secrets could mean the difference between life and death. At first I thought those historical experiences accounted for my relatives' evasiveness, until I realized I didn't know families of any race or ethnicity that encouraged frankness to explode like a grenade among their members. But people of color often edit ourselves while speaking or, on occasion, consider it prudent not to speak at all. We feel extra pressure to protect our plans, our personal affairs, and our inner selves from the scrutiny of the dominant group. We suspect they won't understand our perspective or agree with it. In my family, that need to hide information was so strong that it translated into secretiveness even *within* the family. What if the private facts of our lives escaped through the loose lips of a mole among us?

Thus, an embedded tradition among my relatives was lack of candor, downright caginess. A response to a question might be lobbed back like a tennis ball, aimed deliberately out of reach, or it might boldly be ignored.

I should make it clear that nobody would describe my family members as silent or even quiet. They actually were exceptionally talkative. And yet in my adulthood, it struck me that the purpose of all the talking was not to reveal but to conceal. So I shouldn't have been surprised that while I searched for my mother's money, my direct questions were met with misdirection or, more often, silence.

A second peculiar circumstance I faced was that the events I was recording and deconstructing in my memoir were still unfolding. But even though I didn't know the final outcome of my story when I was working on the narrative, I knew what the ending would be. It would address all that I was learning about the history of secrets and silence in my family and the damage they inflicted. *My Mother's Money* is a memoir about my family, shown through the lens of money, a story that emerges from my ancestors' costly silences on the subject of their finances. The effects of that silence were reflected in every step of my search for my mother's money, until finally I was able to ferret out some truths about my family members' relationships to money and to one another.

I sat on my story for years, until I could figure out how to tell it with two central characters who were incommunicado. Knowing I wanted to tell the story, throughout those waiting years, I engaged in compulsive note taking. In addition, in my journal I meticulously documented the obstacles that arose during my fifteen-year struggle with banks and a series of attorneys to track down my mother's money. The journal format determined my choice of a chronological structure for the narrative, which would follow my quest naturally through time. However, in the early chapters, I alternated between forward movement of the narrative and background chapters.

For example, in order for readers to understand my mother's failure to make her children's inheritance easy to claim, I determined that it would help them to know the history of legacies in my mother's family. So one chapter describes bequests my mother's ancestors made in the past, including how an elderly relative of my mother's left a half-sister a strip of land narrower than a driveway, situated between two houses owned by other people. For readers to appreciate the history of extreme silence in my family that my brother in his own way continued (to my siblings' and my detriment), I recounted an incident from decades earlier. My mother and my sister had arrived for a lunch at my mother's highly educated brother's house, to which they had been invited, only to find him wearing a sign around his neck that read I'M NOT TALKING TODAY.

Everything about my family fascinates me, consumes me. Not a day goes by that family members, whether alive or dead, don't haunt my consciousness. And it's this haunting, this obsession, that makes my memoir writing possible, makes it necessary. Pat Conroy, author of *The Great Santini*, wrote, "Some of us are designated rememberers." I would say some of us are *doomed* to be rememberers. But we are more than that; we are *investigators*, uncovering and untangling what many consider better left undisturbed. They'd rather we didn't disinter and deface the past, partly because their memories are at odds with our own, partly to protect the family's image. I didn't want opposing opinions to stifle my point of view.

But fear and doubts tortured me. Growing up, I'd felt as if I lived under a gag order, forced to mute any observations that my mother had not vetted, accepted, or originally pronounced. Speaking the truth about, say, the prominent use of alcohol by both of my parents, not just by my father, was not tolerated for a moment. The habit of having my point of view muffled when I was a child didn't politely take a backseat when, as an adult, I wanted to write about my family. The childhood apprehension I thought I'd overcome skulked about the edges of my consciousness, frequently interfering with my writing, even though both of my parents were, by that time, dead.

I asked myself what I could tell and, more important, what I *should* tell. How much privacy did I owe my characters, who also happened to be my family? Was there a hero, a villain? Was I being fair? Was it okay to blurt out this story about my family and its unflattering financial idiosyncrasies on the permanence of paper? Yet, like a tattletale, there I was, deciding to blab our business all over the place. Would I be ostracized as a pariah among these people who prized secrecy so dearly?

I was beginning to find out how difficult it can be to write the truth.

At first, I mistakenly thought the process of writing a memoir was three-tiered: living the experience, recalling the experience, and *re*living the experience (the last of which seems an unfortunate but unavoidable aspect of the process).

All three phases were distressing. Over years of writing and revising successive drafts, I was often mystified, frustrated, or enraged. Few of us would willingly undertake the grueling task of writing a memoir if we hadn't survived hell to tell our story. That's largely what memoir means to me: living to tell about it. I felt what Rigoberto González described in his essay "Memory Lessons": "Every hardship longed to be documented."

Don't all memoirists consider our past the stuff of stories? If our personal histories were commonplace, there'd be no need to write about them. I certainly wished nothing in my past merited a book. But I suffer from a compulsion to try to derive meaning from intense experiences that randomly fall to my lot—and to imprint my findings on the page.

As I wrote, I found out that memoir writing involves more than just the three levels I'd initially imagined. Besides enduring, recalling, and reliving events through the writing, we memoirists bludgeon our way through the silence that threatens to suffocate us. If we're successful, we not only find the object of our search, as I did, but also gain enough understanding to extract meaning from a complex and muddled collection of events. Our new insights often aren't pleasant; our epiphanies can be excruciating. But ultimately it can be as satisfying for us to make sense of the truth as we see it as it would be to suck air into our lungs after a long submersion in the sea.

For me, writing a memoir was not so much a matter of coming to hard and fast conclusions as it was about exploring and presenting what happened and what it meant.

Before I got down to the task of writing my memoir, I secured critical resources for the journey ahead. Besides reading a dozen fine memoirs—among them *A Three Dog Life*; *Eat, Pray, Love*; *Devotion*; and *Volunteer Slavery* (all by American writers), as well as all those by the British author Diana Athill—I was guided and buoyed by two anthologies about memoir writing. Both focused on writing about family; both were invaluable in providing insight into what others had learned through their own memoir-writing experiences. Most important, they proved that other writers had grappled with—and found ways to resolve—the same issues I would encounter.

Women Writing on Family: Tips on Writing, Teaching and Publishing, which I consider a handbook for memoir writers, addresses craft, finding time to write, doing research, and much more. It even covers ways for writers to handle their ambivalence about deceased family members, as Carol Hawkins shows in her essay, "Telling Our Truth: Writing the Legacy of the Dead." With a total of fifty-five essays, this book also contains a whole section called "Writing Exercises and Strategies," which can act as warm-ups or solutions when you're stumped.

Aware that exposing and interpreting my family's behavior could provoke a libel suit (yes, those can crop up in the production of a memoir), I found Martha Engber's chapter, "Family Secrets: How to Reveal What Matters Without Getting Sued, or Shunned," particularly useful. For those of us who are exposing what others want to obscure, Engber explains the risks memoirists take and the legal protections offered to both the memoir writer and those she writes about. Unsure about how vulnerable to a lawsuit I might be, all during the writing I planned to follow Engber's advice to consult an entertainment or intellectual property attorney before publishing my memoir.

Another important written resource was the book *Family Trouble: Memoirists on the Hazards and Rewards of Revealing Family*, which consists of personal essays that examine the subtleties and nuances of writing memoir, such as ethnicity, gender identity, and freeing ourselves from our fear of exposing secrets. The essays reminded me that what we worry will be offensive to those we write about often isn't. Unfortunately, the opposite also holds true.

In *Family Trouble*, Dinty W. Moore writes in his essay, "The Deeper End of the Quarry: Fiction, Nonfiction, and the Family Dilemma," that "more people have been harmed . . . by secrets and concealment than by candor and revelation." In my own case, I had become weary of colluding in family secrets and silences. I *had* to speak out, and Moore's statement emboldened me.

In addition to critical textual resources, I assembled a loose posse of friends and family members to read drafts and keep me going. Without these friends (one of whom is a writer and editor), my quiet husband, and his outspoken sisters, I wouldn't have been able to muster the emotional stamina to complete the work. They reminded me of incidents I had forgotten. They listened intently to my increasingly surprising discoveries. They leaned toward me over cups of coffee and tea and asked hard, *hard* questions that forced me to confront my own silences on various aspects of my narrative. When working on my memoir started to feel as if it would be my undoing, they actively supported me and cheered me on.

I wrote the toughest parts of the manuscript in short

stretches. My husband used to place his hands on my shoulders and gently steer me back into my study. "Just work on it for five minutes," he'd say. "You can do five minutes." He was right. Even five minutes moved me closer to the finish line.

To keep my commitment to writing my memoir from withering like neglected grass in the heat of August, I glanced again and again at the words by the National Association of Memoir Writers that I had pinned on the bulletin board above my desk: *Be Brave. Tell Your Story.*

It's astonishing how often the word *courage* and its synonyms appear in the same sentence with the term *memoir writing*. During the writing of my memoir, I had to summon courage on a daily basis—courage to tell my story the way I felt it happened, and courage to shatter the silence and replace it with words I hope others can wrap around themselves like a comforting cloak of recognition.

This essay, "No More Secrets and Silence," won first place among all the essays submitted for consideration in The Magic of Memoir.

LYNETTE BENTON's memoir, *My Mother's Money*, was a finalist in the 2014 memoir-writing contest sponsored by SheWrites.com and Serendipity Literary Agency. Her work has appeared in *More magazine Online, Skirt!, Brevity, The Arlington Advocate, Lexington Minuteman*, Purpleclover .com, *Grub Daily, Women Writing, Women's Books*, and many other online and paper publications. Benton also teaches and coaches writing students aged nine to ninety-three. Her advice to writers appears on her website, Tools and Tactics for Writers.

✴ DANI SHAPIRO ✴

Author of *Devotion*

BROOKE WARNER: Memoir is a fraught genre that people seem to love to hate, that's difficult to sell, and yet it's unbelievably popular and you've written two beautiful memoirs yourself that have been widely read. How do you make sense of this push-pull we see with memoir as a genre?

DANI SHAPIRO: Part of the push-pull has to do with some misconceptions about the literary form of memoir. Readers often confuse memoir with autobiography. Autobiography is the story of a life—presumably a life of public importance—that captures the reader's interest not necessarily because of its literary merit (though certainly some autobiographies have great literary merit) but because of fascination with the author. We read because we want to know more; we want—and feel entitled to—all the details of that life. Memoir is something else entirely. Memoir is a story the writer carves out of her own life, hewing to memory as her tool of illumination. There is no presumption that the story is important or definitive. This is why it's possible for a writer to write multiple memoirs.

BROOKE WARNER: What compelled you to write a second memoir?

DANI SHAPIRO: *Devotion* tapped me on the shoulder. One afternoon, I literally saw the word floating in the air in front of me—nothing like this has happened before or since—and I understood that the midlife, existential crisis I was suffering from, as a mother of a young child who was constantly asking me questions about what I believed, was in fact a spiritual crisis. And the only way I know to discover the contents of my own mind is to write my way into it and through it. And so I embarked on a kind of inquiry, detective work, to dig into my own history—I had been raised in a religious home—and my current life, in which I had turned my back on spiritual questions that now haunted me. It wasn't what I wanted to do—I wanted to write another novel!—but it was what I *had* to do. I've learned to follow the most insistent creative urges, whether they're welcome or not.

BROOKE WARNER: How did you come up with the structure for *Devotion*, and did you map it out in advance or, rather, follow the threads where they led you?

DANI SHAPIRO: *Devotion* is structured in a puzzle-like, mosaic way, in 102 brief chapters. The structure also announced itself with great insistence. I wasn't happy about it at all. Up until that point, I had written traditional narratives that followed a largely chronological storytelling form. I knew how to do that. What the hell were these pieces? Honestly, I was very worried and wondered if anyone would want to read this thing. But I didn't feel I had any choice, and I knew enough not to force some other, more palatable structure on the book. I came to understand—much later—that the mosaic structure mirrored the spiritual journey itself: full of starts, stops, doubts, misgivings. To have forced that material into a graceful arc would have been untruthful. The very process of writing it—of stopping and starting, pausing, waiting, cultivating patience, sitting with the unknown—was part of the creative process. But, of course, it's easy to be articulate about this in retrospect. I think most writers would agree that when we're in the middle of a piece of work, we have very little idea what we're doing, and it's only when we're engaged in talking about it after we've finished that we begin to understand what it is we've done.

BROOKE WARNER: What is your advice for people who struggle with their memories while writing their memoir, either because they can't remember or because their memory feels unreliable?

DANI SHAPIRO: Here we have one of the great questions that harkens back to the love-hate relationship with memoir you referred to earlier—and to the prevalent misunderstanding of the form. Let's think about memory for a moment. Is memory reliable? Do we remember the same events in the same way each time they come to mind? Neurobiologists understand the mutability of memory—the way a memory transforms each time we remember it, on a cellular level. So, in order to write memoir, we are already operating on constantly shifting ground. The work of memoir is not to get it "right" but to hew to memory as closely as possible and to discover what happened—or, as my friend Andre Dubus III recently put it, *what the fuck happened*—and, in putting the pieces together, to begin to make order out of chaos, sense out of senselessness, perhaps even beauty out of pain. Remembering begets remembering. The more we incline our minds in the direction of memory, the more we are eventually able to summon—without straining, without forcing, but in a wakeful daydream. I would urge writers who are struggling with these issues to go take a long walk. Seriously. Or listen to music. Or play music, if they play an instrument. Or sit in quiet contemplation on a park bench or in a cathedral. And also to set aside the tormented, self-censoring internal chatter that insists that the whole endeavor is doomed.

✳

BROOKE WARNER: What is the magic of memoir for you?

DANI SHAPIRO: When I dig mercilessly and with great, determined effort into the deepest parts of my own humanness and find the courage to articulate what wasn't accessible to me before—and when that process slowly transforms the mute, the unsaid, into a resonant story; when fear, shame, longing, regret, grief, joy, desire, and fierce love all become tangible; when I spin my life into something larger than myself; when I'm alone in my writing room on a day when I'm managing, in the words of Virginia Woolf, to put the severed pieces together, that's the magic for me.

✳ ✳ ✳ ✳ ✳

DANI SHAPIRO is the best-selling author of the memoirs *Still Writing*, *Devotion*, and *Slow Motion* and of five novels, including *Black & White* and *Family History*. Her work has appeared in the *New Yorker*, *Granta*, *Tin House*, *One Story*, *ELLE*, the *New York Times Book Review*, the op-ed pages of the *New York Times*, and the *Los Angeles Times* and has been broadcast on *This American Life*. She was also Oprah Winfrey's guest on *Super Soul Sunday*. Dani has taught in the writing programs at Columbia, NYU, the New School, and Wesleyan University; she is cofounder of the Sirenland Writers Conference in Positano, Italy. A contributing editor at *Condé Nast Traveler*, Dani lives with her family in Litchfield County, Connecticut.

BE BRAVE AND SAY THEIR NAMES

Kelly Kittel

My husband, Andy, and I met as Peace Corps volunteers in Jamaica, and my mom dubbed us East Meets West, since he hails from the coast of Oregon and I from the coast of Rhode Island. A decade later, when our fourth child, Noah, was born, we had good careers, loving families, and feet planted firmly on the prescriptive path that defines success in our society. We had two girls and two boys, matched sets, and life marched along as expected. Until the dreadful day when fifteen-month-old Noah was run over by my sixteen-year-old niece in my in-laws' driveway. The world crashed over us like a tsunami and spit us out on a foreign shore, gasping for breath. Nine months later, we buried our fifth child, another son, named Jonah, who was stillborn as a result of medical error, and the world rolled right on over us, leaving us crushed in its wake.

I always knew I'd write a book someday, but I certainly never dreamed that life would place this particular tale in my hands. I could barely speak, much less write, so I carried it inside me, cleaved to my heart, while I learned how to breathe again. There's a group for bereaved parents called the Compassionate Friends, and in one of my many desperate attempts to find my voice, Andy and I attended their conference, where I asked a renowned grief author, "How long should you wait to write your story?"

"Ten years," she said.

And so I waited.

I was raised to believe that family is the most important thing. Mine hails from the *Mayflower*, after all, and I spent my childhood tromping around cemeteries behind Mom and my grandmother Mimi. Our ancestors were so much a part of our lives, I half expected them to show up for Thanksgiving dinner each year. I am not a patient person, but life somehow marched on and the story that would become my memoir, *Breathe*, continued to grow. Our niece rejected accountability for her actions, her mother evicted us from the house we were renting, and most of our extended family moved to denial and blame.

I'd always written lengthy holiday letters, and after reading them, my friends and family would say, "You're such a good writer. When are you going to write a book?" And for years I joked, "First, I have to decide how many family members I want to alienate." But as time went by and the story evolved, most of them became aliens without my writing even one word.

If it hadn't been my life, I would never have believed it. And it was no joke, either. *Breathe* is not only a story about losing our sons but also a story about being forced to redefine family and relinquish members who are hurting you.

We moved from west to east and cut our ties, using miles and words instead of shears. I had five miscarriages and gave birth to two more children, Isaiah and Bella. We successfully sued my doctor for Jonah's wrongful death, but our family was also put on trial when my niece sat in the gallery and her mother took the witness stand to testify against us.

My second daughter, Christiana, is now a forester and has taught me that trees self-prune, cutting off nutrients to the branches that are diseased or failing and no longer contributing to the growth of the whole. Likewise, we ultimately had to prune our own family tree.

During that decade of waiting, the ocean became my first audience. I am happiest when I have sand between my toes, and Andy and I took hundreds of beach walks, kicking shells along the tide line as we tried to figure out what had happened to us and to our life as we'd formerly known it. Our voices tumbled out in waves followed by long intervals of silence, ebbing and flowing with the tides. We rubbed the jagged edges of words like death and denial between our bloodied fingers until they were worn smooth like sea glass, until they hurt less.

When the tenth anniversary of Noah's death was at last on the horizon, I set to work. It was Easter of 2006, and it seemed like a good time for resurrections. I figured I had a year to write my story and a few months to edit and publish it, and, in my blessed ignorance, I thought that was a sensible plan. Our medical malpractice trial had been videotaped, so the first thing I did was sit in front of the TV and transcribe seven full days of the proceedings, word by word. Following that lengthy task, I wrote a first draft, which weighed in at over six hundred pages and contained neither one scene nor one line of dialogue. I realized I had an Everest-size mountain of things to learn, so we marked Noah's anniversary by climbing a peak in New Hampshire, instead of heading out on a book tour.

Seven is the most significant number in the Bible, representing completeness and perfection. It took God seven days to make the whole world, and it took me seven years to write and publish *Breathe*. Seven years during which we moved again, to Costa Rica, and again, to Oregon, and finally back to Rhode Island. Seven years during which the story grew inside me, waking me in the wee hours of the morning and demanding to be heard, to be fed, and to be exercised. They say there's no greater agony than bearing an untold story inside you; for me, this was that story. If you have a story like this inside you, eventually you will write it. You will write it when, like me, you no longer have the option not to.

Common advice given to memoirists is to write your story using real names and change them later, so that's what I did. I'm a swimmer, and for days on end I followed the blue line in the pool, back and forth, amusing myself by dreaming up pseudonyms for my family members. But whenever I tried to insert those aliases, it simply stopped being the story of my sons. As soon as I wrote that Noah was run over by my niece, Jane Doe, my story drifted away, dead in the water. But could I use real names?

I read everything I could find on the topic. I listened to webinars. I talked to intellectual property lawyers. "You have the right to tell your own story," they said. "Anyone can sue you for anything. You have to decide whether or not to roll the dice." Ultimately, I consulted with my publisher. These were family members who, after all, had shocked everyone by voluntarily testifying against us during our medical malpractice trial, which had nothing to do with them. My publisher concluded that the names could remain. The trial made my story a public record, and because our family members had inserted themselves into the process, they had become a de facto part of that public record.

Still, I'd be lying if I didn't admit that right up to the eleventh hour I worried about legal liability. Not because I hadn't told the truth. I had. Not because I'd intentionally maligned anyone. I hadn't. In fact, one of my biggest challenges in weaving the story of my sons with that of our family conflict was maintaining the tone of a love story while minimizing vitriol. I worried because I'd already lived through one stressful trial, during which I'd lost ten pounds in one week, and I simply never wanted to do that again. I already had my husband's complete support, and then my oldest daughter, Hannah, said, "Mom, you've had the strength to get this far; I know you can see this through."

My son Micah said, "Mom, be a warrior, not a worrier."

And Anne Lamott wrote, "You own everything that happened to you. Tell your stories. If people wanted you to write warmly about them, they should have behaved better." So I did.

Now that publication is a couple years behind me, I am continuously amazed by the rewards that rolling those dice has reaped. *Breathe* has blown open one door after another, and the journey continues. One of the more surprising things about publishing Noah and Jonah's story is that before this book, the most defining characteristic of their lives was that they'd died. That's the extent of what most people knew about them. But now, reader after reader has learned that they lived. And they hold them in their hearts and they, too, miss them. Since *Breathe* was published, my mom and my mother-in-law have joined their grandsons in the happy hunting grounds. Egyptians believe that to say the names of the dead is to make them live again, so every time I sit in a bookstore and read their voices, it brings them into the room with us. Because of *Breathe*, our moms and our sons have become manifest. I didn't know this would happen, but such is the power of story. And it is a mighty and magical thing indeed.

I have five living children, three of whom were very young themselves when their younger brothers died and two of whom never knew them in this world. So as I wrote my story with my reader in mind, that included my own kids. I was fully aware that I was telling my three oldest children their own story, a story they will always feel but may not have otherwise remembered in detail. Likewise, I knew I was telling my youngest two children the history of our family before they knew us. *Breathe* has given all five of them the gift of their brothers Noah and Jonah returned anew to their lives, and this has meant different things for each of them.

Like children, books take on lives of their own, and for parents there's nothing more amazing than witnessing these transformations. When Isaiah was born after his brothers died, our cries of joy were surely heard in the highest of heavens. I believed that Isaiah was my chance to raise not one but three boys. He is sixteen now, and, as with many teenage boys, I'm not always sure what he's thinking. But in his sophomore ceramics class he sculpted a work of art using the design on my book cover, inscribed with the words my family carves on our gravestones: "to live in the hearts of those we leave behind is not to die." For this, he was honored at his school with a book award and won a Scholastic Art & Writing Gold Key award.

Breathe is structured in three parts: The Book of Noah, The Book of Jonah, and The Book of Isaiah. The prologue is titled "The Book of Kelly," and the epilogue is "The Book of Bella." Bella is my thirteenth baby, the exclamation mark at the end of our family! She's twelve and loves to dance. Her dance teacher read *Breathe* and asked if I would write and record a voiceover of my story for a competition dance she wanted to choreograph. "Can you dance to words like *placenta* and *fetus*?" I asked, and Miss Pam never hesitated. So neither did I.

Thirty-five girls have been dancing my story, our story, for the past year. The dance is complex and lovely, and the music a soothing oceanic instrumental by Ólafur Arnalds, serendipitously entitled "Epilogue," and so, likewise, we named the dance. One of the greatest fears of bereaved parents is that their children will be forgotten. But because of *Breathe* and *Epilogue*, hundreds of people have watched these girls synchronize their movements to my voice, uttering names that are rarely spoken. "When Noah and Jonah had both died, people asked, 'Which do you miss more?' Which would you miss more: your right arm or your left?" *Epilogue* has earned the highest medals awarded, as well as many special judges' awards, with titles like Epic Storytelling and Something Special. *Epilogue* is the transformation of life into art and sorrow into joy.

✳

When your baby dies, you wonder so many, many things, including how you can possibly get through the next painful breath, never mind the rest of your life. Your life without your son, and then without your next son, stretches infinitely on beyond you. You ask all the terrible questions for which there will never be any earthly answers. The whys and the why nots, the why me's and the what-ifs. Somehow, you learn to resign yourself to living without understanding.

But to sit in a darkened theater and watch Noah and Jonah's baby sister, the Epilogue herself, dancing their story onstage almost two decades after their deaths?

Well, you think, *this? Maybe this.*

My wish for my children has always been that they will be the change they want to see in the world, and this holds true for *Breathe* as well. We've long had a refrigerator magnet reminding us to "be brave and do hard things." Sometimes we have to release the words we clutch tightly in our hearts and hands. Roll the dice. Name the names. Then hope that they will march forth and make the world a better place.

KELLY KITTEL (www.kellykittel.com) is an author formerly known as a fish biologist. She lives in Rhode Island with her husband and three of their five living children, but her favorite writing space is in their yurts on the Oregon coast. Her award-winning first book, *Breathe: A Memoir of Motherhood, Grief, and Family Conflict*, is available wherever fine books are sold. She has also been published in numerous anthologies and magazines and has written many notes to teachers. *Epilogue* the dance can be enjoyed at http://tinyurl.com/hxou2j7.

DIALOGUING WITH THE INNER CRITIC

Robert W. Finertie

Howdy. IC here (short for Inner Critic).

"Go away."

I know you don't want to hear from me just now. I can see you tensing up at the mention of my name.

"Yep, I was hoping I wouldn't run into you."

I see you've cleared your calendar so you'd have some time to write.

"Uh-huh."

I can tell by that focused look that you're determined not to let anything get in the way of your writing today.

"That's right."

I'm proud of you. Coffee on the table, pen in hand, a fresh pad of lined paper. Go for it. But actually, before you start, have you thought about who's going to read this crap?

You pause to consider the question.

Meanwhile, IC is smirking to herself. As long as she's stalling, she's not writing.

IC: 1; writer: 0.

You counter with an affirmation: "I am a creative writer. I deserve to be published."

Who says? Where's the evidence? How many of your articles have been accepted?

"I am a creative writer. I deserve to be published."

Are you kidding me? What about all those rejection letters?

"I am a creative writer. I deserve to be published."

Broken record. Sounds lame. Have you thought about what people will think as they read this? Do you really want to reveal all your flaws?

"I am a creative writer. I deserve to be published."

Really? You know what happens in the barnyard: when chickens discover a flaw in one of their peers, they gang up on her and peck that chicken to death.

"I am a creative writer. I deserve to be published."

You'd better keep propping up that image of perfection. Don't let them see any of your flaws.

"I am a creative writer. I deserve to be published."

Once it's in print, there's no turning back.

"I am a creative writer. I deserve to be published. My writing is a search for my truth and the meaning of my life."

I don't think you have the guts to put it all out there.

"I am a creative writer. I deserve to be published."

It's awfully scary to write raw and write real.

"I am a creative writer. I deserve to be published. Others have done it and survived."

Aren't you afraid to let others see how damaged you are?

"I am a creative writer. I deserve to be published."

Aren't you ashamed of some of the things you've done?

"I am a creative writer. I deserve to be published. Yes, I am ashamed, but will I be any more ashamed if they know?"

What if your writing isn't all that good?

"I am a creative writer. I deserve to be published. I will learn my craft and rewrite to make it better."

Eventually, the Inner Critic runs out of things to say. Repeating the mantra helps the writer win. In this dialogue, it took twelve times.

This was a real conversation with my Inner Critic. After she quieted down, I kept iterating my affirmation—twenty-five more times—without any rebuttal. Over time, I begin to believe my affirmation and then to know its truth.

Another success I've had with quieting my Inner Critic is to envision it as my waste bin, full of trash talk. When it's time to write, I light a candle to symbolize the sacredness of this activity. I pick up the bin and say aloud, "I'm busy right now. I don't have time for you. You must wait outside until I blow out the candle."

Then I place the bin outside my study and close the door.

ROBERT W. FINERTIE loves the evocative power of words to touch the heart. A former pastor and psychotherapist, he has worked on being a wordsmith for many seasons and writes something every day. Recently enchanted with the magic of memoir, Bob describes himself as "crazy about that genre." His favorite authors include Cheryl Strayed, Isabel Allende, Fred Buechner, and Anne Lamott. Bob resides in Walnut Creek, California, and loves to hike the open spaces there with his wife, Leslie, at his side and his trusty Canon slung around his neck.

FROM FEAR TO FREEDOM: A MEMOIR'S JOURNEY

Rita M. Gardner

Over a decade ago, when I first considered writing my memoir, *The Coconut Latitudes*, it was for reasons I didn't fully understand. Triggered by my mother's and sister's deaths (my father had passed away decades earlier), I realized my pain over those losses included the awareness that not just life, but also history, was being erased. That history was full of everything that made me who I am. Sooner or later I, too, would be gone, and with me a story that had burned inside for decades. It was like an old photo that had been sharp and clear but was now fading into obscurity. And I wondered, as my own memory begins to fail, what will I remember? Will it be the events recorded by old snapshots, or what lies behind them? And the bigger question was, does it matter at all? Who will care? All I knew at the beginning was that for some reason, I cared a lot. When asked why I wanted to start writing, I could think to say only, "So the past will not be lost." Everything I'd endured was stuffed deep inside, and even when the images disappeared, the impact of them would remain and keep me small and afraid.

And yet—some part of me knew that if I ever were to become my full self, I would have to face what was buried, because even after the picture faded beyond recognition, the past was driving my life into invisibility. My parents, for all their faults, abuses, and failures, chose to live an extraordinarily visible and adventurous life. Their children got to go along for that experimental ride, and somehow we survived. In my sixth decade, I realized two things that made me take action: I didn't want this story to disappear, and I didn't want to be invisible anymore.

I could not have written my story when I was young. Like many others contemplating memoir, we are often keepers of family secrets, whether wittingly or not. It's especially difficult when coming from the position of being a victim of circumstances. And I certainly was that. I acted the part of victim for longer than I care to say. But at some point I had to let that go. I was in a deep pit of misery, and no one was going to save me except myself. And the only way I knew out of that trap was to tell my story. I had to just start a little bit at a time, much like Anne Lamott's advice to her son in her marvelous book *Bird by Bird*. The desire to write my family history had finally become larger than the fear that had held me back from doing so. And so I began the journey into that dark wood, without signposts, aware I might lose my way and unclear where the expedition would take me.

But first, I questioned my sanity. Here I was at the trailhead, facing the inevitable step away from the familiar. All I knew was that I must write a memoir. But even with that insistent prompting from a place deep inside me, I was afraid. How could I, who had perfected invisibility, write a book that would expose family secrets held for decades? And who else would care to read it?

I comforted myself by thinking no one would have to see the finished product if I deemed it inadequate (which I was quite sure would be the case.) After all, I thought, I was already *not good enough*. I didn't finish college, much less pursue that coveted MFA that seems to be de rigueur for *real* writers. So, I thought, I could write about my family, but not about me. But if this was not going to be my story, whose would it be?

I considered a history of my father's risk-taking life— how he found his way to a tropical island after decades of hazardous jobs in remote parts of the globe. I could write how he was seduced by the promise of paradise but how that life also became his undoing. Or maybe I'd tell my mother's story, the one about a young schoolteacher herself seduced by the tall man who pulled her into his dreams. I could chronicle her arrival to the island with two small children and how she began her own sentence of submission. Or maybe I could somehow write about the most difficult subject of all: my sister, the one with secrets she couldn't tell, a cypher who learned to disappear into silence far too young. But I knew I'd never break open the door she kept locked all her life, so how could I betray what little I knew about her?

In the end, I had to face reality. I could tell only my story. My own account was twined with my family's like rivers, whose origins are different but cleave together as one. I'd need to pry apart our separate channels of being until *my* river became its own torrent of words, slicing its singular way forward in its search for truth, secrets be damned—at least for the writing part.

For those writing memoirs and fearing retribution from family members, I acknowledge that is a real stumbling block, which authors have handled in different ways. There is no one solution. I began writing the book when my sister was alive but did not want to jeopardize our relationship, so I knew it could not be published during her lifetime. That did not stop me from the important work I had to do *for me*. And so the writing began. I still operated as if no one would ever read it—it was the only way I could start. But something propelled me on the writing journey anyway, though I knew not what I'd discover. In doing so, I was able to find that small self I used to be, the one who was battered and beaten down. I pulled her into my arms and let her know she would be all right. I cried for her and loved her. And I promised to tell her story—first to me, her grown-up self, and then someday to the world.

Something miraculous began to happen as I stepped off the familiar road and into uncharted territory. I think anytime we take action of any kind, we find others on similar journeys. I didn't know how to construct a memoir; all I knew at first was that I had memories and stories I wanted to put down into words. How they would come together, I had no clue. I figured I should take a few classes on writing and signed up for several local courses. I found like-minded souls also searching for assistance with their writing projects. Whether starting a memoir or penning novels, we all had many of the same questions, doubts, and fears. Most of us worked full-time, so our moments together were precious and valuable. Several of us formed a writing group to support each other. We listened to each other's stories, we critiqued gently, and, most of all, we began to trust each other with our words. It was the first time I dared let anyone hear what I was writing. I learned what worked and what left them confused, and I didn't die of shame.

Each time we ended a meeting, we made a promise about what we would accomplish by the next time we gathered. Whether we actually delivered on those commitments didn't count as much as did the notion that we and our words mattered. We all shared difficult moments, sometimes crying as we read, and our stories began to take shape.

A colleague suggested I apply for a residency at Hedgebrook, a writing retreat for women. I'd never heard of it but took the plunge and applied, since by now I had a loose binder of interrelated stories. I was accepted, and it was there that I laid out all my disparate sections and realized they could be chapters of a real book. I tell this just to illustrate the power of taking action, even when afraid, because we all find some time in life when we *must* do something— and we do it.

That drive comes from a fire that burns within and that moment when it's no longer possible to tamp down the flame. I saw we were all in the same boat, no one of us more courageous than another. Our fears might be like relentless ocean waves, but deep inside, hope lives too.

In a poem by David Whyte called "Out on the Ocean," he writes of being in a bucking kayak, five miles from shore, with waves raging around him as he pulls desperately for home, and how "the spark behind fear/ recognized as life/ leaps into flame." It concludes:

always this energy smoulders inside
when it remains unlit
the body fills with dense smoke.

When I first read it, I could almost feel that restless smoke in my own bones. It was energy, and it was still alive. My own spark ignited in workshops and began to blaze brightly at Hedgebrook. By the time I came home after two weeks of writing, my binder had swelled to become, in Anne Lamott's famous words, a "shitty first draft."

Several more drafts followed. I had to let the writing project stop for a few years because of work commitments that took all the energy I had, but I wasn't disappointed. In truth, I wasn't ready for the next step—publication— until I had more time to devote to the manuscript. I found it very instructional to reread it after shelving it for over a year. Having a space like that between readings highlighted parts that needed more work. Another draft came, and more doubts, but there were also more moments when I realized some of the writing was really good. The book grew up from an awkward child into a fully formed adult, ready to take its place in the world.

Once I announced that my memoir was completed, a friend asked, "Well, now that you've finished writing it, are you in bliss until it gets published?"

At the time, we were slogging along a foggy hiking trail near San Francisco. How to answer her question? All I could say was, "Bliss? Um, no!" Foggy inside and out was how I was feeling as I began the next phase—the path to publication.

She Writes Press would publish my book in 2014, and I soon learned there was a monumental amount of work ahead of me until and beyond the publication date. Once again, I took workshops and classes to learn ways to market and publicize the memoir. Sometimes I felt as if I were on a steep trail, seeing to-do lists as obstacles to anything resembling bliss. And so I scrambled through the fog of concepts like marketing strategies, branding, social media, and platform. Because I was somewhat technology-shy, all these new ideas made my head ache. But I slowly progressed, with help from an editor, a publicist, a publisher, and, of course, my new writing colleagues and friends. I was not alone on that misty trail; I was on the path toward a book in hand.

The day came when I opened my front door to a pile of boxes sent from the publisher—copies of my new book! In shock and disbelief, I signed for the package, and once again a familiar feeling crowded out the elation—fear. The book launch date was coming up soon. As an introvert still expert at hiding, I was now about to expose myself and my story to strangers. I had to release the idea that I should appear perfectly poised and "do it right" at the event. But how?

First, I had a prereading party with a group of friends. I didn't die, and sold about twenty books. Second, I met with an expert in helping people with presentations. She brought a recorder and videotaped me reading. It was torture; I saw myself fidgeting and stuttering, all my awkwardness in full view. When the coach left, I went into my bedroom and curled into a fetal position, thinking, *I cannot do this!*

And yet somehow her instructions sank in beyond the blanket of fear. By the time the big night arrived, I relaxed. No matter how well (or badly) I'd prepared, I had to step beyond the fear and just be myself. I would not be perfect; that was never going to happen. So, instead of fear, I felt relief and excitement. I discovered I actually *had* a self, and she was okay.

What happened next? Unknowingly, by sharing my history, I tapped into others' lives, into their inner worlds, and gave them permission to tell me or others about their past. A lot of readers began to reveal similar experiences of trauma in their childhood, whether an alcoholic parent or other shared incidents. It mattered *to them* that I wrote my story. My project wasn't a narcissistic, navel-gazing endeavor after all. I was no longer invisible, and the world did not end. Instead, it opened up in surprising and joyous ways. I touched people;

they touched me. Discussions became intimate exchanges of ideas. We dove below the surface chatter to what was real. These connections, whether painful or joyful, united us all.

I'm still an introvert with much to learn about writing and revealing truths; it is a lifelong path of discovery. The difference is that my writing journey to date has given me a gift I didn't expect. It has brought me home to myself. I hope this might inspire others to dig deep and begin their journey. Everyone's stories can color their past, shape their present, and sometimes foretell their future. All stories matter, and writing is a courageous act. As we surrender to the process, our flames of inspiration can continue to gather strength. Mary Oliver's poem "The Journey" is a stunning testament to taking action. It starts:

> *One day you finally knew*
> *what you had to do, and began . . .*

Next, she chronicles all the voices that shouted "their bad advice" to us and tried to make us stop, all the obstacles in our way, all the excuses that would keep us stuck. In conclusion, Oliver reminds us, in her spare but exquisite language, of the monumental changes that can occur when we move beyond fear into commitment to do that "one thing" we actually can do.

My heartfelt wish for those who yearn to tell their stories is to surrender to the quest. You can and will face your fears. You'll find unexpected courage along the way. Everyone's path is different, but the writing journey is worth taking, and one with untold surprises ahead. And you just might save your own life.

* * * * *

RITA GARDNER grew up as an expatriate in the Dominican Republic during a repressive dictatorship. Her award-winning memoir, *The Coconut Latitudes: Secrets, Storms, and Survival in the Caribbean* (She Writes Press, 2014), chronicles that experience. In 2015, it won top national awards in the category of memoir: Gold Award in Benjamin Franklin Awards sponsored by IBPA, and a Gold Award in 2015 Next Generation Indie Book Awards. Previously it was selected by the expatriate blog *The Displaced Nation* as one of the best expat memoirs for 2014. Her published essays, articles, poems, and photographs have appeared in literary journals and travel magazines. She was a contributor to *My Gutsy Story Anthology 2*, a book of inspirational stories published in 2015, and will be featured in a literary travel anthology about Andalusia, Spain, to be published by Wanderland Writers in late 2016.

✳ HOPE EDELMAN ✳

Author of *Motherless Daughters, Motherless Mothers*

LINDA JOY MYERS: A major theme in all your books is the mother-daughter relationship. What made you want to write a memoir about parenting your young daughter? What, if any, were some of your distractions and/or challenges?

HOPE EDELMAN: At first, I planned for *The Possibility of Everything* to be a novel. Not that I'd ever actually written a novel before. I'd had such an extraordinary experience bringing my three-year-old daughter to Mayan healers in Belize that I knew I had a story worth telling, but I didn't think anyone would believe it had actually happened as it did. I was also reluctant to put the story out there as a memoir because I'd developed a reputation as a research-based, non-fiction author. Writing about spiritual matters seemed like a radical departure from my previous work. And, of course, I considered the privacy issues surrounding writing about my daughter and my husband, insofar as they'd be able to read the book one day. Was writing the book fair to them? I was in a writing group in Los Angeles at the time, and I wrote the first few chapters in the third person, creating a fictional character to stand in for myself. When the group's assessment was that something about those chapters wasn't reading quite right, I considered that maybe the problem was that I had no idea how to write a novel, at least from a third-person point of view. This was right around the time I was turning forty, and I was starting to think about how much time I'd spent writing what was expected of me, or what could sell. And I started feeling the pull to spend the coming decade writing stories that were important to me, as well as ones that would (hopefully) be important to readers. If the narrative that had unfolded in Belize had really unfolded as it did—and it had—maybe I needed to get out of my own way and just tell the story. I reworked the first chapter with a first-person narrator and handed it in as a memoir. At our next meeting, the other writers said, "This is a *completely* different book. It works now! What did you do?" I said, "Search and replace." Seriously, all I'd done was change "she" to "I." This taught me an important lesson about the pitfalls of trying to write a memoir as a novel. The demands of the two genres are very different, as are the expectations that readers bring to the texts. All of the exposition about the protagonist that was slowing down the story as a novel became crucial self-reflection in the memoir, helping readers feel as if they understood the main character's interior world. The underlying consciousness of my narrator had always been that of a memoirist telling a true story, rather than an invented one. Once I was willing to claim the point of view as my own, the process went very quickly from there.

✳

LINDA JOY MYERS: Many memoirists debate whether writing a memoir is healing or therapeutic, or don't want that label applied to their work. What is your take on this debate?

HOPE EDELMAN: Of all of my books, writing the first one, *Motherless Daughters*, had the strongest healing component to it. The book was part memoir, part interviews, and part research. The memoir sections required me to go back and reexperience some of the most painful episodes of my adolescence surrounding my mother's early death, and to reconsider them from a more adult perspective, ten years later. Doing that gave me a great deal of compassion for the teenager I'd once been and helped release me from some of the self-blame and guilt I'd been carrying during the intervening years. But really, the women I met while writing that book and the readers I met afterward were my main form of therapy. I discovered a large population of women with similar stories and learned that we formed an unofficial sisterhood. This was incredibly significant because, for more than a decade, I'd felt so marginalized and alone as a result of my experience. I've also been teaching memoir writing for about twenty years, and I've seen extraordinary personal transformations occur in the classroom when a writer engages with his or her story in a new and different way. I'm reluctant to apply a blanket "healing" label to the process of memoir writing, though, because simply writing down one's story is not what helps an author come to new insights about the self. To achieve that kind of insight requires a level of engagement with the story that goes beyond an episodic accounting of events and involves a willingness to identify, explore, and reconsider some of the long-held beliefs about oneself and one's story.

✳

LINDA JOY MYERS: Most memoirists wrangle with their inner critic at times, the whispering voice that tells us not to reveal so much. Does this show up for you while you write? And what do you do to fight back against the voice?

HOPE EDELMAN: I haven't struggled much with personal-privacy issues; I've been an open book for most of my life, for better and worse. My inner critic tends to remind me more of the potential consequences of public self-revelation in the twenty-first century. I started writing memoir in the early

1990s, before the Internet was a household item and when a book would—if an author was lucky—be reviewed in a handful of media outlets and live or die by word of mouth. Readers who wanted to contact an author would have to attend a public event or write a letter to the author care of the publisher. Now, in the age of citizen reviews, social media, and author websites, publishing a memoir means receiving immediate feedback from readers. I love hearing from and corresponding with readers, and the majority of e-mails, messages, and online reviews I receive are positive and want to discuss the work itself. But a small portion of them get personal and even downright hateful. There's a tremendous amount of free-floating rage in this culture right now, and a memoirist whose story triggers a response in a reader will occasionally wind up on the receiving end. I'd like to be the kind of author who can say, "I write what I want to write, and to hell with the haters." But if I'm completely honest, that's not who I am. I sometimes find myself in the middle of writing a memoir, with my fingers poised above the keyboard, asking, "Do I really want to put this sentence out there, knowing what may come back in response?" And because I write about family matters, I'm reluctant to expose my husband or daughters to unwanted public criticism, based on how I've depicted them for the purpose of telling my story. My inner critic and I go back and forth on this a lot.

LINDA JOY MYERS: What is the magic of memoir for you?

HOPE EDELMAN: It's the moment when a personal story touches a deep and resonant universal chord—when a sentence in a memoir slays me so deeply that I have to put the book down and think about how my entire internal world just shifted a millimeter to the left because of what I now know to be true that I didn't know four seconds ago. I tell my students not to worry about writing a book that wins awards, or a book that's a best seller, or even a book that will get published. I tell them to focus on telling a story that will touch one reader so deeply that it will alleviate a moment of suffering. To write a book that inspires a random moment of kindness. To tell a true story that gives someone a brief, fierce explosion of hope.

* * * * *

HOPE EDELMAN is the author or editor of seven books, including the best sellers *Motherless Daughters*, *Motherless Mothers*, and *The Possibility of Everything*. Her work has been published in fourteen countries and has been widely anthologized. She has been teaching nonfiction writing for twenty-one years, most recently at Antioch University Los Angeles, and has been a visiting writer at the University of Iowa, Ohio State University, and the University of North Carolina at Wilmington. As a creative coach, she helps authors excavate and write their life stories. She lives in Los Angeles with her husband and two daughters and can be found every July at the Iowa Summer Writing Festival in Iowa City.

I STILL HAVE A STORY TO TELL

Robert Hammond

When you're all alone in the dark, you can either close your eyes and go to sleep or look for the light.

I entered the department store and tried my best to look like a real shopper. Something told me they were watching me. *Maybe it's just my drug-induced paranoia.* I half-convinced myself. I picked up a pair of slacks, folding them neatly over my arm. I turned and headed down another aisle, this time deftly slipping a belt and a handful of silk ties beneath the pants. I then headed to the dressing room to do my dirty work. I entered an empty stall and wrapped the belt and ties around my waist, covering them with my shirt. I tucked the shirt in carefully and straightened out my jacket, making sure nothing was bulging or hanging out. Then I exited the dressing room and put the pants back on the rack where I had found them.

They're watching you. Eyes piercing your soul. You're naked for everybody to see. Don't you know that everyone is watching you now? You can't hide anymore. They all know. They all see you. They hear your thoughts. The sound of your pounding heart echoes over the loudspeakers as all of the store employees and all of the real shoppers stop and listen. They turn toward you and watch you with accusing eyes, penetrating eyes that burn with laser-like intensity through your naked soul. No place to run. No place to hide. It's over now. They know what you've done. They know who you really are. They all see you. You're naked.

I was in a movie, watching myself play out that final scene, but I couldn't change the script. I was trapped in this moment of destiny. I watched from the audience as two security guards tackled me just outside the front door. Like on a video recorder, the action stopped and then replayed itself in slow motion. I watched as they cuffed my hands behind my back and dragged me into the security office. I saw the police officers come in and place me under arrest and haul me down to the station.

The next thing I remember is looking up at the ceiling. A white light glared down at me. The room was white. A man in white looked down at me and laughed. He put his face close to mine and stared into my eyes mockingly. He turned to his assistant and said, "Hey, you want to see what a black guy with jaundice looks like?" I couldn't see who he was talking to at first, but I knew that someone else was in the room. I whispered, "What's going to happen?"

"Looks like you'll probably be dead by Christmas," the man in white jeered.

Dead by Christmas. It was Thanksgiving. I closed my eyes as I slipped in and out of consciousness.

This memory is one of my tamer ones. After spending more than half my life in and out of jails, rehabs, and prisons while battling heroin addiction, I was a dead dog on the road of life.

By the time I entered the recovery house, I was already a successful author, having written several books on personal finance, identity theft, and consumer issues. I had appeared on hundreds of radio and television talk shows as one of the nation's leading credit experts. Writing was an essential part of my life, but something was sorely missing. I needed to do something different. I needed help.

As part of my treatment plan, my counselor arranged for me to write out my moral inventory in the form of a memoir. For more than an hour a day, I poured out all my thoughts and memories and was frightfully surprised as rivers of poetry, mixed with secret crimes and lovers, bubbled to the surface of my soul and spilled out onto yellow legal pads. The result of this process was a catharsis that led to emotional healing and spiritual insight, transforming my life with a deep and permanent Light.

After several months of editing and revisions, I found an agent, who shopped the manuscript to New York publishers. Unfortunately, he passed away before any offers were made, and I struggled to find another agent. Discouraged and over-whelmed, still struggling with rebuilding my life, I put the manuscript on a shelf and focused on other priorities.

After a brief stint in law school, I changed course and earned my master of fine arts in creative writing, with an emphasis on screenwriting. I wrote more books and screen-plays and began working as a creative consultant and part-time screenwriting professor. Knowing the power of story to transform, I realized I was ready to share my own story with the world.

Then came the controversy about James Frey's memoir,

A Million Little Pieces. Projecting worst-case scenarios and future fantasies, I imagined the accusations people would hurl at my story—that it wasn't true, even though I knew it was the true account of my life as I remembered it. At the same time, I was fearful of exposing my previous life of crime and of possible retaliation by some of the people whose true names and crimes I also included.

I ultimately decided to rewrite my memoir as a semiautobiographical novel. Working with several editors, I spent about a year rewriting the entire manuscript. I changed the perspective to third person, combined characters into composites, and fictionalized many of the places and specific event details, even though the essence of the story remained true to my own life experience. The resulting novel, *The Light* (New Way Press, 2013), was transformed from memoir into a mystical odyssey that followed Abel Adams, a brilliant but troubled young misfit seeking freedom, love, and spiritual enlightenment while battling drug addiction, dark forces, and strange temptations.

The Light was a surrealistic adventure tale about redemption and recovery. Abel Adams was essentially my alter ego, an allegorical amalgam of all of us who have gone astray at some point in our lives. Even though many people have since shared their deep identification with Abel's desperate desire for deliverance from darkness, I sometimes regret having fictionalized my original first-person narrative.

Decades have passed, and my life has changed dramatically since the events revealed in *The Light*. I have survived many more misadventures and have learned many new lessons. I am now embarking on a journey to tell my true story, a newer and truer memoir. I still have a story to tell.

✳   ✳   ✳   ✳   ✳

ROBERT HAMMOND is an award-winning screenwriter, producer, and author of a dozen books, including *Ready When You Are: Cecil B. DeMille's Ten Commandments for Success* (2012) and *C.B. DeMille: The Man Who Invented Hollywood* (2012). His bestselling book, *Life After Debt: Free Yourself from the Burdens of Money Worries—Once and for All* (2000) sold over one hundred thousand copies. Hammond holds an MFA in creative writing and is a sought-after speaker on personal achievement, storytelling, and Hollywood history. He provides creative consulting services to business organizations and governmental agencies and lives with his wife and two rescue pets (a dog and a cat) in Northern California.

MY TWENTY-THREE-YEAR PROJECT

Marina Aris

A good piece of advice you will hear often is that you should wait to write memoir until you have enough time and emotional distance from the events you are writing about. Honest reflection takes a while. By writing memoir, you almost always assume the role of underdog, and if readers hook into your journey, they will really want to know: how you navigated adversity, trekked across wicked mountainous trails alone, loved and lost and loved again. If you do not begin writing at the right time, you will have little to offer. It will be difficult to identify the path of your journey, since you will likely still be mired in it.

I know, because I began writing my memoir at the worst time in my life. When I began, twenty-three years ago, I was a nineteen-year-old, unwed, and unhappy mother of a newborn. The adversity I suffered as a foster child led to my running away at sixteen and finding myself without a home, a family, or a sense of identity. I stumbled into motherhood, in part because I wanted someone to love who could in time love me in return.

The first year of my son's life, I learned that despite the abuse I suffered as a child, I was incapable of hurting him. The maternal wiring within me was somehow intact, and I knew what to do. In caring for him, I began to learn how to care for myself. And caring for myself meant making time to write. Even then, writing was instinctual, and necessary. It was the only way I knew of to cope with what I could not understand. It was a way to reorder the world around me and the emotional chaos within me. It was the only way to find balance between hope and hopelessness.

I didn't have a proper writing space. I tapped away the details of my childhood and the worries that plagued me on a machine that was a cross between a typewriter and a word processor. I could see only one line of text on a sliver of a gray screen above the keyboard. I sat on a black leather sofa that sometimes stuck to the undersides of my bare thighs while the bottom of the machine heated my lap. I wrote often, but without direction or focus beyond the emotional pain I was in. There was no way I could, at that time, produce a memoir worth reading.

Those early attempts only offered value in terms of my growth as an individual. With every draft, I unloaded the weight of my memories. The pain lessened, and I began to see the events of my personal history within a new framework. I realized that my story could help others, but only if I could learn how to write myself out of dark corners and into the light. Where was the light? What had I learned? What rewards had my extreme resilience granted me?

Even on the darkest days of my life, there was a glimmer of hope. Hope that I could amount to something when no one expected anything of me. Hope that growing up alone and unwanted didn't mean I would live that way for the rest of my life. I needed to dig more deeply than the surface scars to find that glimmer. But more than anything, I needed to be brutally honest and realize that at some point I would be neither victim nor hero of my own story. I would simply be a narrator, a guide, and the bearer of good news.

By God, there is no emotional wound deep enough to kill you! That realization alone is enough to slash at the soul a thousand times. You may end up broken and scarred, but the well within is deep. There is always more to give. And with that glorious realization, I faced the blank page time and again, so that I could slice open the vein of truth and give from the deepest parts of myself.

It did not take me twenty-three years to understand the rules of memoir writing. But it took nearly all of that time to understand that what happened to me, although painful and tragic in its own way, is not in and of itself a story. The story could come only from years of living in the aftermath of neglect and abandonment by my biological mother. I needed to answer one important question: Why was my story worth telling? Could it really make a difference in a world where every day people die for useless causes? Where every changing season we worry about how much land the sea will swallow beneath its surface? The events I survived more than twenty years ago seem to dim in comparison. What did I hope to accomplish?

The only answer I could come up with is that stories have a power we may never fully understand. Stories can touch people in places that are still wounded and help them heal. Stories can provide hope and offer perspective. Stories can connect people to causes that matter and to one another. I had to believe, then, in the power of story, and expect nothing in return.

THE QUESTION OF TRUTH AND MEMORY

The question of truth never bothered me. I was committed to writing the truth even if it caused me to wrestle with a misplaced burden of shame. What bothered me was the question of memory. Is memory unreliable? I don't think that is the question we should be asking. The real question is, what kind of memory are we writing about? Some memories are visual, some auditory, others traumatic. It depends on how the little machine in your brain records things, and how it then files away moments so that specific triggers can help your recall.

When I wrote about traumatic experiences, I opened a door inside myself and became a child again. The memories came to me intact and alive, with all the pain, fear, and confusion I felt when they first occurred. I remembered who and what and when and how. I remembered every emotion, so much so that it wasn't unusual for me to cry or tremble or curl into my own body in the middle of writing.

What I don't remember is what I was wearing, the exact time of day or night, all the words I may have spoken, since during my most traumatic years I was forced to comply with a vow of silence. When it comes to facts, there is no denying that there are holes in my memory. Every so often, I'd hit a wall. The chronology didn't make sense, or I simply struggled to place events in the correct order. My mother owned several lemons that wound up smoking on the side of the road, but what color or make or model those vehicles were, I couldn't say. I remember only one car, an emerald-green Mustang, but that was because it was tied to a specific person, my mother's sugar daddy, a World War II veteran named Bill. I made long lists of what I remembered. Sometimes random but specific things came to mind. My mother's long nails polished a deep red. A stuffed Santa doll, the first and only toy I had an attachment to. The deep blue, almost purple color of an alarm clock I never heard rattle alive. The vinyl album sleeves my mother owned, dusty with cocaine residue.

It is fair to expect memoirists to write about their experiences truthfully—that is, to write about memories that haunt them without giving in to careless speculation or crossing the line into fiction. I believe that most memoirists, especially writers of traumatic experiences, are capable of tapping into the emotional core of their memories. And through writing my own memoir I learned that if I could not bring myself to relive my past on the page, the writing would be flat and lifeless. In those instances, I was only skimming the surface of my experiences, and that provided little value to me as a writer and to the work as a whole.

THE INNER CRITIC

Almost every writing book I have read talks about how to deal with one's inner critic. I usually skip over that chapter, because the only thing my inner critic has ever said to me is that I should be writing. I have learned, through years of shying away from the help of a therapist, that writing, no matter the quality, is good medicine. Writing is affordable and accessible and can almost always help you arrive at the best answer to your most troubling quandary. Not writing feels wrong to me. Not writing is the equivalent of not breathing. Perhaps my childhood taught me how to live on the page. How to sort out the parts of me that are wounded from the parts of me that aren't. If the blank page, then, is the white door of possibility, it can lead only to self-discovery. And if you can associate writing with discovery, then the writing becomes an adventure that you crave and relish.

If my inner critic decides to show up and speak its mind

about how much I have yet to learn about the art of writing, I have no qualms about telling it to shut up so I can go on with the process of learning. Writing, like most things, is best learned by doing.

STRATEGIES FOR WRITING

The word *memoir* defines only the finished product. There is no word for the gut-wrenching process required to finish one. We can label it an act of courage, persistence, even foolishness, but that does not define how it's done. How it's done is not as simple or as complicated as I imagined it would be.

Putting my thoughts and memories on the page was easy. Framing those thoughts and memories in a way that respected the rules of storytelling, that was difficult. I had to learn how to shape true life events into the elements that make up any good story. But mostly I had to accept that my past self was the protagonist and that labeling someone or something as the antagonist was not the same as stating that I was good and the other was not.

As a genre, memoir allowed me to drag my readers through the muddy waters of emotional turmoil, but by the end I had to deliver them to the calm shore of resolution. Memoir may be one of the only forms of writing that requires you to push through a complete narrative arc that doesn't end badly. Not all memoirs are traumatic in nature, but almost all of them will require you to take breaks. Breaks give you mental space in which to reflect and, when necessary, to recover emotionally. The strategy of viewing and treating your past self as you would a protagonist creates distance from which to honestly reflect on the events you're writing about.

In film school I learned about setting a scene and using a 16 mm camera to record the action. If you can imagine looking through the small hole of a camera lens, you will more readily see the color and shape of things. You will ground yourself in a specific place and world. It's too easy to delve only into feelings and emotions when writing memoir. You need to force yourself to think back to other sensory details, specifically those in the setting you're writing about. For me, that was 1970s New York. I don't remember the corner prostitutes or the loose garbage floating in the wind, but I do remember the lights of Times Square and how I marveled at them.

THE EFFECTS OF MEMOIR WRITING

As far as others are concerned, I can rest easy knowing that I have written my truth and that I have not set out to hurt anyone. When it takes more than twenty years to complete a memoir, you learn that justice cannot be your aim—that's what the legal system is for. There is no justice to be found by way of memoir. Words can teach, they can inform, and perhaps sometimes they can bring justice, but if that is your aim, you are more than likely to miss your mark. No one cares to read a memoir set in the limiting victim perspective. At some point, you need to realize that victimization, although terrible, is only temporary.

It took a long time for me to learn this, to feel in my bones when I was writing from a place of frustration and anger, instead of a place of acceptance and curiosity. Acceptance brought me gratitude for the fact that, despite all the suffering, I am still here, attempting to alchemize negative experiences into positive outcomes for myself and others. And curiosity helped me to realize that all I wanted was to learn from my past. The more I wrote, the more I learned about compassion and humanity, and the more I understood the value of adversity and what it had to teach me.

On bad writing days, I produced either words that were flat and devoid of emotion or words that moved me to tears. I had to learn how to work within those two extremes. I couldn't just skim the surface of my memories. Skimming meant I was trying to protect myself. It meant I wasn't keeping the memoirist's promise to share my truth. I had to learn how to ride the tidal wave of my history and still reach the shore of my current life unscathed. I'd write for months and then abandon the work altogether. When I couldn't write, I recovered.

While I wrote, I thought about my children. How would my story impact them? Would they be able to handle the details of my past? Would they be plagued by the same sense of shame I carried most of my life? I concluded that they should know the truth, if only so they could have answers to questions they might never think to ask until I am long gone. How were the withered and broken branches of our shared family tree formed? Who were those damaged people who lived long before them and long before me? If I could trace our shared family history back to the initial point of breaking, would that make my children whole in some way? Would it make them love and understand me, as a person, more or less than they already do? Or would they, like I am, be relieved that I was able to create a wall between the past and the present? That I managed to keep out what could cause us further pain?

In this way, memoir becomes a labor of love, a testament to the maternal oath I have taken: to love, to nurture, and to protect. But memoir can also serve as a testament to human resilience and how it is about more than survival. When resilience stops being about survival, it becomes a tool by which to achieve personal growth. My younger self struggled with wanting to know why things happened. My older self was concerned with how to make peace with what happened, regardless of why. People change when their perspective changes. I needed my perspective to change in order to fully see myself as the victim before and the whole woman after. Memoir allows acceptance of what was in order to alter what is yet to come.

Through memoir, I have come to accept that I am absolutely the sum of all my past experiences. I am now a wife and the mother of three children, but I am also an impostor. I have never fit into society's mold, and I never will. The child I was remains very much alive in my mind, and it is still difficult to reconcile her frailty with my strength. I am immune to loneliness. Solitude means safety and space in which to experience the rich inner world that is part writer's mind, part survivor's glory. Large social settings are stressful, but I can connect deeply with someone one-on-one. Out in the real world, I sometimes feel like a human lie detector. I am hypervigilant, my brain ready to submit to the slightest trigger that sets off my post-traumatic stress disorder. I care deeply about children or those who cannot fend for themselves.

All of these facts equal me the person, but what readers really want to know is whether or not I have made it. Am I, despite the experiences that have shaped me, a normal, functioning individual? And when I say yes—that despite the residual effects of early trauma, I am someone who loves and is loved, someone who fails but also succeeds—then, only then, is my reader going to be satisfied with the journey I have labeled memoir.

At the heart of it, memoir is the study of how the past shapes us, how we guide one another through overcoming adversity, conquering fears, or even letting go of a great love. But reading and writing memoir is about only one thing: human connection. And as a writer I can't think of any greater reward than to know my words have connected me to another human being. To know that my thoughts have traveled the wire of transcendence and rested in the heart and mind of someone who might, just might, understand me, if only a little.

* * * * *

MARINA ARIS is a native New Yorker and author of the forthcoming memoir, *Running Into The Night*. Marina spent her childhood years in the care of strangers and two years in the care of her mentally disturbed mother. Since 2007, she has spoken publicly about the adversity she suffered in childhood, and has presented at Columbia University and the Hunter College School of Social Work. As a former member of Toastmasters International, she won several awards and honors for speaking about child abuse, foster care system reform, and overcoming adversity. In addition to writing, speaking, and advocating for youth in care, Marina is the host and organizer of the Brooklyn Writers Project Meetup, a dabbler in art, poetry and photography, and the very busy mother of three. You can learn more about upcoming releases and see her latest creative experiments on her website at www.MarinaAris.com.

WHERE'S THE JUICE?

LaDonna Harrison

For many years I was a college teacher; now I am a reader and a writer. As a writer, besides all the usual challenges of finding time and solitude to write, managing insecurities and excuses, and that horrible fear that I have nothing of worth to say, I want with all my heart to write a memoir that is beautiful and authentic.

My memoir, *The Prayer Diver*, focuses on a life-changing experience of trauma I had as a young woman. The subject is uncomfortable and painful, not beautiful at all, but I want the writing to be beautiful. I want my readers to feel, to experience, and mostly to be changed in some way. I know I cannot accomplish this without authenticity, and that I cannot write authentically without immersing myself, reliving a painful experience and expressing it in words. Further, and perhaps most difficult of all, I have to be ferociously open about my own behaviors and motivations. My tendency is to want to be the good guy or even a victim and to skim over the parts that show me as anything else, but the life breath of a piece of memoir writing is in the deeper truth. That's where the juice lies.

As a reader, I want and need to be pulled into a juicy experience, rather than to be told about an experience. Last night, as I do every night, I climb between my sheets, luxuriating for a moment in the slick coolness of a four hundred–plus–thread count cotton sateen in the desert. I'm picky about the feel of sheets. I turn on my elderly Kindle, the one with a blue leather cover that opens like a book, and pull out the hidden book light. In that moment, I feel just a little apprehension because I am starting a new book. I am in that uncertain stage between grieving the ending of a book I loved and beginning the unknown. I'm considering three options. I will decide after I've read the first few pages of each. Like my sheets, the read has to feel right and authentic. I don't want polyester, "man"-made fabrics with pretend softness. I want my sheets to breathe through real fibers.

One work I consider is written by a well-known author, so I have high hopes. I read the first few pages and because of the author's reputation keep reading, hoping the words will come alive. They don't, even after I've read more than 12 percent of the story. (I know this because my Kindle tells me.) The problem for me is not really the past-tense telling of the story; it's in the distance I feel between and among the characters and me. The experience is not satisfying, though I think it could be with some revision. I'd like to see what present tense would do. Also, I want the writer to slow down, take me deep, and give me time to get to know the character. There is movement in the plot, but I can't seem to care because the characters are flat. They have no flesh, no texture, no fabric, and no juice.

Then I try an unknown work that begins with exposition disguised as dialogue. I feel hoodwinked, so I move on. It happens just about that fast, too. I don't like to be manipulated and won't sit still for it for long. I don't want a whole backstory in a paragraph, no matter how it is described. Let me discover the character and develop understanding and sympathy, or not, but let me do it on my own, through the character.

The third option is not a subject or setting I'm very interested in—war—but as I begin to read, I sense a breath of real life. Immediately, I am transported. I am with a young woman on a Japanese island beach as she collects star sand. I see her long, straight black hair held back off her face with a traditional hairpin. I feel the grit and smell the sea. I'm wondering how old she is and why she is alone on this stretch of deserted beach. I'm wondering what star sand is. I'm anticipating what might happen next, because I know it is wartime. This is my next read!

Most of us have been told in beginning writing classes to "show, don't tell." I've said it to students myself. This is nothing new, but what does it mean and how do writers accomplish this simple directive in order to make characters, real or imaginary, complex and even complicated? Sometimes telling a writer to "show" is not enough. Writers must be shown how to show! Inexperienced writers often tackle memoir with the idea that the form is an easy one, not overly reliant on imagination or education. All the writer has to do is tell the story in chronological order, but *telling* itself implies a distance from the actual experience, a looking back at and reiterating what happened in the past. One way to *show* a scene in words is to re-place yourself—to bring the past experience into the present and relive it.

The following example from my past takes place in present tense:

I am at a writing workshop in Idyllwild, California, doing an activity to demonstrate phenomenological writing with a student in the class. I turn my folding chair toward her and look into her face, noticing the smoothness of her brown skin against her blue-green beaded earrings. Her eyes are a soft brown; her hair, I see now, is slivered with silver. I'm nervous, because I've never done this before in front of others and I'm not sure whether the activity will work. I take a breath and begin by asking her to choose a scene from her memoir and talk it through with me.

She is a girl, just coming of age, in Costa Rica, at a family gathering. She begins telling me about family members and food being served. I stop her and ask her to take me with her into the scene. Where is she specifically? What is she doing? What does she smell? What does she see? What colors? What does she hear?

The student begins reliving the experience. I can tell she is going deeper, immersing herself. Her eyes close. I see her take a breath, inhaling the aroma of fried plantains. The men sit drinking bottles of Imperial; empties clutter the makeshift table. Laughter rises and falls in waves, mixed with women's voices as they tease and joke.

Palm trees suddenly replace the pines outside the Idyllwild classroom. The air becomes heavy with humidity. I ask the student what she is wearing, and she smiles. I see her sway a little as she talks about her new flowered skirt and the feel of the cotton fabric swishing against her thighs. Little puffs of dust rise up from each step she takes in her rubber thongs, swaying to the rhythm of the music from the radio.

What is unexpected about this encounter with the past for the student (and for me) is how the skirt emerges as essential and symbolic. The skirt comes alive in the scene as the girl, coming of age, is noticing her body, her movement, her clothes, wondering about who else is noticing her. The skirt can become memorable in the reader's mind, something to develop further.

Entering a memory or a piece of writing in this way, as it is happening in the moment, is what I think of as phenomenological writing. Experiencing the process of writing as a phenomenon invites the muses to breathe life into words for both the reader and the writer. Phenomenology is the study of structures of consciousness as experienced from the first-person point of view. It has been practiced in various guises for centuries but became more popular and acquired some credibility in the early twentieth century in the works of Husserl, Heidegger, Sartre, Merleau-Ponty, and other philosophers.

For the practical purposes of considering the experience of writing a phenomenon, let's define *phenomenon* as:

- an object or aspect known through the senses, rather than by thought or intuition
- a temporal or spatiotemporal object of sensory experience
- a rare or significant fact or event

Instigating a phenomenological experience supports authentic development of a work.

- Imagine a scene from your story, a snapshot full of narrative.
- Enter the scene.

- Slow down and *be* in the scene with all of your senses. Look outside yourself, inside yourself. Smell, see, hear, taste, and feel what is present, and let that experience take you to other experiences connected to your memory in your mind and in your body.
- Write what you experience. Imagine leading readers into your world.

Here is an example of a phenomenological description of a claustrophobic reaction I have on an airplane: I am on a plane in Minneapolis, about to fly to San Francisco for Christmas. It is the last flight of the day out of the city, because of weather conditions. We taxi onto the tarmac, and the pilot begins talking to us: "I'm sorry for the inconvenience, folks, but the weather in San Francisco is forcing us to delay our flight for about two hours before we can take off. The good news is that we will be offering, free of charge, the movie *The Grinch Who Stole Christmas*."

My physical senses assess my situation. I see, my eyes darting this way and that, all the people around me; they are talking, resting, reading, pulling scarves around their necks against the cooling air. Some passengers in window seats pull down the shades to better view the movie. They seem calm, while my movements stiffen with intention to appear normal. I see the inside of the plane, the blue-gray walls, and the coordinated seat cushions. I hear the engines shut down and the quiet descent. I hear voices around me less clearly when I carefully move my arms and hands to put on the headphones to listen to the Grinch. I smell the cologne of the man in front of me as he reclines his seat back toward my lap. I feel my breathing become shallow and quick. How far back will he recline? I have no space. I have no air. The air feels solid. I feel my mouth becoming dry, my throat constricting. I want out. I want out now.

My mind leaps to reasoning in order to soothe and dissipate the solidification and create more space. The mind gives imperatives: *listen to the movie; focus on your hands, your fingernails, on anything but where you are being restrained.* Contained has become restrained. My senses are heightened. Voices get louder, people get larger and multiply, taking up more space, breathing more air. I will be here forever, unable to breathe, flopping about like a gasping walleye in dry dock. I am a mummy wrapped tightly, entombed. I am a bird in a cage with her wings clipped. My breath becomes shallow and constricted; a boa constrictor is tightening its thick, muscled body around my chest and my throat. I grab the snake, pulling with all my strength, trying to escape the potent grip. My heartbeat becomes faster and shallower. I fight for air. I fight for control of my life while I am held down, confined, prevented from moving. My muscles tense, straining to be free; my blood vessels tighten, constricting the flow of blood. I am trapped in the backseat of a car, unable to get out. I am held hostage on a jet. I am stuck in an elevator. I am imprisoned in my body with "locked in" syndrome. I am buried alive within the element of time and place. I am out of my element, overcome.

My element is no longer mine. In my heightened state of anxiety, I do not have control over my surroundings. I need to gain control over my space, since I do not have control over the place I am in. If my symptoms do not fully inhabit me and I am able to gain control over my space and hold the control long enough, it will ease my attack symptoms, I hope.

In the cabin of the jet, the captain opens the door to the cockpit, and I can see out through the windshield of the plane. I see the sky, the runway, and the terminal in the distance. I imagine we are getting ready to take off. I anticipate the movement. One way to gain some feeling of control over place is through the retinas. I feel my body begin to relax.

Whew! That was not fun to relive, but I see now in reviving the experience how the element of control dominates a panic attack and emerges as a theme. I find that the most exciting part of experiencing the writing process as a phenomenon is the unexpected. The practice, though unimaginably difficult at times, allows the writer to see what has been hidden. It is a poetic approach to prose that creates a space for metaphor, analogies, connections, themes, and insights into motivation that may not have been fully comprehensible in the moment of the lived experience. What seems ordinary and easily overlooked can become extraordinary—a skirt, for example.

Writers must become not only sensitive to language and the way it speaks to us, but also sensitive listeners to and observers of the lived experience. We need to be able to read between the lines and listen between the notes of the music of language in order to absorb and transfer the deeper rhythms and tones and vibrations of our juicy experiences to others through writing.

Since she retired from a teaching career as both a college writing instructor and a seminar leader-trainer, LADONNA HARRISON has been writing creative nonfiction and a memoir, entitled *Prayer Diver*, about the effects of trauma on young adults. She facilitates writing workshops at the Spirit Mountain Retreat Center in Idyllwild, California, where she has a cabin to escape the summer heat of the desert in Palm Springs, California.

✳ INTERVIEW WITH AZAR NAFISI ✳

Author of *Reading Lolita in Tehran*

BROOKE WARNER: I first read *Reading Lolita in Tehran* in 2004. It was one of the earliest memoirs I read, and I was captivated, as tens of thousands of other readers have been ever since its publication, by your voice, your blend of the personal and political, and your commitment to principle, feminism, and education. Yet you wrote this book long before the so-called Memoir Revolution. Can you talk about what you knew of the genre when you wrote and published *Reading Lolita*, and what you think of memoir today, well over a decade since your first memoir was published?

AZAR NAFISI: To start with, when I started writing *Reading Lolita*, I had no idea that it would turn into a memoir. What drew me to writing the book was the fact that I needed to tell these stories. It seemed as if all the things that were happening were happening not just to me, but to my country and my people, and none of it would become real until I talked about it. Until I told the story. So that was how it all started. Once that urge came to me, I was already fascinated by the intersections between what we call fiction and what we call reality. And so, in my personal memoir, there were intersections between fiction and reality and intersections between history and personal history. That was very seductive to me, and that's how I ended up writing *Reading Lolita* as a memoir. Memoir has many of the same features as fiction. You need characters that are authentic; you need to be able not only to convey your own voice but to convey the voices of others, and sometimes others whom you don't like. What I discovered when I was writing my memoir was that you have to become almost naked. You have to face the truth. You have to be able to create and therefore understand even those characters in your real life who were villains. For me, the process of writing has always been about discovery—discovery not just about the world, but also about myself. Sometimes I don't like what I see in that mirror, but that's how it is. You can't go about this in a cheap way.

BROOKE WARNER: Your online bio says you are involved in the promotion not just of literacy, but of reading books with universal literary value. Can you talk about this particular form of advocacy, and your feelings about reading and writing, and what seems like today's trend of writers' wanting to write without being true readers of their genres?

AZAR NAFISI: In my life, there has never been a moment when I have separated reading from writing. I always mention that before I became a writer, I was a reader. You need to read stories, and I'm not saying that as homework. It is just that in any profession, you need to be proficient and you need to be passionate about that profession. You need to get that vast experience that writers—and not just your contemporaries, but writers thousands of years ago—have provided for you. I think of reading as nourishment, as food for writing. In terms of advocacy, reading and writing break all the boundaries that reality imposes on us. They create a space where we must confront one another as human beings. I think it's very dangerous to celebrate only our differences, without understanding what we have in common. The worst crimes of humanity have happened because we have said other people are different from us.

Slaves are different from slave masters, so if we beat them, they don't feel the same way. Jews are different, so if we put them in concentration camps, it's okay. Literature creates for us a universal space, and it creates connections that go beyond boundaries. It's also very empowering. We need to know about our past through fiction, and those universal moral and emotional and human events that writing provides us, in order to see ourselves as human and as humane.

BROOKE WARNER: *Reading Lolita in Tehran* is, according to your own website, a book about the "exploration of the transformative powers of fiction in a world of tyranny." Given the current political polarization of the United States, do you see literature as a vehicle that might save us, or at least help us?

AZAR NAFISI: Definitely. When I was writing *Reading Lolita in Tehran*, I was already thinking of *Republic of Imagination* (my most recent book), because at the end of that book I talk about America, and how what my students in Iran knew of America was either through the regime's mind, which was demonizing America, or through their reaction to that demonization, which made them love America. Also, they idealized a democratic country like America. I wanted them to see how fantastic democracy is but at the same time to see how dangerous it can be. That freedom is also an ordeal. The question I pose in *Republic of Imagination* is: Can a democracy exist and survive without a democratic imagination? And of course the response is no. What's happening in our political process now, with Mr. Trump, is that we're looking at someone who's not just intolerant, but someone who cannot accept voices other than his own. Freedom of choice, that idea of freedom of voices, is one way literature can save us.

*

BROOKE WARNER: You've written countless other articles and several other books since *Reading Lolita*, including another memoir, *Things I've Been Silent About.* What is it like to have written a book like *Reading Lolita in Tehran*, which is such a smashing best seller, early in your writing career? Has it been a hard act to follow, or did it provide a fertile foundation for future work, or something in between?

AZAR NAFISI: You write because you have to, even though writing is one of the most difficult things in the world. When I wrote *Reading Lolita in Tehran*, I had no idea that it would be read by so many people, never mind become a success the way it did. I wrote it because I was obsessed, and because, several years before I came to the United States, I wrote numerous diaries about what was happening in Iran, and I was dying to be able to articulate those thoughts. Some of my friends and close colleagues told me nobody would read this book because we were entering a war with Iraq, because nobody was interested in Iran, and because I was writing about these dead white authors about whom nobody cared. But then people read the book. I am thankful for that success because it gave me space to be able to write whatever else I wanted to write. It connected me to all these people who shared my passion. I never in my wildest dreams could have imagined that I would connect with so many people the way I have. So that has been reward enough.

*

BROOKE WARNER: What is the magic of memoir for you?

AZAR NAFISI: The magic for me is that it's for me. I understand that some people are antimemoir. But for me, memoir has this magic of constantly looking at reality through the eyes of the imagination. When I write memoir, I see how important both reality and imagination are to one another. How, if we want to survive, we need to go to that other place and keep a distance from our own reality. I can see the world through eyes that mix the personal with the public, history with personal history. I love the flirtation between those concepts, so I'll keep doing it until I'm sick of it.

* * * * *

AZAR NAFISI is best known as the author of the national best seller *Reading Lolita in Tehran: A Memoir in Books*, which electrified its readers with a compassionate and often harrowing portrait of the Islamic revolution in Iran and how it affected one university professor and her students. The book has spent over 117 weeks on the *New York Times* best seller list, has been translated into thirty-two languages, and has won diverse literary awards. Nafisi is a visiting professor and the executive director of Cultural Conversations at the Foreign Policy Institute of Johns Hopkins University's School of Advanced International Studies in Washington, DC. She has written for the *New York Times*, the *Washington Post*, and the *Wall Street Journal* and is also the author of *Anti-Terra: A Critical Study of Vladimir Nabokov's Novels*, *Things I Have Been Silent About: Memories*, and *Republic of the Imagination*. She lives in Washington, DC.

WHY I DON'T FIND WRITING MEMOIR CATHARTIC

Jill Smolowe

Twice I've written memoirs that detailed painful periods in my life. The first, *An Empty Lap*, published in 1996, dealt with my husband's and my contentious road to parenthood as we struggled to overcome a sequence of hurdles that began with disagreement over whether to have children, moved on to infertility, then (happily) culminated in the international adoption of our daughter. My second memoir, *Four Funerals and a Wedding: Resilience in a Time of Grief*, published in 2014, explored what kept me going as I cared for, then (devastatingly) lost four loved ones—my husband, sister, mother, and mother-in-law—within a seventeen-month period.

After I completed each of these memoirs, the question I encountered most frequently was "Did you find writing the book cathartic?" I confess I find the question odd.

For me, the memoir form has two valuable purposes. It gives the writer in me the opportunity to reflect on an experience in a mindful manner that helps me to unearth meaning and extract lessons from a period of turbulence. It enables the communicator in me to share an experience through a focused narrative that aims to offer insight and reassurance to those who are going through similar turmoil, and also to their loved ones, who often feel uncertain about what to say or how best to help. To be sure, all of this can be very satisfying.

But it carries steep costs. If you are to touch hearts and minds with a compelling story about an upheaval in your life—the natural terrain of memoir—you must reimmerse yourself in the painful details of that period. You must trespass the boundaries of your privacy zone. You must lay bare some of your most closely guarded thoughts, comments, and actions. Come the day you dream of (you know, the one where your memoir hits bookstore shelves and people queue for blocks—no, wait, miles—to buy it), you confront another cost. You must surrender this intensely personal narrative to readers, who will then dig in to dissect, discuss, judge. Since this story is stripped from your life, you may feel like they are dissecting, discussing, and judging you.

Given all that, I do not embark on this exercise lightly. Before I can make the commitment to breaching my privacy and spending considerable time revisiting a painful chapter in my life, I need clarity on two points: *Why* do I want to tell this particular story, and *how* do I plan to tell it? The *why* question demands that I be clear about the message, the bit of hard-earned wisdom that I find so compelling that it supersedes my intense instinct to safeguard my privacy. The *how* question demands that I identify the lens through which I will tell my story. If I am not clear on these two points, I am at risk of becoming endlessly mired in a growing mound of anecdotes that, no matter how poignant, painful, or moving, will never have shape or purpose.

For me, finding the answers to these two questions requires detachment and emotional distance from the events. As a result, I do not find the writing of a memoir cathartic. Nor do I approach the task with a hope or expectation that the process will in some way heal me. Instead, I am propelled by my belief that there is a book missing from the shelves— one that would have been helpful to me in my time of turmoil, one that I hope may now be of use to others.

That's not to say that writing can't be therapeutic. When I want to alleviate tension, stress, or upset, I regurgitate my experiences into a journal. Raw and unfiltered, these entries provide an outlet to vent. Sometimes that act of writing helps to calm my roiling emotions. Sometimes the writing even serves, yes, a cathartic function. Later, those entries are invaluable. They offer a snapshot of what I was thinking and feeling at a given moment, provide the surrounding interpersonal and sensory details, recount snippets of dialogue. All of this is just the sort of material that helps bring a memoir scene to life. But is such undigested writing the business of memoir? To my mind, no. It's not even the first draft.

Instead, by the time I arrive at a working plan for a memoir, I have gained sufficient distance to approach the writing with a clear eye and a measure of dispassion. Sure, emotions occasionally bubble to the surface as I re-create them on the page. Sometimes I bring myself to tears, tears that, if I write the scene vividly enough, perhaps the reader will share.

But that is not my purpose. My purpose is to communicate my message. In *Four Funerals*, for instance, I aimed for readers to come away with an understanding of why the cultural script surrounding grief is limiting, misleading, and often an obstruction to healing. While writing, I kept my lens trained firmly on exactly what got me through so much illness, loss, and grief. If an anecdote served that purpose, I used it. If not, I cut it, no matter how poignant.

For me, the work of memoir writing is selecting, culling, honing, shaping, rewriting. Rewriting. Ruthlessly chopping. Rewriting once more. The driver is my intellect, not my emotions.

If there is any catharsis to be had, I find it comes later. It lies in the letters I received from couples who wrote to say that *Empty Lap* helped them move past a marital impasse (complete with a photo of their newly adopted child). It rests in the e-mails I continue to receive from widows and widowers who share their stories of loss and thank me for depicting, in *Four Funerals*, a grief trajectory that they recognize. It can be cathartic indeed to know that one's pain has meaning for another person and is helping them to navigate a similarly dark passage.

✷ ✷ ✷ ✷ ✷

JILL SMOLOWE is the author of the memoirs *Four Funerals and a Wedding: Resilience in a Time of Grief* and *An Empty Lap: One Couple's Journey to Parenthood,* and coeditor of the anthology *A Love Like No Other: Stories from Adoptive Parents.* An award-winning journalist, she has been a foreign affairs writer for *Time* and *Newsweek,* and a senior writer for *People.* Her articles and essays have also appeared in the *New York Times,* the *Boston Globe,* the *Washington Post Magazine, More, Money, Red* (UK), *Woman & Home* (UK), *Bark, Adoptive Families* and the *Reader's Digest* "Today's Best NonFiction" series, and on the *Time, Fortune, Highlights* and *Next Avenue* websites. Visit Jill at www.jillsmolowe.com and facebook.com/jillsmolowe.author.

THE GIFT OF LOSS

Alison Dale

I stole my way into the world of memoir at age seven, while attending a three-room school surrounded by cornfields. I loved the wide-open space and longed for recess, when I could run free. An introvert who was ahead in my schoolwork but not allowed to skip a grade, I was often intellectually bored and socially overwhelmed at school. I would finish my work early and long to get away from the confines of my noisy, bustling classroom.

One afternoon, I told my teacher that I wasn't feeling well, and she gave me permission to go rest in the nurse's room. I wandered in and lay down on a small cot, covering myself with a soft gray blanket. The sound of the droning teacher and murmuring children receded into the background, and I felt a warm silence rub up against me like a cat. Immediately, I felt relief. After lying there for a few minutes, I sat up and looked around. The office doubled as a supply room, and above the cot was a long white shelf, stacked with pale green notebooks. I reached up for one and opened it, inhaling the scent of fresh paper. The blank pages thrilled and beckoned me. They were like the wide-open space around the schoolyard, only more private.

I managed to smuggle the notebook into my school bag and off school property at the end of the day. The vague unease I felt about my "theft" gave way to excitement at the thought of having all those pages to myself. I'm sure I could have simply asked for the notebook, but then the teachers would have known I had it. Their knowing would have intruded on my newfound private space. I loved words, and reading. I hadn't yet tried writing, but now I had somewhere to put my own words. This urge to write felt very private, even secret; it seemed like something that should go undetected by the people around me. The notebook would become my first primitive journal, and writing would become my favorite hideout.

Perhaps this urge to create in a shroud of secrecy had something to do with my having been born to an unwed mother, who'd disappeared from the prying eyes of society to create me covertly before relinquishing me for adoption. Perhaps, while developing in hiding, I picked up the message that creative acts should be concealed. Or maybe the urge to create in secrecy was a reaction to my adoptive mother's need for privacy. My parents were going through a divorce at the time—one of the first couples in our community to do so. To my mother's great dismay, I often blurted out sensitive family matters to complete strangers. I thought our life was worth talking about. The message was: don't.

Though a writer herself, my mother steered clear of self-revelation, preferring the more veiled language of poetry. She also wrote book reviews, and occasional articles for the local newspaper. With three children to care for, she was too busy to navel-gaze and didn't wish to draw attention to her own angst. Instead, she used writing to build a new identity and voice beyond the shadow of my departed father. I was proud that my mother was a published poet who had pieces in the local paper. Many years later, I would meet my birth mother and discover that she, too, had been a newspaper journalist. I would follow in both their footsteps until my feet walked me back in the more compelling direction of memoir.

The year after I made off with my first "stolen" notebook was the year I learned cursive writing. Suddenly, writing became an art form, and learning to form letters that flowed into each other gave me a sense of momentum. It also brought me a sense of calm. I felt rooted and in touch with myself as soon as my pen or pencil touched the page. The connected flow of cursive writing amplified this effect, and to this day, I still get tremendous relief from the simple act of writing by hand.

I was destined to become a memoirist, because as much as I loved the idea of writing fiction, my plot lines always fizzled out and I'd come back to my own musings. Yet I loved stories and all the things it took to tell a good one.

Eventually, I abandoned my fictional urges, but I still studied the techniques of fiction. I then became a freelance journalist, contributing to newspapers and the occasional magazine. I profiled new businesses, community agencies, artists, and musicians and wrote frequent music reviews and an arts-and-entertainment column. The pressure of next-day deadlines honed my craft immeasurably. I would stay up all night to get the words just right and be rewarded by the sight of my work in print the next day.

Newspapers gave me a forum and a following. They helped me develop my style, but I longed to write more deeply. I wanted to write about the world *behind* the eye, which mystic and medical intuitive Carolyn Myss calls the realm of *homo noeticus*. The word *noeticus* comes from the Greek term *noesis*, which means "understanding, perception, and clear mind." My ongoing practice of personal journaling strengthened all three of these states. Years of doing it gave me great ease with language and a direct connection to my inner voice. I wanted to take it a step further and fashion stories out of the raw material of my life.

I have found memoir writing to be like the process of making pottery. I take the raw clay of my life and work it through my hands until it starts to take some kind of shape. When I start a piece, I never know quite what it will become, but the process turns me on. My face often gets flushed from the presence of my muse, and from the heat generated by the kiln-like process of rewriting and refining. It's a total workout for body, mind, spirit, and emotions.

Memoir writing could be seen as a narcissistic endeavor, but I see it as a process of making the most of my life, then offering that to others. I've had to fight the critical voice that tells me it's self-indulgent, self-centered, and small-minded to write about my own life, but, as memoir coach Denis Ledoux puts it, "It's true, and it happened to you." That's reason enough. Maybe it was true for someone else, too. My inner critic says things like, *Oh, no one cares about* that, *dear. Don't think you're so special. You shouldn't bring attention to these things, anyway. It just makes people uncomfortable.*

I recall my mother once saying, "You don't have to bare your soul to the world, you know." Well, actually, I do. Yet it's such a vulnerable thing, putting my most sensitive self out there for the world's consumption.

The act of writing memoir is as deep a practice as any meditation, with all the attendant distractions. It's hard just to stay put and write. I squirm, because the act of writing memoir is often gut-wrenching. I'm digging into the guts of my life and pulling out things that are deep-seated and deep-rooted and that sometimes prefer to be left alone. Writing dredges things up. I sometimes feel as if I'm lifting an anvil from the bottom of a swampy ocean, and get so tired I have to lie down. At those times, I remember that I'm actually diving into shady shipwrecks full of buried treasure, and that there's a lot of pressure when you go down deep. Emotions come up and head me off at the pass. I experience powerful cravings for things that promise to relieve the stress (usually food). But if I can stay at the page long enough, the emotions that surface end up being the treasure I'm seeking. These feelings are the heart of the story. They are the bridge between writer and reader. When I finish a piece, I feel enlivened by the creative process that transformed raw life into art. When I share it, I sometimes want to run for cover, but sharing it is an act of bravery every time, and a risk worth taking.

In the movie *Shadowlands,* author C. S. Lewis shares the expression, "We read to know we're not alone." Though I must be alone to write deeply, the time spent finding precise words to describe a situation, combined with meaningful reflection, offers a bridge between lives. This practice of articulate honesty, revelation, and reflection gives so much value to inner experience, which is often not so different from that of other people. They just haven't necessarily put it into words. If they *have*, and I have a chance to read it, then I get to see the world behind *another* person's eyes. The quietness of the page allows me to savor a phrase, an insight, a perspective, and feel soul-to-soul nourishment. As humans, we are more alike than different, yet we have imaginations as distinct as our fingerprints. This is what delights me most about other people's writing—the specific way they put things, in the way only they can do.

In my own first piece of published memoir, I wrote about the reunion with my birth mother. We both loved to write, and the first letter I received from her was ten pages long. Her handwriting looked like mine. Her sentences flowed like mine. I could hear a surreal kind of echo in every one, and I literally jumped for joy until I read:

"Unfortunately, the breast cancer I had two years ago has come back and has spread to my spine. I'm sorry that we're in this time bind. We'll just have to do the best we can."

My heart went into shock, disbelief, and then panic, as the clock suddenly started to race. We arranged to meet as soon as we could. Three buses and ten hours later, I arrived in Stratford, Ontario, and walked into the open arms of a tall, striking woman with short gray hair and glasses. When we hugged for the first time at the bus station, our bodies fit together so naturally it was like we'd never been apart. We then drove to her place, where we sat eating green grapes and cashews, sharing our stories and feeling our way into this new-yet-familiar relationship.

Carol was gaunt and looked tired. At one point, she asked if I would mind rubbing cream on her back. The radiation had made it itchy. I followed her into the bathroom, where she kept her cream. In a trance of incredulity, I rubbed it into the brown patches left by the radiation, touching my mother's skin for the first time.

A few days later, we went to a psychic for a channeling session, wanting some spiritual guidance on our situation. The psychic told Carol that she was needed on the other side but could go whenever she was ready, without a lot of pain. She told *me* that my greatest breakthrough would come through loss. Somehow I knew this would be true, but the impact of hearing this during our first week together translated into two words: *hello* and *goodbye*. It was extremely upsetting.

The time bind, as Carol had called it, made everything more intense and vivid for us. I'd never connected this deeply with anyone, and it was overwhelming to think of parting again. The psychic had called us "twin flames," and we were, in so many ways. We had the same books, the same music, even the same hands. Most notably, we were twin *rainbow* flames, preferring the company of our own gender. To have this in common was perhaps the most stunning miracle of our reunion. We'd both grown up in very religious families who condemned same-sex relationships, mostly out of ignorance and lack of exposure. A relative, when he found out about my orientation, had said to me, "If they ever prove it's genetic, then maybe I'll accept it." Whether or not it *is* genetic, there we were—two birds of a rainbow feather, grateful to have found this hugely healing kinship.

Thankfully, we were given more time than we thought we'd have at first—four years, in fact. Carol was fifty-five when she died. I was thirty-two. The beauty of our time together was exquisite, and the loss was equally profound. I carried our story inside me for years, not knowing how to get it out but wanting to share it with the world. Finally, a contest created the perfect conditions to bring it forth. The Canadian Lesbian and Gay Archives was having its first-ever writing contest and sought submissions for an upcoming anthology. This was my chance to add our story to Canadian LGBT history and to mark the ten-year anniversary of Carol's death.

Summing up our relationship in 2,500 words was intensely challenging. I sifted and sorted through memories until a few key vignettes surfaced. The process was a true labor of love, and tears often obscured the words on the screen. They were tears of pure grief mixed with complete wonder. At those times, I would think about what the psychic had said—that my "greatest breakthrough would come through loss." When I printed the finished draft, I held my story as if it were a newborn child. Carol had named me Joy when I was born, so I called the story "Finding Joy." Here is an excerpt:

We were healing mirrors for each other—both shadow and light. I alternated between being a fountain of love and a deer in the headlights of oncoming loss. I was scared to get close and then lose her. Carol had gone through the same thing while she carried me, deliberately detaching so the pain would be less.

One night, I took a bath at her house. She knocked gently on the door and asked to come in. After a minute, she asked if she could wash my back.

"You look like you are seven years old. I feel like I've missed so much." She kneeled by the tub and rubbed the washcloth over my skin. It was like traveling backward through time.

Another day, she took me shopping for winter boots. We stopped at a coffee shop in the mall, where she said, "When I gave you away as a gift of joy, I never expected you to come back and be that very thing to me."

Carol died four years after we'd met, in her home, on Mother's Day. I was the only one in the room with her at the time—the same room where we'd sat talking that first night. As she prepared to leave the shrunken cage of her body, she let out a huge honking sound, like a great bird taking off. I stood in awe, and cheered for her freedom.

A few days later, I borrowed a rainbow kite to fly in her honor. Had it been mine, I would have let go of the string, as she had with me, trusting that someday we'd meet again.

Through our relationship, I learned the greatest lesson: that joy is in the finding, not the keeping.

This chance to love and let go was truly my greatest breakthrough, and writing the story allowed the loss to become the gift it was meant to be, for me and for others.

* * * * *

ALISON DALE lives in Stratford, Ontario, where she juggles her time between music and writing, listening for the rhythmic pulse in each art form. A former freelance journalist, she now concentrates on memoir, loving its authenticity and candidness, and the sheer joy that comes from making beauty and value out of raw life experience. She sees writing as a transformative personal practice, and one that leads directly to well-being. For this reason, she keeps her hand on the page as much as possible, while encouraging others to bust into their own story vaults and dig out the treasures buried there. When Alison is not writing, she is riding her motorcycle, playing instruments, and working as a music care practitioner, helping people with special needs express themselves through the language of sound.

THE POWER OF WORDS

Vanya Erickson

In the middle of the night, I was awakened by a familiar breathless urgency. Scenes of my father swirled in and out of clarity in that half-awake state, heating my chest, pinning me to the damp sheets. Countless atrocities materialized with such vividness I knew I'd never escape. But then something shifted. Light shimmered at the edge of his image, softening his features, and for the first time, I shouted back. "Enough!"

The sound of that word woke me up, although, surprisingly, not my sweetheart, who was snoring on the other side of the bed. I reached for my glasses and laptop, my fingers shaking, my belly an empty pit. I looked over at the sleeping man I loved and wanted to wake him. I wanted to tell him how grateful I was for his kindness, and how he was a great father.

But the claws of the nightmare were still in me. I tiptoed to the couch in our tiny studio and began writing into the darkness of that October night. My face, a disembodied mask illuminated by the laptop screen, hovered like the moon over my keyboard. *Shouldn't I be over this by now? After all, Dad's been dead for thirty years—he can't get me anymore.* But as I typed, I heard the impatient pacing of his cowboy boots scraping the linoleum and my fingers began to stab the keyboard. *If I do this, will he finally go away? Will I ever heal?*

Within a few years, I had dozens of Dad stories—tight, tense scenes from my childhood that brought relief when I read them aloud. They electrified readers. Literary magazines published some. I now had a regular posse of writing pals hating my dad. But the memories didn't stop. They surprised me like stray bullets while I drove to work, or when I was helping my students, or as I sat in meditation. There was no telling when they'd appear.

In response, I kept writing as if it could save my life. I carved large swaths of time from my day like an addict, waking at 3:00 A.M. to write before work, saying no to everything social except the most crucial family events. I became a lousy friend. Such was the urgency to purge my past.

Then came the "oh, shit!" stories I'd long since buried—the hell of self-damage I had crawled away from a half a century ago and had never imagined putting on the page. Immersing my body in a nightly bath of scalding water, pain searing every orifice, my suffering euphoric; staring into the mirror, blind to my skeletal reflection, taunting my haunted body. I held my breath and exposed these, too—reliving each moment, weeping as I wrote down every last motherfucking word.

This was followed by days I wanted to give up and throw my manuscript away. Days I didn't give a shit what anyone thought about my work, followed by days I wanted to be told that my writing was brilliant, that I'd made someone cry.

Days I avoided everything—choosing to drink, shop, or get lost in the black hole of the Internet. But none of it worked.

Every time I quit, an internal signpost nagged at me, gently at first, then relentlessly. Then I'd begin again. I started with the softer, nearly forgotten memories: my horse nuzzling me in greeting, the scent of oats on his breath; the warm breeze moving through pines like a whisper; my body dancing like liquid, music in every pore; my mother reciting poetry, her face lifted in rapture.

Finally I had both sides of the story. I had pushed through the denial, hatred, and fear and discovered what really mattered: I could choose happiness. I could choose compassion. I had found a way to put the truth on the page—both the trauma and the beauty—and found that with kindness, I could contain them both, cupped in my hands. Now what holds me to the page day after day is the contrast of all life's beauty braided with the ugliness—and the power of those words strung together to heal.

* * * * *

VANYA ERICKSON is a veteran writing and performing arts teacher and has spent her life helping children stand up and be counted. She bears witness to the transformative power of words on a daily basis. Her work has appeared or is upcoming in *Oxford Magazine, Gulf Stream Literary Magazine, Evening Street Review, The Delmarva Review,* and *Sweet: A Literary Confection.*

✳ DAISY HERNÁNDEZ ✳

Author of A *Cup of Water Under My Bed*

BROOKE WARNER: In the introduction of your book, you beautifully articulate what I think a lot of memoirists want to achieve with their writing. You write, "I wanted, too, to testify. To say: This happened." And there is so much here—coming of age in an immigrant family, defining your sexuality on your own terms, socioeconomic concerns that are a source of anxiety and even obsession for your mother and aunts, your father's alcoholism. Did you worry about tackling too much, and how did you approach the subject matter when you first started writing the memoir and deciding what it was going to be?

DAISY HERNÁNDEZ: I didn't realize I was writing a memoir! I started by writing into the questions that I had: Why did it irritate me so much that my auntie called me *una india*? What did being *una india* even mean? Why had my father's Afro-Cuban religion made so much sense to me as a child? Why did the murder of one transgender Chicana teenager haunt me? So each chapter was originally a stand-alone essay. After years of writing, I took stock of what I had written and saw that a memoir had happened! I also clearly saw three themes emerging: culture, sexuality, and class. Having that triad helped me to remove certain pieces from the book. It also helped me to write the opening and the last chapter. While the memoir and the structure found me, I did read a lot of books that struck me as a fusion of memoir and essay or as unconventional memories. These include Julie Marie

Wade's *Small Fires*, Abigail Thomas's memoirs, Brenda Miller's essay collections, Luis Alberto Urrea's *Nobody's Son*, Julia Alvarez's *Something to Declare*, and bell hooks's *Bone Black*.

✳

BROOKE WARNER: You've been honored with so many awards for this memoir, and a notable one, in my opinion, is from Lambda Literary. In an online review, they specifically call out the section on sexuality. They write, "Hernández talks about sexuality with grace; her deft hand with language, imagery, and emotion create an internal world that is both intimate and achingly beautiful." This is amazing. Can you tell us about writing about your sexuality, and what you hoped readers would glean around the topic of your bisexuality?

DAISY HERNÁNDEZ: The memoir actually started with the section on sexuality. I was in my twenties and trying to understand my experience, and I had been blessed with Latina feminists who had pushed me to read the work of Audre Lorde, Cherríe Moraga, Gloria Anzaldúa, and James Baldwin. These writers had all turned to writing to make sense of sexuality and race and their communities, so I figured I could do the same. I quickly found out that for me, writing about bisexuality means writing about my immigrant parents, my two languages, and my childhood in a working-class community. Sexuality is an experience that's intimately related to race, ethnicity, and class—not to mention gender. The only hope I harbor for readers is that my writing opens a door for them. Maybe they've never read a story from a bisexual Latina before. Maybe they read my memoir and part of it feels like their story or their sister's story or their daughter's experience. I hope it opens a door that the reader needs in her own life.

BROOKE WARNER: Titles are difficult to come up with in memoir. You want them to tell a story but not be cliché, and the trend is so much toward pithy, evocative titles these days. I love *A Cup of Water Under My Bed*. What's the story of this title, and how did you land on it as the title of your book?

DAISY HERNÁNDEZ: I had a different (very boring) title, and my editor at Beacon Press, Gayatri Patnaik, called and asked, "Are you married to the title?" With as much of a deadpan voice as I could muster, I said, "No, but we're seriously engaged." Then she gave me wonderful instructions: spend an hour or two with the manuscript, and make a list of words or phrases that jump at you. I did that, and I sent the list to her and the marketing department. They picked the title. Then I emailed my closest twenty friends and asked them to pick between the new title and the old one. The group was completely divided! That's when my amazing friend, the novelist Carolina DeRobertis, stepped in to argue for the cup of water—for the fact that it's an image, and an intimate one, but it also speaks to the larger efforts of the women in my family to take care of me. The moment I heard her say how layered the title was for her as a reader, I knew it was the right one.

BROOKE WARNER: What is the magic of memoir for you?

DAISY HERNÁNDEZ: The novelist Doris Lessing famously wrote that the novel allows the "small, personal voice" of one writer to speak to many readers. I don't experience that with novels, but I do experience it with memoirs. In fact, I spent last month "binge" reading memoirs for a seminar that I'm teaching on memoir as social criticism, and even though I was reading so many memoirs, each time, I heard the small, personal voice of the writer. In hearing that voice, I also heard the voices of entire communities and of specific moments in time. People often chide memoir as an insular genre, but memoir springs from people being in relationship to each other. Every memoir in some ways is a community story told with a small, personal voice that is, hopefully, unforgettable.

✳ ✳ ✳ ✳ ✳

DAISY HERNÁNDEZ is the author of *A Cup of Water Under My Bed: A Memoir* and coeditor of *Colonize This! Young Women of Color on Today's Feminism*. The former editor of *ColorLines* magazine, she has written for the *Atlantic*, the *New York Times*, and NPR's *All Things Considered* and *CodeSwitch*, and her essays have appeared in the *Bellingham Review*, *Dogwood*, *Fourth Genre*, *Gulf Coast*, *Hunger Mountain*, and *Tricycle*. She teaches creative writing at Miami University in Ohio. To see more of her work, visit www.daisyhernandez.com.

JOURNEY TO A MEMOIR

Sonvy Sammons

Mom planted the seeds that would become the first sprouts of my memoir when I was a child living on a small farm in Montana in the 1950s and '60s. As I watched her journal daily, I knew writing was helping her to survive her life of isolation, illness, four children, and an alcoholic husband. And, in spite of working long days, she wrote dozens of poems and stories late at night, based mostly on her childhood years on a Wisconsin farm in a Norwegian immigrant community. Blessed with an amazing memory, she wrote stories of her extended family and ancestors as they'd been told to her, gifting my brothers and me with an irreplaceable written history.

Three important awakenings in my life have shaped and inspired my memoir. The first of these was the feeling of being "commissioned" by my mother's example. At a young age I, too, found writing letters and journaling helpful in sorting my thoughts and feelings and calming frustration and anger. It seemed boastful to think I could ever write family stories as beautifully as Mom did, but I promised my ten-year-old self I would someday give it a try.

The second awakening that helped launch my memoir writing happened when I was a young adult, after I'd left my childhood home for college and marriage. Growing up with an alcoholic father, I was socially isolated and had little opportunity to observe other families' behavior to compare with my own family's frightening brawls. Once I was on my own, I visited others' homes and realized how bizarre things had been at mine. When I shared childhood anecdotes with people, I often heard, "You have a compelling story, and you should write about it." More than once, I went home thinking, *Maybe this story really is supposed to be written.*

As a young girl, I always thought the things I hated about myself were nonnegotiable personality traits I had inherited from my Norwegian parents, Dad especially. At that time, I would have been described as stoic, shy, independent, and unwilling to reveal my true feelings or trust anyone. I was almost forty when I read *It Will Never Happen to Me*, by Claudia Black. In writing of alcoholism and its effect on families, she said adult children of alcoholics (ACoAs), in order to survive, learn three coping skills: don't talk, don't trust, don't feel. *She's describing me*, I thought, feeling exposed by someone I'd never met. But somehow I felt less alone and unworthy, and, for the first time, I understood why I was the way I was. It was a revelation that started me on a marathon to read every book that was written by and about ACoAs. It made me believe I could break free of my past.

I, like most ACoAs, was unwilling to reveal my problems to others, especially a counselor I didn't know. But Claudia spoke to me through her book. Books are safe. I was willing to turn to a book for discernment, comfort, and help in solving my problems. Books don't judge you, sense your shame, or talk back. The collection of books by and about ACoAs helped me immeasurably and were my therapists, my inspiration, and my comfort throughout a hard time in my life. I dreamed of writing my own story, sharing how I'd found so many answers and so much healing in others' life stories, adding what new insights my similar but different journey had presented. Maybe I could be a helpful voice to someone else.

The third awakening was similar but more urgent. Earlier, I had been focused on my own self-discovery and healing, and how much I had learned from books written by and about ACoAs. Later, I became painfully aware that my own family, children, and grandchildren are today very much at risk. The findings of researchers and writers Michael Windle and John Searles in *Children of Alcoholics: Critical Perspectives*, and of Richard Towers in *Children of Alcoholics/Addicts*, haunted me then and still do. Windle and Searles state, "ACoAs are four times more likely than children of non-alcoholics to become alcoholics themselves, and perhaps as many as four out of five ACoAs marry an alcoholic." Towers estimates that "eighty percent of adolescent suicides are children of alcoholics." I already had concerns about my brothers, as we had all shared the same dysfunctional household. But now I was startled to realize my own children were at risk as well, even though I was rearing them in an alcohol-free home.

Dad's alcoholism was the biggest factor in the too-early deaths of two of my brothers. The alcoholic in the family usually gets all the attention, as everyone tiptoes around him to keep peace. All the other members fend for themselves. Sammy, unable to do that, committed suicide at age twenty-nine.

Thirty years passed before my second brother's drinking raged out of control, his brilliance in writing and music pushed aside, his marriage in trouble, and his gifted young son watching his father drift away. There was nothing the rest of us could do as the ripple effect of Dad's alcoholism took another brother's life. I felt as helpless as I did when I was a child with no power in a scary environment. The family's story is not pretty, but it must be told.

I felt powerless to influence the alcohol use of family members of my generation, but my motivation to reach my daughters, nephew, and grandchildren is strong. I hope to write my story so that these younger ones might know their risks and family history. It's not just the alcoholism but also the negative coping skills that get passed along, even when there's no more drinking. Knowledge is power, I have always believed, and I will not give up trying to break alcoholism's deadly cycle in our family.

So, what made me finally start writing my memoir? I give Dr. Barbara Finan, a teacher in a pastoral ministry MA program in 2000, credit for that, as I pondered writing my life story as part of my colloquium–thesis project. I thought I'd write it in such a way as to encourage churches to be more aware of ACoAs and offer informative discernment programs in their outreach efforts. Barbara, however, said, "Write your personal story. It is one of redemption that will inspire, as well as teach. Write to show how your experiences shaped you as a person and as the pastoral minister you now are." My memories, which are now being reframed into a memoir, were first put on paper in that graduate program.

Writing down those memories for the first time, I sat at the computer and poured out my heart and mind, living hours on end in that other childhood world. It was an emotional marathon, from 4:00 P.M. until 6:00 A.M. sometimes, but it became a whole new chapter in my own healing. Thus, I discovered one of the best reasons to write your memoir:

for clarification and catharsis in your own life. The colloquium format was more rigid and formal than what I now envision in my memoir, so that document serves as a bank from which I pull significant ideas.

Reading my original story again, I am surprised by the deeper layers of feelings and details that emerge. I am now completely reshaping and blending those memories into a memoir as creative nonfiction, enriched by the new insights and tools I bring to the table. My daughters are now on their own, and I am no longer working full-time. It is, at last, the right time to deal with the dozens of memories that have been bouncing around in my brain, yearning to be set free. I aim to set them free, and myself as well.

Liberating my memories will involve telling the stories of quite a few people other than me, and I do have concerns about respecting their privacy. The fact that both my parents and two of my brothers are now dead makes things a little easier; nonetheless, I want to try to show all sides of people, the positive and the negative. My one remaining brother said, "Sis, it's your story. Tell it as you wish, but just remember, I have to go on living here."

Good advice, I think. The adage "do unto others as you'd have them do unto you" sounds like a plan. Unless someone has told me I'm free to use their name, I plan to use pseudonyms.

I don't want to completely demonize anyone in my story, as they all are mixtures of good and bad. I thank members of my writing group for showing me how I'd demonized my father. Just from what I'd written about Dad and his drunken misbehavior, the group expressed hatred and scorn that shocked me. I had succeeded too well in making him a villain. I knew Dad was a brilliant, gentle, compassionate man whose drinking didn't escalate to the point of alcoholism until I was in sixth grade, and I don't want my children and grandchildren to get the same feelings my fellow writers did when they read my story. Some revisions were in order.

I added some backstory to show Dad's innate goodness and the emotional wounds from his mother's dying young, his father's harsh, demanding nature, and his emigration to America alone as an eighteen-year-old-boy. After knowing more of his story, in spite of hearing of Dad's drunken rants, they could still see him as a person with his own scars and frustrations. It has helped me acknowledge that the alcoholism that changed him so dramatically was not so much a character flaw as it was an illness—indeed, a family weakness and an attempt to salve an emotional wound. My changed perspective helped both my readers and me see Dad with more empathy and understanding.

Comments from my writing group have taught me I am doing more than writing a memoir. I am bringing my family members and significant others to life, defining them for all the world to know, love, or hate in ways that may endure through generations. I must choose with care the words I write and speak, for they have the power to lift up and inform or to create unintended hostility, damage, or pain.

The task of translating memories and significant events into a story is a challenging one. I always loved English classes and could generally write grammatically correct sentences, but the notion of painting pictures with words is on the agenda. That is a whole new skill set for me, one I am loving to learn—but unfamiliar none the same. Good advice on writing interesting stories, however, is amazingly available. I have taken advantage of instruction and encouragement in books, writing journals, webinars, and college minicourses, and input directly from other writers, especially in several writing groups I attend. Some of the most significant advice includes to use dialogue frequently to bring characters to life; to create a scene of each chapter or incident so your reader can really "see" it; to use the five senses so readers can experience what you are telling them.

Way back when I was first starting to write my memoir, my first "eureka" moment came when I stumbled across Denis Ledoux's website, The Memoir Network. His comments on "show, don't tell" jumped out like a neon sign, and my writing was changed forever. I was like a kid with a new toy as I waded into scene after scene, challenging my memory to bring back details I needed. Now, instead of *telling* my reader Dad was drunk or angry, I have learned to *show* him stumbling, slurring his words, or slamming a door, or with a fiery red face. What a difference. I am most grateful for my great teachers, including Ledoux, Joan Dempsey, Brooke Warner and Linda Joy Myers, and Jane Friedman.

Being in a writing group that meets weekly keeps me writing at times when I would otherwise make excuses not to. It forces me to make time, and I am finding that is a big part of writing a memoir. When the other writers in my group like a story or are moved to tears or laughter by it, it keeps me hanging in there. Likewise, if they don't understand the story the way I intended, I know other readers will feel the same. One week, I pondered taking out a short backstory about my brother Sammy's depression and events before his suicide. However, several in the writing group felt the story would heighten awareness about people who suffer in similar ways, just as it could also help the parents or caretakers of those sufferers to feel less alone. So it stays in, for now.

After I wrote my first draft, one challenging observation from an early reader changed my story more than almost anything else: "You have told me of many things that happened. I want to know more about how you felt when it happened, the impact it had on you and your life, and what you think or feel about it now."

I went to work, writing more to reflect that new awareness, and the results sometimes surprised me. As I focused more on how an event affected me emotionally, the story pulled me in and seemed to come alive. And each time I revised the writing of a particular event, I recalled something I hadn't remembered before, including feelings I had buried. Sometimes it was scary; other times it was poignant and I ended up in tears.

Such a time was when I was working on a chapter that tells of the dark, concrete basement of our farmhouse, and how I, then twelve years old, hated going down there alone. The family's freezer was in an interior room of the basement, and when Mom sent me to get food out of it, I had to walk past Dad's workbench and tool cabinet. It so happened Dad had chosen a dark corner down there, hidden by his bulky tool cabinet, in which to sit on a stool and drink beer or whiskey alone every night.

One time he surprised me down there, on my way to the freezer, by suddenly lunging out of the darkness, trying to grab me and pull me close to him. I can still see him leering at me with a drunken smirk, his hands groping. I'd met that look a couple times before, and I fled in a panic, running back upstairs, taking two steps at a time. As I revised this chapter, expressing feelings and memories I'd not previously noted, I uncovered more anxiety and fear than I had felt in a long time.

Picture me, sitting at my computer in my writing-music studio with the door closed. I am deep in thought and emotional angst as I revise the basement story, pulling long-ago-buried feelings and fears from a space deep inside me. I wipe tears away from time to time, reliving what that little girl went through, mourning the fears and losses she already felt and would only add to in the years ahead. From where I sit, the entire house is silent. I am alone in my small room. My husband is out in the living room, watching television, the sound turned down low.

Ka-boom! All of a sudden, a thunderous noise echoes outside my window. All the lights go out. I am instantly paralyzed with fear. I cannot see my hand in front of my face. I reach out to touch the computer cabinet, almost surprised that I am here in my studio.

There's no light anywhere, no sound at all. My heart flip-flops as I stand up, feel my way to the door, and pull it open.

I can hear my husband rustling around to get a flashlight in the kitchen. At last, I can breathe again. Richard's close by, and I feel safe.

"Here you go—a flashlight for you," he says. "Transformer, maybe. They'll fix it soon, I'm sure." I cradle the flashlight tenderly, glad for its welcome glow, grateful for Richard's calming strength.

This was one emotional surprise in writing my story that I will never forget.

I was there. In that basement. Perhaps I really can take my readers there, too.

SONVY SAMMONS is a wife, mother, daughter, friend, and animal lover who has finally retired from working for an income and is now writing a memoir. She received a BA from Montana State University and an MA from St. Mary's University of Minnesota.

In her previous life, she taught elementary school, junior high, and high school. After following her husband, Richard, all over the country during six years of military service, she settled in Bismarck, North Dakota, and became liturgist–music director of Corpus Christi Church. Over the next twenty years, she and her Richard reared two wonderful daughters, five dogs, and two cats.

Today, Sonvy keeps busy with writing, quilting, sewing, reading, teaching piano and guitar lessons, walking her Gordon setter, Nellie, and traveling to Minnesota and Michigan to visit her daughters and three grandchildren, all of whom she adores.

IT WOULD NEVER HAPPEN TO US

Laurie Prim

My twenty-five-year friendship with Carolyn ended in 2015 with a two-sentence text: *Sorry, but just don't feel like talking right now. Your book hurt my feelings, and I don't want to say hurtful things to you, so it's better if I just keep my distance for the time being.*

I don't mean it was the beginning of the end, that, despite numerous tearful conversations and the hard work of trying to rebuild trust, we couldn't salvage the soul-sisterhood we'd shared through college, graduate school, and beyond. It was, literally, The End. *Time being* was a euphemism for *forever*, and we've never spoken again.

I thought we'd survived my reproductive trauma. True, there'd been strain; there nearly always is. It's one of the universals of fertility support groups: friends' pregnancies wreck us, they feel hurt, and we torture ourselves with the guilt. Lots of friendships are destroyed, but, even living two hours apart, Carolyn and I were different. When she sent me an e-mail of her first ultrasound, I wrote back telling her I was happy for her but that since I'd seen my first baby with no heartbeat at twelve weeks, it was really painful for me to look at ultrasounds. I attached the pages I'd written about that experience, and she empathized and didn't send any more ultrasounds.

When she once mentioned my "hormone pills" during an IVF cycle, I sent her a picture of my kitchen table covered with vials, syringes, needles, pills, patches, suppositories, and a red BIOHAZARD sharps container. She gasped that she'd had no idea, and I assured her she couldn't have. When I asked my friends for space while I clawed my way through the darkest days of my life, she gave it to me, even though I'm sure it felt disappointing and bewildering. She did her best to support me, and I let her know how much it meant to me. It sucked for both of us, but we were no ordinary friends, and ultimately we got to celebrate each having a son.

Four years later, trying for a second child, I had my third miscarriage. Two months after that, I was still reeling, yet trying to prepare myself for my upcoming fourth IVF cycle—my last chance—when Carolyn had her second baby. I called and left a message of congratulations, hoping she wouldn't hear the shaking in my voice. (After all, people told me, I had my son. I should be fine, right?) She replied with an e-mail about how amazing her new baby girl was and attached a picture of the two of them gazing lovingly into each other's eyes in the hospital bed.

I went ballistic. "How dare she?" I sobbed, punching pillows, cursing her and my whole brutal journey, and I spared no ugly detail when I wrote about that day. Was that the death knell of our friendship? Or was it some culmination of everything, and her finally being done with my emotional fragility and largely unapologetic self-care? Or something else altogether, something I am destined never to know?

But by the time she read my (yet-unpublished) book, I had had a second baby and Carolyn and I had been as close as ever for three years. In fact, that was why I gave it to her— my reproductive struggle completely reshaped my life, and she was someone I wanted to share that with. She'd had her own share of trauma in the past several years, including the grueling death of her other best friend and then her father. I felt, to some extent, like we were healing together. I was trying to work up the courage to dip my toe in the waters of fertility support and advocacy, but at least with Carolyn I was safe.

I was driving when I got the text, after weeks of unanswered calls and texts of my own. I immediately pressed her name in FAVORITES and bawled into her voice mail while trying not to veer out of my lane. "I'm sorry, Carr. I didn't . . . I wouldn't . . . I thought . . . I thought you would understand things in the context of what I'd been going through. I'll give you whatever time you need, the way you did me when I couldn't talk. I love you."

The next day, I texted: *Forget it. I miss you already. Please let's figure out how to make things right with us.*

In the ongoing silence, my own anger settled in. This was not about *her*. This was *my* memoir, my truth.

What happened to her supposed understanding? She'd previously sent long texts about how much she loved my book and how she was so sorry for everything I'd been through and how she had a true understanding of fertility struggles now. She was even excited to start incorporating it into her new counseling practice, and I gave her my copy of *Reproductive Trauma*, by Janet Jaffe and Martha O. Diamond.

Maybe she was right. Maybe we both needed some time to process our feelings. But when four more silent months passed, I sent another text: *Wondering if we're not going to make it through this. NEVER saw this happening to us.*

Crickets.

Another month. *I'm really hoping we can talk about things. Please let me know if you are willing, whether through text or e-mail or phone or getting together.*

Nothing.

I texted again, asking her to send back my Jaffe and Diamond book, saying I was starting a support group. (Which was true, but I was also worried I'd inadvertently done the fertility community a scary disservice; it was clear by now that this was not a person who should be counseling us.) I got the book in the mail a day later, no note, no nothing, and that was it, the engagement of the deadlock on our friendship. I could see her brushing off her hands at the mailbox—twenty-five years over, without a single discussion.

Here's the thing: when I got that package, I brushed off my hands, too, and it wasn't nearly as hard as it should have been. She was entitled to her reaction to my memoir, but her response to that reaction, just to cut me off like a necrotic appendage, was beyond all reasonableness. This was not on me.

Oh, I grieved. I cried, and I cursed, and I pitied myself to some extent, but mostly I remained more shocked than I'd been since the Twin Towers had gone down. For a long time after 9/11, I'd sometimes stop dead while reaching for a glass or tying my shoe and think, *Wait, did that really happen? Are those buildings—all those people—really* gone? It was the same now: I simply could not believe Carolyn had opted out of my life as abruptly as if she'd been in those towers, and yet acceptance came fast. In the course of having my two children, I'd grieved the lifetime of three lost babies and huge parts of my own self, and a part of that grief would live with me forever. Turns out the grief for a self-centered friend who loved me conditionally doesn't rate much after that. Instead, most of what suddenly surfaced were the times past when I'd thought she'd acted without integrity and I'd given her a pass simply because she was worth it.

Of course I questioned my book. I had to. Was I unfair in my telling? Did I have to be *so* nakedly honest? Should I have just kept it under the bed, as I had for two years? Was it unreasonable to have thought Carolyn would respond with empathy and compassion, or at least a sad understanding of my perspective at the time? A major theme of my book was to show how reproductive trauma turns a person inside out and infiltrates *everything*; was I *that* bad a writer? If I could take it back to have Carolyn again, would I?

Honestly, I didn't grapple with these questions for all that long, either. I think it's fair to expect more sensitivity than knowingly sending a picture of a newborn to someone still raw from her third miscarriage. Furthermore, the meltdown I had was in the privacy of my own bedroom, and, fair or not, it was the reality of everything I'd been enduring for *years*. I acknowledged that Carolyn hadn't meant to hurt me, and I didn't begrudge her her happiness; I was simply incapable of witnessing it because I was broken.

During the months when I was still hoping to hear from Carolyn, I became involved with RESOLVE: The National Infertility Association, as well as some online fertility support groups. Supporting others going through what I had felt so alone in was something I'd long wanted to do. What I didn't anticipate was how supported and grateful and inspired I would feel there myself. I had, at long last, found my community.

Not a day goes by when there aren't stories and posts about how difficult and painful it is to navigate friendships with people who haven't experienced infertility. If I were to take my book back, to deny my truth, I'd be denying the truth of every woman in that community. Every day, these strong, resourceful, resilient women let me know that my story gives them hope and encourage—and urge—me to keep talking.

What I do regret is having underestimated how hard or hurtful it might have been for Carolyn to read the parts of my book that included her, and not having had more of a discussion about it beforehand. I'd lived with all this for so long that it had become part of my natural landscape, and I hadn't foreseen how jarring it would be to read about it for the first time. Carolyn must have felt totally blindsided, and that was not my intent. When I gave her my book, I told her there were some "tough and ugly" parts and that I hoped she would read the whole thing, because I truly thought she would understand my feelings and reactions within the context of what I was going through. I didn't elaborate further, because I stupidly didn't even realize I needed to; I honestly thought this was so within the nature and trust of our relationship.

I am now left to consider who else might react similarly to my book, should I publish it. My sister, who had her fourth baby when I was struggling to have my first? My niece, who would learn that I considered asking her to donate eggs? My health care providers, whom I praised when they were good but called out when they were horrid?

After much thought, I have decided I am willing to deal with any repercussions of telling my truth as it was, or really, what is the point? *This* is what reproductive trauma does; this is how shattering and destructive and invasive and corrosive it is. This is the reality of what we go through month after month, year after year, and it shouldn't have to be silenced or watered down because it doesn't suit people who don't know what that feels like. The only person who gets a say in whether I publish my book is my husband, because it's his story, too.

That said, Carolyn's response to my book has undoubtedly been one of the hardest parts about my "coming out." I often long to climb back into the comfort and safety of the self-imposed cocoon I lived in for so long while I fought to build a family. But a feeling of needing to tell my story and be a voice in this community keeps jabbing me, like an elbow on a crowded plane, and I just keep telling myself that I am strong enough again to handle anything. I will always be glad for the friendship Carolyn and I had, and sad that it's gone, but my direction is firmly, happily forward.

Practically every day, I hear someone say she's grateful for her journey through infertility or reproductive trauma; it's made her stronger, more compassionate, a better mother. I will never thank reproductive trauma for anything, and I blame it for plenty. But I don't blame it, or writing my truth about it, for the end of a friendship I held dear. People who have babies with a wish and a screw don't get to hijack the stories of those of us who struggle violently, just because our agony hurts their feelings. I don't want it to be "us" and "them." I want it to be all of us women in this together, striving for mutual sensitivity, compassion, and support. Even when the process is tough and ugly, that's the magic of memoir.

LAURIE PRIM is a writer trapped in a chiropractor's day job. She writes memoir, women's fiction, and chick lit, and blogs about reading, writing, and reproduction at laurieprim.com and on Facebook. She is an advocate for infertility and reproductive trauma awareness and support, and hosts a RESOLVE

Peer Led Support Group for infertility and pregnancy loss. Laurie is a baseball fanatic, and loves running so much she talks to it like a friend. She lives in South Florida with her husband and two children, who hang the moon, sun, and every star in between.

WE ARE ALL WRITERS

Ashley Espinoza

M y parents and I were always close growing up. My mom called us the three-headed monster. I was an only child until age fourteen, and we did almost everything together. Since my parents have always been my best friends, when my mom called to say, "Come over. Dad and I have something we want to share with you," I knew it would be truly special.

It was a warm summer day, and when I arrived at their house, I knew they would be outside. I walked up the ramp, onto the porch, through the empty house, out the back door onto the deck my dad had built, and down the ramp. I found my parents raking.

I offered to help, but they turned me down; instead, they said, they wanted to tell me their plan.

My mom spoke first: "We shared our story this weekend with an audience for the first time together, and we decided it's time to write a book."

I grew up knowing my parents' history and had heard them speak to audiences before, but they had always done so separately. My mom told of becoming pregnant at age thirteen and giving birth to me a few months after she turned fourteen. She usually spoke to kids around that same age to encourage them to wait, and let them know the consequences of their actions. My dad also usually spoke to teenagers, but to share his troubled youth and tell them about what led his to being shot multiple times and becoming paralyzed from the waist down.

The previous day was the first time they had brought those two stories together and realized how powerful they really were.

My dad spoke next and said, "We want you to help us write a book."

Ever since I had moved back to my hometown after college, I had tried to figure out what I was going to do with my life. I had a degree in psychology that I didn't use, and my plan to attend graduate school hadn't ever panned out. I had a job, but it was just a job. Suddenly, I knew *this* was my life's calling. Of course I would help my parents write a book!

I started writing a memoir before I even knew what that meant. I simply knew I had a story to share and needed to get it down on paper. Three years passed while I wrote silently and secretly. I told very few people because I knew the pressure would get to me and the doubt would start to sink in. The more people I told would only mean more eyes on me, more people to tell me I wasn't good enough, my story wasn't good enough, my writing wasn't good enough. I was fearful of becoming one of those people who say they are writing a book but don't actually write anything.

I sat my parents down individually and recorded them telling parts of their stories. I listened and jotted down notes.

Afterward, I went home and transcribed the recordings. The next phase was turning their speech into structured prose. I did this for months, until I had chapters that sort of told a story.

After a year of interviewing and the beginning phases of writing, I began to structure my book more formally. I realized I needed some guidance. I surfed the Internet and bought books about writing a book: *You Should Really Write a Book: How to Write, Sell, and Market Your Book*, by Regina Brooks, and *Memoir Writing for Dummies*, by Ryan Van Cleave. Only then did I realize I was writing a memoir. I wanted to find information not only on how to write one but also on other people who were writing them. I needed to see their process and whether they were successful.

I knew I needed a theme. I had a book on two amazing stories, but how was I going to entwine them, and how could I create a sellable book? The answer came to me: love. It was a love story: a love story of two people who survived bullet holes and paralysis, all while trying to attend high school and raise a child. Their love endured all. Once I knew that love was the theme, I began writing from that place, trying to bring love into my story as much as I could.

After three years passed, I decided I had my own story to write—my own memoir, about being raised by the two unlikeliest people. I call it *My Path to Ordinary*. I began writing to share that even if your parents have a past, they can still rise together and create an extraordinary, ordinary child. My parents didn't let their obstacles hinder me when I was growing up. Instead, they helped me to see life in a different way and to be truly grateful for who I am. They taught me that I could do anything with hard work, which is why I have worked so hard on their book and mine.

I started to write my memoir. I placed my fingertips on the keyboard. Before I actually typed out words, I had to be sure it was the right time of day. The sun shone through the window beautifully and wasn't beating down on me. I had to make sure my tea was the ideal temperature. I placed essential oils in a diffuser in case I needed a nice aroma to get me into the perfect writing mood. I wanted to be fully prepared to share my own story. It was different than sharing my parents' story. I had to dig deep inside myself.

When I began to dig deeply into my memoir, the world around me changed. I began to view almost everything as a memory. Now, when I made an egg sandwich and sat down to savor it, immediately my brain jumped to my childhood, when my dad always made me egg sandwiches. That sandwich was a little reminder of who I am and how something as simple as a dish can bring up everything you used to be as a kid.

Exposing the hard truths or secrets in a memoir is one of the hardest factors to overcome. When I tried to keep things out of my writing, it was evident to me that they were missing. My book screamed at me that my readers needed some explanation for the parts I was leaving out. The worst thing it did for my writing was to keep me closed off. By refusing to write about certain parts, I knew I was holding back. My thoughts weren't free until I wrote down the words that kept me quiet about certain parts of my past, the things I kept locked down deep inside me for years.

Keeping a secret from yourself and hiding who you truly are as a person can weigh you down, even when your secret is small, like mine is. I wasn't abused or mistreated, but I've always felt as if I've lived a double life. My parents split up when I was a baby, and when my mom married, I started calling her husband Dad. The dad in this story is technically my stepdad, but *stepdad* is not a word I use when I talk about him—he's simply Dad. It was a secret I kept from my biological dad because I knew he wouldn't want me calling my mom's husband Dad. I kept my worlds separate and never wanted them to collide. In fact, I avoided writing about my dad dilemmas so much that I left my dad out of my writing altogether.

Still, it was clear that he was missing whenever I allowed others to read my work, because they always asked about him. "But what about your real dad?" they would say. I always shuddered at the word *real* as much as I did at the word *step*.

I tried to dismiss this question, but eventually I had to write out those words. I had to speak my truth. My dad who gave me life was always part of my life, and he is part of my memoir. I originally didn't write about him because it seemed confusing at first, until I realized that feeling confused at times and having to explain my family history was part of my story. Sometimes you have to write down those words that feel most confusing or hurt the most to free yourself from them. That is the biggest lesson I learned: write your truth, whatever it may be. Write who you are and how you became that person. My life is out there in the open now; I no longer have to hide part of it.

After years of writing in secret, I decided to reveal the truth. *I am writing a book!* was the statement I had to shout to the world. It was hard to say at first. Instead of telling my friends and family that I was writing, I used to pretend I was staying home to read, so much so that I became a social recluse. But when I finally began to tell people the truth—that I was spending my weekends writing—it was freeing.

I surfed the Internet and read as many memoir books and articles I could find when I came across the National Association for Memoir Writers. I listened to a free teleseminar in which John Kremer said the same thing I already knew: I needed to start a blog. The day I launched my blog was the same day I first admitted I was writing a book. From that day on, I have continued to write my own story and help my parents write theirs, and now we all share a blog.

Then I became braver and allowed a few friends to read some work. That was when my inner critics, disguised as outer critics, started to creep in. Those critics took the form of silence. When I allowed someone to read my work, I gave them a piece of my soul and I wanted people to fall in love with my story. When they didn't, I took it to heart. If someone wasn't telling me they loved my book, I thought they weren't supporting my goals. It was the worst kind of criticism to allow myself to have. I should not have put words in other people's mouths, yet I did. Now I remind myself that I am the person who will love my book more than anyone else and that I can't make my writing move people. I remind myself to keep pushing and that my friends are constantly, openly supporting me. It is simply my own mind that tells me they aren't.

And then there are the real demons: *You're not a good writer. No one will read your story. What will people think of you? Do you honestly think you'll make it as a writer? No one will publish you! You've wasted four years on this project for no reason.* These are the phrases that haunt me until I tell them to go away. I know that we all have doubts and that those doubts are what keep us going. We have to prove to ourselves that we are worthy and our stories are worthy.

I write my story and my parents' story because I know they need to be told. I know there is a teen mother out there who needs to hear that she can be brave and raise her child to grow up and be successful. There is a teenager out there who struggles with staying out of trouble and needs to know that he can get on the right path. There are kids who grow up with stepparents and split homes who need to know that others have lived that, too. There are people everywhere struggling to find their way in the world. Most of all, I continue to write because we all have a story to tell. We all have something to share, and we are all writers.

∗ ∗ ∗ ∗ ∗

ASHLEY ESPINOZA is the creator and editor of The Wheels of Grace, a blog she created with her parents to share their stories of being teen parents, living with a wheelchair, adoption, and walking with God's grace.

Ashley helps her parents write their memoir of love enduring parenthood as teenagers, gunshot wounds, paralysis, fertility issues, and adoption. Ashley is writing her own coming-of-age memoir to share her unconventional childhood. Even though Ashley was raised by teenage parents and a dad who was in trouble most of his youth, she was given so much love and was taught that anything in life is possible, even when faced with adversity.

Ashley cannot live a day without coffee, books, gum, or sarcasm. She loves to travel and convinces others to let her tag along on their vacations. Ashley believes the best way to know who you are is by telling yourself through writing.

✳ INTERVIEW WITH MARK MATOUSEK ✳

Author of *The Boy He Left Behind*

LINDA JOY MYERS: Why did you write your two memoirs?

MARK MATOUSEK: I wrote *Sex Death Enlightenment* at a time when I didn't expect to be here for long. The prognosis was two to three years. I wanted to tell a story about spiritual discovery but for worldly people, in a way that hadn't been done before. I'd been a magazine editor in New York, working for Andy Warhol, when I hit the wall, got a bad diagnosis, quit my job, and hit the dharma trail. I traveled around for ten years, waiting for the ax to fall, but it didn't, and I had a kind of mortal awakening that I wanted to describe to other people—a conversion, in the sense of being turned around. I'd gone from being a cynical, selfish, atheist obsessed with his career to being a seeker who saw the world from a diametrically different perspective. I wanted to tell that story to a mainstream readership, to say, *If this happened to me, it could happen to anybody*. No one had really done that before; it was years before *Eat, Pray, Love*, and I was obsessed with getting it done. I wrote *The Boy He Left Behind* because the ax didn't fall, I survived my illness and decided to hire a detective to find my father right before my fortieth birthday. He disappeared when I was four, after he came back to kidnap me but couldn't, and I never saw him again. In the course of the detective's looking for him, I realized that the search for me had less to do with actually finding my father than it did with looking for the man in myself, the father, I'd never been able to quite put my hands on. The memoir was as much about manhood in general, questions of masculinity, the epidemic of the absent father in our culture, as it was about finding Jim Matousek. These were deep themes that I wanted to explore in the writing. I never knew my dad, but he'd haunted me since I was a kid. Writing the book helped to close that chapter.

LINDA JOY MYERS: Was one book more challenging than the other?

MARK MATOUSEK: I'd have to say *Sex Death Enlightenment* was more difficult to write because it was my first book. I also thought it would be my last. I rented a basement office and wrote seven hundred pages in a year, which were a mess, of course, and needed a huge amount of cutting and shaping. *The Boy He Left Behind* is much more compressed. The story is tighter, also because I had already learned how to write a memoir.

LINDA JOY MYERS: One of the things you teach is writing for healing. It sounds like, in both cases, your memoir was healing to you, so let's talk about this—how you understand it and how you approach memoir as healing or therapeutic. Some people, by the way, say, "Oh, no—don't use the words *therapeutic* or *healing* in connection with memoir!" Have you heard people say that?

MARK MATOUSEK: Oh, sure. I hear people say that writing is therapeutic but it's not therapy, and I think that's true. For me, writing memoir has been a way of working through difficult, confusing, and complex experiences. Both of my memoirs have been quest books—quests for some kind of knowledge, some kind of wisdom, and some kind of healing. That became the model for how I approach memoir writing, whether or not the writer is dealing with serious crisis or trauma. Every memoir needs to be asking a question; there needs to be some kind of urgent inquiry driving the narrative. What are the stakes for the writer? Why does he or she need to tell this story? What truth(s) does the writer hope to uncover? The process of self-inquiry often brings healing. For me, writing has always been a way of staying sane, ever since I was a little kid. I grew up in a dangerous home with a lot of trauma, loss, and violence. Writing about what I saw and felt helped me survive the pain and confusion and gave me a new way of looking at things. Writing is where I could tell the whole truth and bring some clarity to the mess. It taught me an important lesson: that when you tell the truth, you see more clearly. I like to tell students, "When you tell the truth, your story changes; when your story changes, your life is transformed." That's the essence of my work as a teacher and writer.

✳

LINDA JOY MYERS: There are a lot of very personal confessions and details, and your inner self, that you reveal very deeply in both books. What was it like for you to think, *Oh my gosh, all these people I don't know are going to read this*?

MARK MATOUSEK: For me, it's a paradox. In my life, I'm an introvert and fairly private. But in writing, my shyness falls away. So does my shame. There's no need to prevaricate, hide, cut corners, or worry about what others will think. When a memoir involves other people, it's important to respect their privacy and boundaries, of course, and ask permission before sharing intimate details. But for myself, I feel like an open book. Writing has been a practice of reducing self-consciousness by dropping the mask and telling the truth.

LINDA JOY MYERS: What is the magic of memoir for you?

MARK MATOUSEK: The magic comes from taking the raw materials of life, however confusing, painful, or shapeless, and creating something beautiful (and meaningful) to share with others. When you can make a story out of loss or pain—or any mixed-up experience that comes with being human—there's a kind of redemption that happens. Nothing is wasted if you take time to write it. It's a way of transcending the limits of unexpressed pain. We story to cope with mystery, I think. We may not know who we are, why we're here, or where we're going. But at least we can put it into a story.

✳ ✳ ✳ ✳ ✳

MARK MATOUSEK is the author of two award-winning memoirs, *Sex Death Enlightenment: A True Story* (an international best seller) and *The Boy He Left Behind: A Man's Search For His Lost Father*, as well as *When You're Falling, Dive: Lessons in the Art of Living* and *Ethical Wisdom: The Search for a Moral Life*. His work has appeared in numerous anthologies and periodicals, including the *New Yorker*, *O, The Oprah Magazine*, *Harper's Bazaar*, the *Saturday Evening Post*, and *Tricycle: The Buddhist Review*, among others. A popular lecturer and writing instructor, he is on the faculty of the New York Open Center, the Omega Institute, Esalen, Hollyhock, and Kripalu, teaches Writing to Awaken workshops around the world, and is the creative director of

V-Men (with Eve Ensler), an organization devoted to ending violence against women and girls. His new book, *Writing to Awaken*, will be published in spring 2017.

FROM CHINA'S RED STONE BRIDGE TO SAN FRANCISCO'S GOLDEN GATE BRIDGE

Jing Li

" **I**s my English good enough to be accepted into your Writing Salon class?" My Chinese-accented voice came out trailing off inside the vast warehouse of the crowded 1999 book fair at San Francisco's Fort Mason. My sense of inadequacy kicked into high gear. Even the word *salon* sounded intimidating. I'd just been finally able to tell it apart from *saloon*.

It was a journey of its own to transform my brain from Chinese to English: memorizing a reservoir of vocabulary words; conquering the rapid flow of everyday conversations; stumbling over culture shock–related misunderstandings; being overtaken by tiny, powerful prepositions, as in *on sale* and *for sale*; tackling the look-alike, sound-alike triplets *persecute, prosecute*, and *prostitute*; breaking out a sweat before saying words like *anise*, for fear its sound-alike cousin, *anus*, would come out!

"Do you accept someone like me, whose first language is not English?" I took a step closer, asking Jane Underwood, founder of the San Francisco Writing Salon, a middle-aged, elegant woman with a pleasant smile. She was sitting alone in her booth, offering to teach people life-writing skills.

Despite my BA in English from China and my master's in pedagogy theory on America's school education, which I hurriedly earned within a year in 1990 from Southern Nazarene University in Bethany, Oklahoma, I'd never taken any writing courses. The essay writing for my California teaching credential examinations was the last portion I passed, after math and reading.

"Why, yes, of course." Ms. Underwood was encouraging. "Anyone who wants to write is welcome."

A great sense of relief and gratitude flushed over me. So heavenly to be accepted and approved. For, you see, acceptance and approval for me, a born-unwanted peasant girl from Old World China, were as rare as food, water, love, and affection in my growing-up years.

The minute I came out as a girl, instead of a gold-valued boy, as her first grandchild, my fiery-tempered, loud-voiced grandmother put on a long face and walked around on her three-inch bound feet, doing her chores without saying a word, for two days.

My mother left me when I was two months old to be raised by this very same grandmother, who threw her own newborn baby daughter into the urine pot to drown just eleven years before her rival daughter-in-law, my mother, gave birth to me.

"Not another cheap, flat piece female," cried Grandmother, wanting another male baby, like her firstborn child, my father.

The baby survived to be my aunt Er Gu. It was her father, my grandfather, who dashed up to snatch her out of the urine pot, dripping wet and choked silent. "Why, you wretched woman!" Grandpa, usually quiet and good-natured, yelled at Grandmother. "It's a life. Let her live!"

Er Gu, who's turning seventy-one this year, 2016, grew up timid, like a scared rabbit, passively taking in her mother's explosive smacking and quietly accepting her father's frustrated yelling. Er Gu had a soft heart and a childlike, innocent smile. The near drowning in urine took away her sense of smell permanently. She wasn't as tidy and neat or quick and bright as her sister and brother, my father. Growing up with her, I followed everybody's example in the family, calling Er Gu a "dumb idiot," even though she helped take care of me when I was a baby.

I wasn't any more special in Grandmother's eyes than Er Gu was.

"What an untameable, disgraceful, wild spirit!" Grandmother's yelling at me when I was a small child, while tossing me her dirty looks, still rings in my ears today. "Just like your bad-omen, ugly mother!"

"My darling Mei-Mei." Grandpa, on the other hand, would beam, chuckling and laughing, praising me to anyone and everyone. "Brightest child ever!" In Grandpa's adoring eyes, I could do no wrong, even when I threw a hot-tempered, childish tantrum, yelling and hitting his daughter, my aunt Er Gu, who just smiled on, loving me.

As a small child, I learned who my parents were from the one-by-two-inch black-and-white photo on the sod wall of my grandparents' one-room house in my birth village of the Red Stone Bridge, 赤石桥, nestled in central-northern China's deep pine forest mountains, picturesque but impoverished.

Grandpa toiled all day in the commune's cornfields, from the first rooster's crow till darkness blanketed the sky. Grandmother, too, on her painful three-inch bound feet, toiled many days a year, on top of taking care of everyone in the household, cooking, cleaning, hand-sewing clothes, embroidering, mending socks, making shoes from scratch out of worn-out rags, milling grains into flour. She turned me loose as soon as my little legs could carry me.

As far back as my memory goes, I was always running around alone outside in the wilderness, on the hills, picking pink trumpet flowers and blue lilies, singing at the top of my lungs: *bao-bao-bao-hua-hua*; playing barefoot in the small, clear-watered creek; racing by the roaring river at the foot of the majestic South Mountain; chasing after the rare sight of a jeep or truck, flying through the village in rolling clouds of dust, to smell the exotic gasoline; making mud cakes by the village's dirt roadside with my two little friends Ai Lan and Fen Hua. Together, we giggled and laughed like wild birds, selling our mud cakes like the adult villagers did at the annual street fair on June 23 of the lunar calendar. When, in the summer of 2015, I went back to visit my aunt Er Gu, the person in the world I missed most after Grandpa's passing, we three childhood friends got together. We giggled and laughed crispy-loud, just like when we were small children.

Amazingly a happy child, I was blissfully ignorant of the dire poverty and misery all around me while I grew up in the midst of China's man-made famine years (1959–62), my stomach growling loudly, my face and hands unwashed and blackened by dirt and grime, my hair uncombed, tangled, and matted with lice and ticks.

At age five, I became a first-grader after Grandmother argued with the principal, Mr. Yang WenBing, insisting that I wasn't too young to start school.

My very first teacher, Mr. Shih, was a three-feet-tall dwarf in physical size but a giant in enlightening, cultivating my young child's mind, instilling in me my lifelong love of learning, reading, and math. Today, over half a century later, I can still see his toothy, thousand-watt smile and hear him praising me in front of the class, telling the awed-eyed little boys and girls to be diligent and do excellent work "just like Li Tsai-Mei 李彩梅."

In his pale, long-fingered hands, Mr. Shih held his teacher's whip, twice his height. And the half-room-size mud-and-brick platform, *Kang* 炕, was our teaching and learning arena. Standing authoritatively in front of the small blackboard was our teacher, with his square body, baby-like arms, and stubby legs. And sitting in the circle, fanning out around our teacher, were a bunch of runny-nosed, raggedy kids, offspring of China's second-class citizens, the poorest peasants, over 80 percent of the nation's population. Our backs straight, legs folded, hands in our laps, our eyes were filled with sparkling respect as we looked up at our teacher. The entire front side of the wall in our classroom was the pinewood-checkered window, with soft, off-white paper, instead of glass, pasted on the frame. Echoing out into the schoolyard, our voices repeated after Mr. Shih the math signs in rhyme. How the naughty boys in higher grades laughed at us for our "baby learning" at recess time!

When I turned eight, Grandpa took me on a 400-*li* (130-mile), three-day journey, first in the village's straw-cushioned, horse-drawn wooden cart, then on a standing-room-only livestock truck with tall, splintered pinewood fences that swayed violently along the mountain trails, and, finally, on a crowded train. He dropped me off to meet and live with my parents and two younger brothers at their one-room city apartment, where water came from a thin, three-foot-tall iron pipe sticking out of the ground in the middle of the crowded dirt yard and hundreds of blue-collar families shared open-sewage, squat-toilet outhouses.

Grandmother said it was time for my mother to love me. Mother was expecting me to be her household helping hand and a babysitter for my brothers.

✳

初生牛犢不怕虎。 *chu-sheng-niu-du-bu-pa-hu.* Like a newborn calf thinking itself the equal of a tiger, I burst onto the writing scene upon discovering Jane Underwood's Writing Salon, my crafting skills next to none, my English descriptive vocabulary words scarce as the watery millet soup that was my staple food in my childhood famine years.

Like a true "born stubborn dog," as my illiterate but brilliantly intelligent grandmother called me when I was small child, I kept on writing my life journey, *From China's Red Stone Bridge to San Francisco's Golden Gate Bridge*, at the pace of the tortoise in the race, determined to learn to write my own book in English, my beloved foreign language, by my own ability.

Awakened was my adrenaline-charged ambition. I'd been losing my grip on my self-worth as a battle-fatigued classroom teacher in America's chaotic inner-city public school system. I was dying to achieve something meaningful. I was thirsty for knowledge, like a seedling in the earth is thirsty for rain.

To improve my reading speed, I watched *Jeopardy!* and turned on captions on my TV. To fill in my ongoing patchwork quilt with background knowledge on Western literature and American history and culture, I read extensively. Reading well-written books on crafting and writing, as well as well-known memoirs and real life stories, helped to hone my writing and fine-tune my storytelling skills. Two childhood memoirs resonated deeply with me: Frank McCourt's *Angela's Ashes* and Maxim Gorky's *My Childhood*. The universal resilience in both men's early childhood suffering in their Old Worlds mirrored my very own—except that I was a girl, from the opposite side of the earth, speaking an alien language of an alien culture.

I also took writing classes and attended critique groups, workshops, open-mic events, and writers' conferences. I found myself thriving on these supportive writing communities. Their insightful feedback gave me refreshing perspectives, opened windows for me to view my childhood and make meaning out of my life.

Your mother never smiled at you as a child? How terrible. I was startled, my heart touched, by my fellow American writers' sympathetic feedback in my defense. For sympathy was a rare gem in my growing-up years with my parents and two brothers in the city of Taiyuan.

Writing my memoir was an emotional challenge, at times debilitating. It curled me up on my couch in flowing tears and sent me down onto my knees, praying for serenity. Lurking in the depths of my heart were my mother, looking at me out of the corners of her small, almond-shaped, silent eyes, and my young child's longing for the happy-sunshine smiling face she reserved for my brothers. She echoed in my ears, telling me I was a coldhearted wolf just like my despicable, dead-man-walking father, who, in turn, kicked and slapped me, yelling that I was a dumb idiot, like an elm tree stump, and that he couldn't stand looking at my face, a carbon copy of "that bad-omen, slut mother of yours!"

To prove my self-worth to my parents by always striving for the best became my lifelong mission. My perseverance prevailed. Coming of age, I became one of the very tip-top few among my wasted-into-semi-illiteracy generation during the civil-war Cultural Revolution, rising from the ashes to catch the last bus as soon as China restored its merit-based college admissions policies in 1977. I competed my way against thousands into Taiyuan Teachers' College and became a famed high school English teacher in my early twenties for producing the highest academic-achieving students, above the 90th national percentile, a milestone usually marked only by outstanding veteran teachers double my age. I was on top of the world, enjoying the same social status as physicians and rock stars, in Shanxi Province. I went on to secure admission to China's best foreign-language university, in Beijing, in 1983, and eventually became the runaway number one, among hundreds of my high-school-teacher colleagues, to come to America as an international exchange teacher in 1986.

"If only you had been a boy," sighed my father, "you would've brought real pride and glory to my Li family name."

"Well, just don't think too much of yourself," my mother said to me, the corners of her mouth pulled down into a faint, sneering smile.

Why was your mother like that? many of my fellow writers asked me. Their probing question made me think hard, searching for answers myself.

"Mother, please tell me what happened to you before I was born." I dialed China from my San Francisco home in 2007. As I gripped the phone receiver, my heart throbbed with anxiety, my mind raced with uncertainty. *What could have happened to make my birth, the birth of her daughter, permanently chill my mother's heart?*

I crossed my fingers, hoping that my $10,000 had softened her heart enough to grant me an answer to my burning question. She had recently half guilt-tripped and half sweet-talked me into refinancing my mortgage to give the fortune to my brother Mount Tai, her favorite child, who, at age forty-nine, was unemployed, overweight, recovering from a stroke, and still living in the same crowded, blue-collar dirt yard he was born into.

I was surprised with delight, secretly relieved, when my mother didn't resist. With an awkward, lighthearted chuckle, she told me over the phone, across half the world, how the beginning of my life ended her lifelong dream to become a writer.

My twenty-year-old mother was horrified to discover her pregnancy with me. She was all set to go on to college, and about to divorce her husband, my twenty-four-year-old father, who had started out as her stepping-stone but was now in her way.

My desperate mother secretly pushed a thick pinewood washboard against her pregnant belly, trying to abort me. Abortion was illegal in 1950s China.

What a miracle that I survived at all, born almost two months premature, with my brain intact!

Writing my memoir was healing. It offered me a profound understanding that my life story was but a broken-off link in the chain of human spirit of endurance through four generations of unwanted girls in my family, having survived the five-thousand-year-old, female-bashing Chinese culture.

My grandmother was the prettiest and brightest child in her maiden village, but her parents bound her feet and sent her brother, not nearly as bright, to school instead. My mother, orphaned at age five, contracted herself, at age fourteen, into a marriage in exchange for her education. When my own daughter was born during China's brutally enforced one-child-per-family law (1979–2015), my father-in-law, a medical professor, pressured me to have my infant baby injected and killed so I could try for a male child.

How my heart is at peace today that I've created a bright future for my daughter in America, the best part of the earth.

"Did you write in Chinese?" asked my high school Mandarin Chinese language students, wide-eyed in disbelief, when I won second place in California's Jack London Writing Contest in 2007.

"Did you write in English?" people asked me, eyebrows raised, when I won first place in the California Writers Club/ Redwood Writers memoir contest in 2015.

Writing each segment of my life story was like starting a sophisticated knitting project—say, a cardigan—with no pattern to follow: a lot of unraveling and countless restarting. It was also like traveling across a rope bridge hung over the gulf between two drastically different languages, Chinese and English. And on that bridge was I, a tiny, scurrying ant, shouldering larger-than-life loads, searching tirelessly to mediate between the two cultures.

✳ ✳ ✳ ✳ ✳

JING LI lives in San Francisco. She enjoys her daily five-mile walking/jogging in the City's refreshing, lung-cleansing cool fog. Grateful living in America, her beloved new home country, her food-paradise, she's perfected in cooking from scratch varieties of her Shanxi-specialty pasta, with fresh garlic and ripe fresh heirloom tomato sauce. Jing's homemade *jiao-zi* 餃子, potstickers, claim many enthusiastic fans among her fellow writers at Redwood of California Writers Club.

Jing still does her own 1040 taxes in good-ole-fashioned way, with pencil and paper and the mental arithmetic skills she learned as a child in China. Passionate about her dream-teaching after exiting America's disheartening public school system, Jing's recently completed her three hundred-page book, *Mental Math for Kids*, aiming to teach America's young children to add, subtract, multiply, and divide in their head and calculate money without using a calculator.

I CALLED YOU A MEMOIR

Nancy Chadwick-Burke

I considered creating you after I read *Summers with Juliet*, by Bill Roorbach, and realized how a memoir could be so inspiring and magical while understated in innocence and adventure and complements to nature. I had something uplifting of my own to express, as I knew I could communicate my personal experiences, drawing connections to places and people and home, despite my disconnections, and share my story to provide hope for others.

So here you are, sixty-six-thousand-plus words of soul-baring, journey-taking memories recalled in vivid color and pronounced action. We started ten years and seventy-five thousand words ago, when I reported on my life, beginning with my birth and passing through grade school, my teens, and decades thereafter. Discontent, anger, and sadness were thrown in for drama. I knew it was too much. One's auto-biography does not a memoir make! So I tossed you into a drawer for incubation, hoping scenes would work among themselves in covert darkness and magically assemble into something I could call a story. Yet I still could not claim you as a memoir.

I persisted. I massaged the words bound within your walls, peeling away the layers that did not belong. I honed every draft to submit you to a professional for assessment, and there were many such drafts and many such professionals. I combed your paragraphs, grammar, verb tenses, and dialogue to ease the knots and elicit clarity. Your last critique said I had strayed from your theme often, and that I had contradicted myself, and that the shift from your voice of innocence to your voice of experience was confusing. It also told me I didn't delve into hinted-at deeper issues.

You challenged me most when I didn't know how to apply these comments to you, despite my intellectual understanding of them. My self-doubt about not being a good enough writer won over my grasp of your thematic development. My work stalled; I couldn't turn you around. I countered your suspension by focusing on what I could do to enable your progress. Instructional study of the craft and reading other memoirs became my teachers. Stories by Dani Shapiro, Mary Karr, Elizabeth Gilbert, and many others were encouraging models as I scrutinized their structures; however, their themes were unlike mine.

You saw the obstacles and adversity commensurate with my growing years, and I showed you faith, life, and connections. I didn't ask you the meaning of life, but I showed you how I embraced mine by offering wisdom and solace through my words in a pure, ordinary way. Remember the story I told you when you we were just starting out, the one where my self-discovery started at fifteen, when I wrote a poem and I realized I had a place in this world? I had grown to know a particular young birch tree, had developed a kinship with it. We shadowed each other through the years; seeing a birch tree spurred memories of home when I found myself with the unfamiliar and told me I was in the right place.

I shared one of my best memories with you when I obliged Mom after she insisted on taking my photo on my first day of kindergarten in front of the house's picture window. My birch buddy was nearby, standing tall and arabesque, as if to say, *Look here and smile.* But my dress was too small; the sleeves didn't meet my wrists, and the skinny elastic around my forearms left an indented pink ring on my skin. My chubby feet were crammed into blood-red Mary Janes; Mom had struggled to pull the strap just to the first hole on the buckle. I stood at attention with my feet together, hands folded in front, heels brushing against yellow marigolds in full bloom. A toasty sun overhead pushed its beams through my birch buddy's arms ushering a smile onto my face and a squint into my eye on that Indian-summer day, diminishing my immediate discomfort. I thought life could not have been any better.

I was reminded of my innocence, my connection to home, and the little spot I had in a big world when I recalled that day. I told you I would always find home and that life was truly good. That's why I wrote you, where I found meaning in you. I was once eager to find complicated significance in what I now see as simplicity. I didn't have to turn you into something you would never be; I had to turn you into something you always were. I reclaimed my goal—to discover an emotional truth, a universal truth, to my experiences—and connected the dots to see a clear picture emerge.

You will be published one day. I can see your cover; I run my fingertips over your inviting photo and speak your title. I don't expect you to be famous, but I hope that whoever opens your bindings and feels my words printed on paper will embrace the warmth and wholeness of belonging, of having home in mind and heart. I will remain diligent in working with you, polishing you like a gem among the other fine cuts of memoir.

And through sharing you, I hope those who will take you in their hands and me in their arms will find their connections to home and will see that life is truly good, too.

I called you a memoir because of all this.

*   *   *   *   *

NANCY CHADWICK-BURKE got her first job at Leo Burnett advertising agency in Chicago. After ten years there, she couldn't get to where she wanted to be so she turned to the banking industry. Then, after another ten years, she realized she wasn't a banker. She quit and started to write, finding inspiration splitting her time between Chicago and San Francisco. Her memoir, *Under the Birch Tree,* is currently under construction and is getting to where it wants to be too. Her essays and blog posts have appeared on TheMemoir-Network.com, TheDiaryBank.com, SheWrites.com, and in other local publications. She and her husband enjoy traveling, cooking fine dinners, and chasing their beagles in circles.

AS IF YOUR PARENTS ARE DEAD

Dhana Musil

P rone on the carpet, pen in hand, I was ready to freewrite
into the deeper, darker parts of my memoir, the parts I'd
been avoiding—namely, the backstory of my childhood.
I'd hoped a little time away from my domestic life would
free me to dive deeper into that daunting realm, but instead
of mind maps and scene ideas, what flowed from my hand to
the page, in big, underlined letters, was: *I don't want to ruin
my parents' lives!*

In my memoir, I write about running to Japan at nineteen
and becoming a hostess. I write in detail about my time spent
messed up on drugs in the trenches of Japan's underground.
I admit to marrying a yakuza (gangster) I didn't love. But
exposing these truths is *nothing* compared with how afraid I
am to divulge the backstory of why I made the decisions that
led me to those situations.

My backstory equals my childhood and has the potential to devastate my parents. But it's through my childhood

that I explain the motivation behind the decisions, right or wrong, that the young adult of my memoir makes. Skipping over painful and awkward memories of the puzzle that is my life means not including the parts that will breathe the most vitality into my tale.

Am I spilling family secrets out of spite and revenge? Absolutely not. Do I want to offer up my parents as sacrificial lambs? Hell no. Am I willing to write a mediocre book? No. But does this mean I have to shelve my story until they are no longer alive? I could ask my parents not to read my book. But even if they don't, the fallout will reach them. How can it not?

My book won't land my parents in jail, but it will cause tears, discomfort, and friction. Hell, it may even cause a family rift. Am I prepared for this? And how to write with this burden constantly upon my shoulders?

Author Angie Abdou gave me her advice when I interviewed her for an article about juggling motherhood and writing.

"To write anything well," she said, "you've got to write as if your parents are dead."

I was taken aback. I didn't want to imagine my parents dead. That sounded gruesome and extreme.

"Censor nothing," she said. "Write it all down as it happened. In full, Technicolor detail. Then, later, when the book is in the editing stages, decisions can be made about what can stay and what can go."

Angie doesn't write memoir; she's a fiction writer. Even so, with each book she publishes she worries that her mother may disapprove of the risqué scenes, or perhaps read a negative aspect of herself into one of the characters. If a fiction writer has to pretend her parents are dead to write an authentic novel, what about a memoirist?

My stomach churned. Fear crept in. What if, for the sake

of my memoir, I pretended my parents were dead and jinxed them? What if they suddenly did pass away, naturally or otherwise? I'd never be able to live with myself. Yet I'd never be able to live with myself if I didn't write my memoir.

I repeated that sentence to myself. *Write as if your parents are dead.* With trepidation I did what Angie said, wrote as if there were no chance of their ever finding out. I felt like a traitor with each sentence, but essential backstory scenes emerged, I was able to link my childhood to my young adulthood, and the story almost began to write itself.

I'm three-quarters of the way to the end of my book, and I cringe every time my mother asks me how my story is coming. Luckily, she never asks to read any of it. Maybe she senses not to.

Though writing as if my parents are dead has helped me craft my memoir, it hasn't alleviated any of my guilt. In order to grapple with that, I light a candle before each writing session, ask forgiveness for wishing my mother and father metaphorically dead, pray for their love and understanding. Then I sit my butt in my writing chair and tell myself to keep writing the truth. All the way to that glorious finish line. Let the rest unfold once the last page has been written.

DHANA MUSIL arrived in Osaka, Japan, when she was nineteen years old. Though only planning to stay for six months, she ended up spending over a decade living in the seamy underbelly of Japan, and eventually married a Japanese *yakuza* (gangster). *These Little Earthquakes* is the memoir she began to craft while a student at The Writers Studio at Simon Fraser University in Vancouver. Her creative nonfiction has won several prizes and has been published in numerous anthologies. Dhana resides in North Vancouver, BC, with her partner, two girls, a cat, and a dog. She hopes that her writing may land her in a place of perpetual sunshine, warm sand, and clear water.

✳ INTERVIEW WITH ✳
SUE WILLIAM SILVERMAN

Author of *Love Sick*

LINDA JOY MYERS: One of the things that people struggle with when they write about abuse is memory. Was what happened easily on your mind, or did you have to search for your memories?

SUE WILLIAM SILVERMAN: If I had tried to remember specific details about my past just by sitting around thinking, it would have been difficult to recall memories with any real degree of specificity. It was in the writing process itself, however, that I was able to discover tangible details and images that convey specific memories. What I do, when writing, is sink into a sensory place in order to remember details. It is through these sensory images that memory emerges. When writing, I'm constantly focusing on *what did that moment smell like or taste like or feel like or look like or sound like?* In short, the senses come first and then, from the sensory details, the memories become clearer and more accessible.

✳

LINDA JOY MYERS: Some people talk about the war between the idea that writing a memoir is a therapeutic or healing process and the idea that writing is about art. What do you think?

SUE WILLIAM SILVERMAN: For me, memoir is taking one's life and turning it into art. This means making your story universal by writing metaphorically—in the way a poet or a novelist writes. Metaphors are the way that we connect with readers. For example, let's say you read my first book about growing up in an incestuous family, but you haven't had the same experience. If I had *not* written it metaphorically, you wouldn't be able to relate to the experience in a deep or significant way. But, through metaphor, readers engage with narratives regardless of their own background. Sure, the book is about incest on its surface, but metaphorically, in a deeper way, it is also about loss of identity, alienation, isolation, and, ultimately, finding a voice—themes to which most people *can* relate. If you're writing for therapeutic purposes—say, keeping a journal—you'd be writing for yourself. And there's nothing wrong with that! But when writing metaphorically and thematically, you're writing for an audience of readers. And, as I say, the way to do that is by discovering the metaphors for any given essay or memoir.

LINDA JOY MYERS: How did your memories and your memoir develop from draft to draft? And how does the epigraph of the first book reflect the theme?

SUE WILLIAM SILVERMAN: With each draft, my writing deepens. In a first draft—and this is true for all my books—the writing is a bit superficial, as I'm mainly trying to get down what most readily comes to mind, which is usually "what happened to me." But then, as I continue, draft by draft, and I sink deeper into that sensory world, the memories clarify and I'm able to present them in a much more textured, tangible, and metaphoric way. Ultimately, then, I'm able to convey not just what happened to me but *what the experience means*. Also, I don't begin with a predetermined theme or set of metaphors. Rather, I allow the book to evolve as it wants to. It's like following a whisper. And if I listen carefully, I can follow the language, the themes, and the metaphors wherever they lead me. The epigraph of the first book is a quote from Wittgenstein: "The limits of my language mean the limits of my world." Growing up, I had no spoken language about incest because it was a secret. I couldn't even speak the word *incest*, because that, in and of itself, would have been too scary. Frankly, I didn't even fully understand what the word meant. And we can't speak that which we don't know. The same is true of my sex addiction, what I wrote about in my second memoir, *Love Sick*. I didn't even know the language or the condition of sex addiction, so here, too, I remained mute, with no voice or words, even as I was actively acting out the addiction with emotionally dangerous men. That's why writing memoir is so important, so . . . well, magical. In other words, until we discover and write the language of an experience, I think we're trapped in it. Writing—language—provides an understanding of this darkness in one's life. Through writing, I was finally able to discover a language and "speak" the truths of my life.

LINDA JOY MYERS: You made a difficult topic bearable to read about. Were you conscious of needing to do that? And now that you've written three memoirs, what was your process of moving from book to book?

SUE WILLIAM SILVERMAN: Thank you! I did want to write a book that would convey universal themes, and to bring the reader inside the world of a lost child. So I'm grateful if I succeeded. I think, for any writer, one of the best ways to bring the reader into your world and to make the narrative and the themes utterly clear at all times is to maintain a tight focus on the material. And this is why I've written three memoirs. It's impossible for any given memoir to convey a whole life. Rather, each memoir depicts only a slice of a life. In my first memoir, for example, I focus on growing up in an incestuous family. In my second memoir, I focus on recovering from sex addiction. Even though there's an obvious relationship between incest and sex addiction in real life, it was impossible to merge these two things when creating art. In the first memoir, the voice is that of a young, wounded girl. In the memoir about sex addiction, the voice is tougher and edgier. So the two experiences wouldn't fit together into a single book—different voices, different themes, different energy. The third memoir, *The Pat Boone Fan Club: My Life as a White Anglo-Saxon Jew*, is about my ambiguous relationship with Judaism while growing up. This ambiguity arose because my Jewish father was sexually molesting me. And here, too, I needed an entirely different, new book in order to fully explore this particular narrative and theme. So with each memoir I switch focus, voice, metaphor, theme. We all have more than one story to tell, in that we all have lots of different aspects to our lives. We're mothers and fathers; we're sons and daughters; we have professions and jobs; we travel; we have religious experiences; we have fears, and on and on. So, when writing, I look at myself from as many different angles as possible. And each angle is a different story, a different essay or book.

✳

LINDA JOY MYERS: What is the magic of memoir for you?

SUE WILLIAM SILVERMAN: The magic of writing memoir is that I discover myself. The magic of reading memoir is that I also discover myself.

✳ ✳ ✳ ✳ ✳

SUE WILLIAM SILVERMAN is the author of three memoirs. *The Pat Boone Fan Club: My Life as a White Anglo-Saxon Jew* was a finalist in *Foreword Reviews* 2014 IndieFab Book of the Year Award. *Because I Remember Terror, Father, I Remember You* won the Association of Writers and Writing Programs Award in Creative Nonfiction. *Love Sick: One Woman's Journey through Sexual Addiction* is also a Lifetime TV original movie. Her craft book is *Fearless Confessions: A Writer's Guide to Memoir.* As a professional speaker, Sue has appeared on *The View, Anderson Cooper 360, CNN-Headline News,* and at scores of colleges and nonprofit organizations around the country. She teaches in the MFA in Writing program at Vermont College of Fine Arts. For more about Sue, please visit www.SueWilliamSilverman.com.

THE AFTERMATH OF MEMOIR

Crystal-Lee Quibell

Should we allow the possibility that someone might be upset with us for telling our story to silence us? Silencing yourself because you're afraid of how people will react to what you have been through does a disservice to you and to the people you love. Writing can be therapeutic, difficult, triggering, and healing. Writing memoir for me at times felt like open-heart surgery without the anesthetic. But the journey as a whole has been worth it, not only for the healing but for the perspective I have gained on how to write honestly. Truly letting down your guard and allowing the whole, ugly truth out onto the page can be pretty life-changing. You don't write memoir and not learn a thing or two about perception, perspective, and perseverance—and how those concepts relate not just to you, but to everyone you've ever interacted with.

You become a keen detective of your own memory process. Referencing journals after I'd written certain passages,

I learned I remembered things differently than I had recorded them years prior. I was grateful for my meticulous journal keeping so I could fact-check my work. I gained great perspective on the truth, on how our memories work, on the smaller details we may remember and on the larger ones we gloss over in time.

Working on my first draft, I found myself paralyzed by the fear of what would happen when these words were no longer between the page and me. Would I lose friends? Family? What would my husband say? How would I share my abuse with my parents? Should I even include the abuse in my memoir? Was this the right time to write about it?

I decided to write everything that had mattered to me, both good and bad—it was time to shed light on some harsh truths. The first draft was simply an outpouring of years of grief, anger, and resentments. Not every story makes the final cut in your completed work, but it does facilitate space for better writing—the kind of writing that can propel your story forward with life lessons others can gain wisdom from. I learned, through editing others' work and my own, what should stay and what should go. Did I achieve some sort of vengeance by writing something unkind about a former lover? That hit the cutting-room floor. Did I believe that anyone could benefit from my sharing something in my overall story? Then it stayed. Anger always gets the cut, and sometimes even joy, and some pieces of writing are just for us. And it's all worth it and necessary. You must write passionately and without question at first. That's what your first draft is—messy and angry and an all-in commitment to purging your truth and your lies.

My truth seemed to make many people around me uncomfortable. As I pored over thousands of words written about suicide attempts, sexual abuse, triumphs, and tragedies that involved the people I knew and loved the most, I became keenly aware of how my truth made them squirm. Worse yet, they'd interject their opinions without having read a word I'd written.

"That didn't happen like that!" my sister scolded when I recalled one particular suicide attempt I was writing about.

"You weren't even there!" I protested. Yet she became increasingly angry every time I brought up the book, some of it about sexual abuse I'd suffered as a child and had not yet disclosed to my parents. My siblings were supportive over-all, except for her. And it hurt, because she's my only sister and I love her dearly. Of course I wanted her approval and support, but sometimes the truth can trigger things within someone's past that they aren't ready to face, either.

There were some intense moments when I had to take responsibility for the roles I played throughout my life, from homeless, pregnant, teenage adulteress to spoiled heiress. I didn't want to be perceived as a victim—I wanted to be real, and I knew that with realness comes honesty and that I wasn't always a good person. I sometimes even deserved the misfortune I had run into. Unfortunately, that meant I had to risk revealing my whole self, not just the shiny, happy, social-media version we all frequently try to cultivate in our online lives. I had to make peace with the victim I'd clung to at the beginning of writing my memoir. I had to stop play-ing small, stop being afraid of what people would think, and sacrifice some privacy and comfort to get the real me onto the page, warts and all.

I would sometimes sit down for hours and write, but when it came to writing about others involved in my life, I'd get scared. I'd tuck the manuscript away and blame a major life event as the reason I hadn't continued. But eventually the weight of my own secrets became so heavy that I knew I couldn't avoid writing them down any longer. I had to commit to finishing the book, even if it ended up being only for me.

So I sat down and finished writing the entire thing in six months. My manuscript was a beast, at over 209,000 words. Prematurely, I decided to attend a writing conference and see if any literary agents were interested in it. I'd edit it when I got home, I told myself; for now, I had to take a leap and give myself a boost of confidence.

When I shared the exciting news that I was off to New York City to pitch my memoir, people's reactions ranged from thrilled and supportive to disappointed and confused. Some had assumed I'd never actually finish the book, but now I had and they were nervous. Had I written about them? Had I shared their deep, dark secrets?

I ended up with several requests from agents at the conference. I was elated and on a high when I flew home to share my news. But the news wasn't met with a big hurrah. People I loved and trusted became distant and moody. Eventually I heard through friends or other family members the fears they were sharing among themselves. No one ever actually approached me and asked what, exactly, I had written about. In the wake of assumption lay all of the friendships and family members I'd held so dear.

Even if you write lovely things about us, didn't you for a moment consider we don't want to be written about at all? my sister texted me. She hadn't even read a word I'd written yet, so how could she react this way? But she had some valid fears about privacy, and, despite my assurance that I'd taken every precaution to protect hers, she didn't believe me. Our communication ended abruptly, and we haven't spoken since. Perhaps when my memoir is published she will read it and realize her assumptions were wrong. Regardless, I couldn't write for anyone else. The writing had to be through me, about me, for me, or it would mean nothing to me in the end. I couldn't leave things out to appease anyone else; I had to share my story in my words, the way I remembered it, or it wouldn't be a memoir.

You can't write for other people if you want to tell your real story. You can't spend your time worrying about who will be offended—because someone always will be. You can't waste your time assuring everyone that it's going to be all right, because even you don't know what will happen when the story is released to the public. You can fret about being sued or losing friends and family, but I assure you, there comes a certain sort of freedom in setting your truth free. And for all the people who exited stage left in my life after I finished my first draft, many more wonderfully supportive authors, agents, and literary friends have come forward to offer support and kindness I could never have imagined. Writing memoir led me to my people but also, more important, to myself.

Writing a book, especially one about yourself, is no easy task. Despite all the unfortunate arguments I had, all the money I spent on poor editors with no qualifications, I learned so much about the publishing industry and about myself. It was akin to pregnancy: just because everyone has an opinion about it doesn't mean they have a right to dictate how your story should be told, how to birth your book into being.

As with childbirth, we tend to forget the pain of writing memoir because we're hardwired to block out trauma. If women could actually remember the pain of childbirth as acutely as they felt it in the moment, no one would ever have another baby again. The same holds true for memoir: there are times in that birthing process when you beg for drugs, an escape from the pain of bearing down and getting the job done. But in the end, when you look at your completed manuscript and kiss it and hold it and have your *holy shit, I can't believe I did this!* moment, that is what makes it all worth it. Because you made that; you crafted every word, carefully editing what needed to be said and abandoning what was better left unsaid.

Telling my story healed me. It carried away years of shame, regret, and suppressed anger and also showed me who I really am as a person and as a writer. I wasted far too long worrying about people's reactions, fretting over their feeling hurt if they weren't included or angry if they were. When I finally sat down to explain to my parents that a distant relative had abused me, their reactions floored me. They were supportive, caring, and compassionate—and relieved to see that I'd survived and thrived. I explained to them that if I didn't tell this story, reveal the secrets that were making me sick, the burden was going to kill me.

My mother's response shocked me: "I don't care if you told the world we're ax murderers. We love you, and we want you to be happy. If writing this book makes you happy, that's all we care about."

That's the amazing thing about memoir and telling the truth: it doesn't just set you free; it also opens doors to previously unimaginable conversations with people you love. I think my brother Billy said it best: "I think it's wonderful, kid. If only everyone had the guts to tell their story, I think it would heal the whole damn world. I'm so proud of you."

That's why I wrote my story. To heal myself and, I hope, the whole damn world. And that's why I know you can, too.

CRYSTAL-LEE QUIBELL is the host of Literary Speaking, a weekly podcast dedicated to helping writers learn inside tips from best-selling authors, literary agents, and publishers. Founder of The Magical Writers Group, a private teaching forum for writers specifically focused on memoir, Crystal-Lee is a champion for the written word, student of publishing, and an obsessive book collector with a serious case of wanderlust. A self-described mermaid and witchy woman for life, she believes that life is better with books, chocolate, and the occasional cheese board. Follow her travels and book-publishing journey at www.crystalleequibell.com.

LIFE INVERTED

Apryl Schwab

$\int$ tanding steps away from the Inverted Fountain on UCLA's East Campus, I sobbed uncontrollably while thousands of people swarmed for the annual *Los Angeles Times* Book Festival. Writers and readers rushed past to their next author presentation while I had a full-blown breakdown.

Mary, a writer friend whom I had met in an essay class, asked repeatedly, "What's wrong? What can I do? What happened?"

Between hiccups and snot pouring onto my lips, I blurted out, "My instructor . . . had us . . . write memorable events . . . one each line. I filled page. Then all read." My shoulders shook and I wailed as if I were alone in an isolated meadow in the Sierra. An exercise from that previous week's nonfiction writing course had exploded my life.

"And so?"

"So . . . in all her years . . . no one . . . not one person . . . had material . . . to write complete book . . . from each line event . . . like me."

"But isn't it good that you have so many interesting directions you can go?"

"But that's it . . . I actually lived . . . every miserable event." More snot, more tears, and choking until I gasped for air.

I had always thought that my life had been tough and unusual, but for an experienced UCLA memoir instructor who had taught myriad students to claim that I had lived the most dramatic writing-worthy life of all sent me into shock. She had spoken slowly and explained that typically students had book-length incidents of only two, three, maybe four events in their entire lifetime, in comparison with my having had one on almost every line of a complete page. So there it was—an impartial expert had confirmed that I had endured a truly fucked-up life.

Tiny, beautiful Mary, by contrast, had lived a charmed life. She often said that she'd had far more of her share of good fortune than seemed fair. She tried to comfort me, but such despair was beyond her realm of reality. She had met her later-to-be husband on her first day as a freshman at UCLA, more than thirty years earlier. Her oldest daughter was at a top Ivy League university, while her younger daughter was a champion diver at an elite LA high school. Mary had never worked, supported as the privileged wife of an extremely successful executive. And if all that weren't enough, she was an incredible writer who completely charmed our Sunday Barnes & Noble critique group every time she read. There we stood, Beauty and the blubbering Beast.

For at least three weeks, I was in a daze, not knowing which way was up. Even the air seemed like a dense fog that I had to press through. But Mary insisted I keep coming to her hillside Beverly Hills oasis for our weekly writing-and-gossip tête-à-tête.

For a while, it was very difficult to face her. We lived on opposite ends of the spectrum of fate. But I eventually calmed down, albeit under a comatose cloak. The sadness was ever present, but Mary's marvelous utopia gave me hope that better times were possible.

The tides turned.

Mary moved to a nine-thousand-square-foot 1920s mansion previously owned by a succession of famous people. On the first day I went to visit, I took along the biggest white orchid plant I could find. The ten-foot-high metal gate creaked open, and I drove onto the huge brick driveway and swung around to a stop in front of the castle-like wooden doors of the multicar garage. It rained on and off all day, and the lights and buzzers and alarms went on and off all day. I shivered in the cool, damp air as I looked around the $7 million home, wondering why it felt like something out of a horror film. Although it was still in Beverly Hills, there was no glorious canyon view, and the previous owner, a forced-out divorced mother, had ripped TVs (which were supposed to remain) out of the walls, leaving exposed wires and an electrical nightmare.

On that first day, Mary was the one who broke down sobbing. She said she had discovered that her faultless husband had been having an affair with a vicious Asian woman whose mission was to get rid of Mary and become the mistress of the mansion. Mary said that her husband had begged her not to let their daughters or family know and had fully committed to being the faithful man she had always thought he was. He had bought her this house (putting it in her sole name, paying cash) as a sign of his devotion. (Or was it a payoff?) She said that he insisted he wanted everyone to continue to see them as a happy family. I did my absolute best to console her. I cried with her for hours, talking through all the details and possibilities.

It was just the beginning. Over the next year and a half, Mary uncovered a pattern of infidelities and an admission of sexual addiction. She couldn't sleep. She couldn't eat. She couldn't stop screaming in fury at how he had ruined their perfect family.

On a beautiful Sunday, typical LA clear blue skies, I checked my e-mails. Mary's husband had sent me a message. Mary was dead. No further explanation. Details of funeral to follow.

If I had ever thought that I had been shocked before in my life, it had just been kicked up a hundred notches. How could this beautiful, middle-aged, healthy, double black belt, vital woman be dead?

Mary had died in her sleep. Not from an aneurism, as was being circulated, and not from suicide, said the coroner, since the low level of prescription drugs in her system should not have been deadly. But since all the heartbreak over her husband's cheating, Mary had said, she had resorted to taking one Ambien per night at nine o'clock in order to sleep. I could only assume that she had done the same that deadly night. But why was she found dead, facedown in her pillow, by her husband the next morning?

Days after Mary's death, her husband e-mailed me a copy of her novel and asked how we could get it published. I wrote back that Mary had stopped writing when all the trouble between them had started, and that she had been in the middle of changing the point of view back from third person to first person, and so it needed major editing to make it consistent. It wasn't ready for publishing. Twenty-five months had gone by, and Mary's unique, hysterically funny yet dramatic novel had not been touched.

We rarely know our future. We can't accurately remember our past, but it is all we have. It is what made us. Good, bad, boisterous, or bland, it is more *us* than anything we materially own. Writing it down is the evidence of our existence in our own distinctive slant. The longer we wait to write, the greater the risk that our memories will fail, or, worse yet, that we will never get the chance to write at all.

A memoir is like the Inverted Fountain. It allows us to turn our lives upside down and inside out. Forget about the crowds rushing past and let it flow, defined solely by your own direction.

* * * * *

Wanting to live an exciting, Tom Sawyer–adventurous life, **APRYL SCHWAB** overshot with more than her share of "gee, this has never happened before" moments. As a CPA in the entertainment industry, Apryl worked for over thirty years behind the veil of the rich and famous in Los Angeles, but her Illinois country-girl roots kept her from embracing the insanity. Apryl's love for travel took her north to Alaska, west to Hawaii, south to Peru, east to Iran, and to many destinations in between. Apryl completed the UCLA Extension Writers' Program, with a designation in nonfiction writing, in an attempt to rewrite her book on her mother's life, entitled *Life Ain't Easy, Get Over It*. No course ever offered an assignment that called for working on that book, so she began her own memoir by default.

WRITING WITHOUT AN AGENDA

Irene Sardanis

A t first, my writing was an act of revenge. I loved hating
my mother. I wanted the world to know what atrocities
had been heaped upon me. I relished playing victim to
my mother's violence. I focused my writing on my suffering childhood. My poor, woeful story. I couldn't understand
why my instructor would say,

"There you go again. Your agenda."

What she was talking about? I couldn't see anything
wrong with my work. I had to tell my sad story with a lot of
dramatic emphasis. I clung to my despair like a security blanket. Who would I be without it? And there my wounded one
just sat. My sorrowful little child self sat there on a chair,
observing me, looking like a rag doll, all floppy and dejected.

"Pay attention to me," my little one said. "Never mind
the other stuff. Just tell them all the bad junk of my life."

I believed that putting it all down in minute detail, exposing all the grizzly, gory stories of my life, would cleanse me

of the filth of my childhood experience. I wanted to magnify the whole production. I wanted to write it all out in flaming color. It was essential to tell the world: *Listen. This is what happened to me, and it was horrific.*

Instead, what has helped is to put the suffering little me on the seat next to the grown part and say to her, "I know you are here, and I know how you are feeling. But I can't have you run the show and take over our story." I pet her little face at this point. "If we're going to do this right, we need to do it another way. Otherwise, people reading our story will become bored and toss the book against the wall. They'll be tired from glancing at the first page, knowing it's going to be someone's poor-me, ain't-it-awful, let-me-tell-you-what-else-she-did-to-me drama."

Yawn. No, that's not going to work. It'll never sell.

The more I wrote, the more I gained another perspective on what happened. I began to see more detail. I smelled the pee and beer in the hallways to our apartment. I saw the cockroaches on the table, the mice in the corner of the kitchen, the peeling paint on the walls. I had to go back into the Bronx apartment, return to the prison of my youth, and be there with my mother. These details added melodrama but also created intensity in my writing.

Describing the beatings and my feelings of powerlessness to defend myself was hard. I searched for the right words to describe fear, rage, and terror. I had wished my mother gone and had terrible guilt about daring to have those thoughts. Better I be dead. Still, I didn't want to be melodramatic about our relationship. I wanted readers to see the scene and be there with me so they could decide what her bizarre behavior was all about.

As I wrote, something surprising happened. When I went under my mother's skin and penned, "My Name Is Maria,"

I immersed myself in her upbringing in a small Greek village. I could see the unfair responsibility she had in raising her six younger siblings at such an early age. My mother was deprived of a decent education, of a childhood. I became curious to learn more about her life. Leaving her homeland to go to America to consummate an arranged marriage with my alcoholic father compounded her tragic situation. Writing in her voice, I began to feel something I had never imagined would emerge: compassion. I felt sorry for the poor woman.

My mother often told me the story of leaving her village, knowing she'd never return. She cried remembering the endless journey on the ship from Greece to America. Add to the mix my dad—the one who preferred other women, ouzo, and gambling to being a husband and a father—and my mother probably sensed his reluctance to marry her right from the start. What a Greek tragedy. How could I not have experienced some sympathy for her story in her own voice?

Although my sisters and brother were around some of the time, I was invisible to them. They lived in their own world and had no interest in what was going on in mine. We all avoided our mother. There was nothing any of us could do to help her feel better. We all treated her as if she were another child in the family. We shielded her from the outside world.

In writing about my mother, I saw her character change from all dark and evil to something else. Before, I refused to see any good in that woman. But now I saw that, in her provincial way, she influenced me more than I cared to admit. When we shopped, she haggled with all the local shopkeepers. I'd turn away from her in shame. But would you believe I learned to bargain and discovered ways to negotiate for everything from produce to theater tickets—just like my mother? She would make a meal from scraps in the refrigerator. At mealtimes, I search the pantry before I cook, a lot like she did. I used to see people in my life as either good or bad. Now I could see other shades of their behavior as well. I could observe their other intentions, different indications of their character. What my mother lacked in intellect, she made up for in simple peasant wisdom and resourcefulness. I learned these things from her.

It took many years of writing to get to this place, but now I've released that victim part of me. It doesn't have to live on the page. That doesn't mean it's vanished. It's still there. But it doesn't take over the entire piece, dominating every paragraph with unhappy gloom and sorrow. I am much more than what happened in my childhood.

Still, as I write this, the wounded one tugs at me and wants to take over again, demanding that I write how we survived all those atrocities. She wants me to share more drama.

"Tell them about how mean she was," she demands. "They gotta get all of it."

I pull her close to me, squeeze her tight, and say no. What is important for readers to know will come out. We don't have to put it all up in neon lights. They'll get it. I'm not going to dwell on all that mess right now.

Through years of therapy, I discovered the gift of expressing feelings on paper. Holding on to resentments has little value to me now.

I've taken many writing classes and attended writing conferences. My instructor reminds me I have another purpose in life: to tell my story honestly, to craft it well, so it might touch others with similar stories. I hope my writing will say to them: *You're not alone. You are stronger than you think. I survived my need to have a sad-story agenda. So can you.* No more *poor me.* Just finding my new voice through writing and creativity.

* * * * *

IRENE SARDANIS was born in New York City. She is a first-generation Greek, and many of her essays depict her life with immigrant parents. Since her retirement as a psychologist, she has become a writer. *The Sun* magazine has published several of her personal essays. She has also been published in *Write For Your Life, Voices: A Hellenic Journal, Invisible Memoirs, The Psychotherapy Networker, Something That Matters,* and other anthologies. She is currently completing her memoir. Her home is in Oakland, California, where she lives with her wonderful husband. You can find her on Facebook.

✳ RAQUEL CEPEDA ✳

Author of *Bird of Paradise*

BROOKE WARNER: You're a cultural activist, and it's clear from your book that you want to highlight the intense obstacles Latinas in our culture face. You write about discrimination, stereotypes, bullying, and many of the other issues Latinas confront as they try to make their way in this society that's innately theirs and yet often rejects them. How central was your activism in the articulation of your personal story?

RAQUEL CEPEDA: The thing that surprises me about the parts of my story that are often dismissed as a monolithic experience relevant only to Latinx people is that significant parts of my story are quite universal while at once uniquely mine. North Americans are preoccupied—unless, of course, they have the luxury of not having to constantly think about and/ or be reminded of their "otherness"—with identity, race, discrimination, and nationhood. I find it ironic that while the Americas began in the Caribbean, on the island of Hispaniola, society still doesn't know how to see people beyond the Black-and-white binary prism that continues to dominate the conversation around race and identity today. I'm simply writing my truth to power, which is less about cultural activism than it is about contributing to the narrative of the immigrant and second-generation experience in North America. Isn't that what it's supposed to be all about—adding our own, albeit scant, narratives to the otherwise nondescript quilt of memoir writing?

✳

BROOKE WARNER: Your book is at its core about identity and genetics, but also about race and what it means to be Latina, as well as the shame and secrecy around the Dominican half of your identity and the process of uncovering this and discovering elements of what makes you you—and, by extension, Latina. Now that you've written this book and put it out into the world, what kind of response have you gotten from your readership, and is this the kind of book that has a crossover readership (meaning that it appeals—and/or that you and your publisher thought it would appeal—to non-Latino readers)?

RAQUEL CEPEDA: *Bird of Paradise* is written in two parts. The first is about my coming of age in Santo Domingo, in the Dominican Republic, and New York City, where I was born. Part of this narrative, in which I learn how to negotiate my Dominican and American identity, was experienced against the backdrop of '80s New York City and a burgeoning hip-hop culture. The story was mostly set in my beloved Inwood section of Manhattan and wrestles with my father's own rejection of his Dominican identity, not mine. The first part of the book sets up the second part of the journey, a genetic adventure I undertake with my father using, in part, ancestral DNA testing to find out where my ancestors came from before they became Dominican and, later, Latina. The journey, a spiritual one, ends up marrying the ideas of *mythos* and *logos*, one that challenges Western ideas of spirituality and one that sets out to decolonize history, specifically what I've been taught about how we came to be American. I knew that my story was universal and intersectional *before* I wrote it, because I lived it. And I didn't live it exclusively within a Latinx bubble. Because of this, I wanted to make this book accessible to everyone. For instance, I wanted to leave the word *Latina* out of the title so that it wouldn't be dismissed as a story intended solely for female readers. However, that wasn't an option. My publishers decided against it. And, well, once a book is explicitly assigned a race that isn't white and a gender that isn't male, it gets sentenced to the annals of a bookstore.

BROOKE WARNER: You've taken a lot of creative liberties with your book, the kind many of writers are afraid to try because they distrust their memories or feel they're breaking convention. Specifically, you imagine your parents' life before you were born. Your birth happens on page twenty-one. Your memoir also has journalistic and even prescriptive elements to it. It's highly footnoted, includes an index, and goes so far as to include DNA kit instructions and an ad for ordering a DNA kit at the back of the book. Can you talk about how, as a writer, you blended these elements of personal story, journalism, and creative nonfiction?

RAQUEL CEPEDA: I knew many of the stories about how I came to be from the time I could remember. I don't know my birth mother very well, and my father and I have had a mostly fractured relationship, but when I interviewed them, their stories fit like pieces of a puzzle. My maternal uncle, who had front-row seats to my parents' dramatic, Shakespearean tragedy, was a major source, as well as other folks who knew my parents in those days. It's highly footnoted, yes, because I wanted to share the writings and bits of history that informed me, and because why not? I also felt strongly about adding the ancestral DNA information and coupon in there so that readers could set out on their own respective journeys if they so chose to. In the writing of *Bird of Paradise*, blending creative nonfiction, memoir, and reportage was simply the most organic way for me to tell this particular part of my story.

✳

BROOKE WARNER: What has been one of the most unexpected things that's come from having written and published *Bird of Paradise*?

RAQUEL CEPEDA: So many positive and serendipitous things have happened during the writing and since the publishing of my book. Some will seem insignificant and make sense only to me, like randomly meeting family members I didn't know existed in a market. And others come in the form of letters and personal accounts from readers—one example that comes to mind was that of a nurse who told me, as I was signing her book, that the morning after she finished *Bird of Paradise*, she found the courage to throw out an abusive partner. If my story can empower someone else in any way, big or small, it means a lot more to me than a positive review or nod. A young public junior high school teacher told me that almost 90 percent of her students chose my book for independent reading, and that meant something to me, because this school serves my community. Young students of color have gotten too used to reading books by dead white men or just by dudes in general. Or, alternatively, schools choose books in which writers of color are "saved," if you will, often by a white teacher or by totally assimilating and acculturating to mainstream society. My book challenges that narrative and empowers people to take agency in their own saving, and, more important, to decolonize everything around them, starting first from within.

BROOKE WARNER: What is the magic of memoir for you?

RAQUEL CEPEDA: I find that magic in quietude. When I'm still, I become in tune with my intuition, a voice akin to a spirit guide that whispers into my ear, *You can do this*, when the world tells me I can't. The world tells me I can't so often that I try to connect to my magic on a daily basis, usually in the morning, before I begin my day. When I'm in the zone, when *mythos* and *logos* are working in perfect harmony, I'm able to tap into the memory I believe we carry in our DNA. And that compels me to articulate my story: the exercise—whether it trickles or pours out of me—is sacred to me. That's magical.

* * * * *

Born in Harlem to Dominican parents, RAQUEL CEPEDA is the author of *Bird of Paradise: How I Became Latina* and an award-winning journalist, cultural activist, podcaster, and documentary filmmaker. Cepeda's most recent film, *Some Girls*, is a documentary focusing on a group of troubled Latina teenage girls in a suicide prevention program who are transformed through an exploration of their roots via the use of ancestral DNA testing. Cepeda directed and produced the NAMIC (National Association for Multi-Ethnicity in Communications) Vision Award–nominated film *Bling: A Planet Rock*, a feature-length documentary about American hip-hop culture's obsession with diamonds and all of its social trappings. She is also a cofounder of *Our National Conversation About Conversations About Race*, a podcast on Slate's Panoply network.

Cepeda's writings have been widely anthologized, and her byline has been featured in media outlets including the

New York Times, the *Village Voice*, CNN.com, and many others. Cepeda lives with her husband, a filmmaker and musician, daughter, and son in her beloved New York City. She is currently writing *East of Broadway*, about gentrification's impact on the members of her community that will be published by Beacon Press. Her virtual address is www.djalirancher.com.

THE UNFOLDING STORY

Jude Walsh

When I made the decision to write my memoir, the story was still unfolding. Even though I was still in the throes of it, I knew I wanted to share my journey. This came from a deep desire to put into print the information that I needed but could not find. I wanted other women to know that one woman survived this experience. I was not sure how my story was going to end, but I was certain my goal was not just to survive, but to thrive. My memoir is about sexual and intimacy anorexia and codependency. It is about relationship PTSD and learning to live well in spite of it.

I believed that I was the happiest, luckiest, most treasured woman in the world until, one terrible day, I wasn't. I shattered. My marriage of thirty years and my illusions came crashing down around me with the discovery of my husband's infidelity and secret life. The discovery of the affair was so traumatizing that I lost my sense of self. A usually assertive person, I became fragile, terrified, no longer believing I had any control over my life or any feeling of safety. I was unmoored. Thus began a long and complex journey back to wholeness.

As a lifelong journaler, I was in the habit of writing daily. I treasured my journals. They were not just writing; I had pasted into them bits of ephemera: tickets, newspaper clippings, photos, programs, lists of books I was reading, projects, my hopes and dreams. What I loved about rereading those entries was that I was transported, viscerally, to those moments in time. The feelings, the smells, the visuals, all came in a rush. They granted me near-perfect recall of the setting and tapped into my emotions and feelings in those experiences. Those journals were what would later provide me with the perspective necessary to examine how I got to this place where I was terrified that my entire life was a lie.

Postdiscovery, I began to journal differently, with a passion and intensity necessary to keep me from total disintegration. I was so traumatized and so easily bullied by my ex that I kept the affair a secret for almost a year. Except for our therapist and two friends who'd had similar experiences, I told no one. I was ashamed and humiliated. How did my life turn 180 degrees in one moment?

In my journals I kept lists of the books I was reading to try to find answers. I began with books on how to survive an affair and progressed to books on sexual addiction and codependency. Next came books on trauma and using creativity to heal. I kept track of the therapy appointments and visits to doctors for medication for anxiety, sleeplessness, and depression. I documented my participation in different twelve-step programs. I kept lists of the various professionals I consulted, from marriage therapist to individual therapist to therapists specializing in addiction and codependency, and then PTSD. As a creative person, I'd always sought out-lets or pursuits that would allow me to focus on something positive, life affirming, in the midst of hard experiences, but for the first two years following the beginning of the end of my marriage, that was not possible. The best I could do was to stay alive.

The years following the discovery were filled with loss. I was too stressed to be effective at the job that was the high-light of my professional career and had to retire early. My mother, an anchor in my life, got cancer and died. My son's heart began to pause, and he needed a pacemaker. I lost ninety pounds and my gall bladder. My husband treated me with progressively less respect and concern and became emotion-ally, spiritually, and financially abusive. I spiraled into depres-sion and anxiety and got breast cancer. I was diagnosed with PTSD. My story suddenly had so many twists and turns that I did not know how to wrangle it into a cohesive book.

I decided to begin with the discovery of the affair, to start there and just write a first draft, spewing the story onto the page. I wrote wildly, without regard for sequence, dialogue, or plot. I wrote it all down. I tried to start at what I thought was the beginning, the discovery, but soon realized the story began long before that. The first craft problem surfaced: How to deal with time, flashbacks? I decided not to worry about that and just kept writing, often crying over the keyboard as I did. I held nothing back, captured the hurt, the anger, the depression, and the wildness of it all. I wrote like the pro-verbial motherfucker on the Rumphius mug. It was cathartic and freeing and produced some bad writing! But the guts of the story were on paper, at least the story to that point. I began to write long before my divorce was finalized, so there would still be much to come. It was my first hint that choos-ing when and how to end a memoir is not always obvious.

Five years later, once the second draft was updated, the writing was less hysterical, less dramatic. Story was coming into play, and a small bit of perspective. Often first drafts of a book where someone has been hurt focus on the meanness, the cruelty, the abuse, and the badness of the other person. When you are writing from a place of extreme pain, that is all you know. It is your truth. It is an excellent way to release and begin to face the trauma. But it does not necessarily make for good memoir. My second full draft was where I began to go back, to look at what it was about me and my choices and beliefs that brought me to this place. There was still anger and pain, but there was also perspective. It was my first step back, my first examination of the story with some detachment.

When I began to revise for the third time, I hit a wall. This memoir was just too big. I didn't know where to end it. I didn't know how to handle backstory or time. I was unsure about how to revise. I began to fear publishing such a personal story. I began to doubt that I could manage to get it into publishable form, and even if I did, who would publish it? I wasn't sure what needed to stay, what was crucial to the telling, and what could be cut. Since it covered a fairly long time span with lots of twists and turns, maybe it was more than one book. If so, what should go where? It was not writer's block—more like writer's overwhelm.

While I had been writing all my adult life—journaling, my dissertation, and professional documents—I was still a novice memoirist. I realized I needed to learn two things. First, what makes a good memoir? What does that look like, read like, feel like? I needed to make explicit what I felt implicitly when I read an engaging memoir. What made it good? I had to look at the memoir as a writer, not just as a reader.

Second, I had to learn craft. Writing a book requires a set of skills I was still learning. I attended workshops and conferences. I joined writing groups and over the years discovered that I was not just writing a memoir but also becoming a writer. I could do fiction and poetry and essay. This was one of the first gifts from the horror, the first hint of something good coming.

Each draft became less angry, less victim-y, had more perspective and less pain. I began to see my part, understand what made me allow mistreatment, tolerate the lack of sex, and not question why I didn't think I deserved better. But even at that point the story was still too large, too scattered. Though I knew what my takeaway, bottom-line message to the reader was, the book was not focused enough.

I needed to learn more craft—how to keep the most important parts, how to focus on the best details and descriptions. What helped most was beginning to write short. I stepped away from the idea of a whole book, a completed memoir, and began to write personal essays, what I looked at as single bites of the pie.

I began to share my writing, to let bits and pieces of myself and my story into the world. The writing helped me not only to process, but also to bear, the pain. It was a survival tool. And it became a place to be creative. I began to write about more than just the life crisis. I was now writing about joy, too.

The twelve-step programs I joined helped me learn the skills necessary to survive and thrive. I needed something to support me as I developed the writing chops I needed to complete a memoir. I found this in national organizations like the Story Circle Network and the National Association of Memoir Writers. I found it by attending writing conferences and retreats. I took in-person and online classes. And in each and every one of those places, I met fellow writers who inspired and encouraged me. I found people to write with, the side-by-side work that Eric Maisel calls Deep Writing sessions. I found a critique group and felt encouraged to submit my essays to literary magazines. Receiving that first acceptance letter was thrilling, the rejections not so much.

It is not a surprise that this memoir is unfolding in a way similar to the one-day-at-a-time philosophy that twelve-step groups espouse. The writing is one word at a time, one sentence, one journal entry, one first draft, one revision, one personal essay, one turning point, one scene, and one story at a time. Just as taking things one day at a time helped me through the experience of sexual anorexia and sexual addiction, one step at a time is seeing me through to the completion of my memoir.

✴ ✴ ✴ ✴ ✴

This essay, "The Unfolding Story," won third place among all the essays submitted for consideration in The Magic of Memoir.

JUDE WALSH writes memoir, personal essay, fiction, and poetry. Her work has been published at *Mothers Always Write, Indiana Voice Journal, The Story Circle Network Quarterly Journal, Flights Literary Magazine, The AWW Collection* (2014 and 2015), and in numerous anthologies. She is a writer at The Good Men Project and Telling Herstories. Her blog, "Writing Now," can be found at her website, www.judewalsh.com. She was awarded a Bill Baker Scholarship to attend the Antioch Writers' Workshop in 2016. Jude lives in Dayton, Ohio. She shares her life with her son, Brendan, and three lively dogs.

TRUST THE PROCESS AND
FIND THE THREAD

Fran Simone

"**A**lcoholism and suicide. Well, they aren't such a big deal." That bomb exploded from the mouth of a workshop leader as we sat down to review the first chapter of my memoir during a summer session at the famed Iowa Writers' Workshop. *Well*, I thought, *it may not be a big deal to you, but it is to me.* His judgment stung. I don't recall anything else said, and my inner critic surfaced.

Returning home, I tucked the draft away. Even though I'd been teaching courses in creative nonfiction for several years, I didn't follow my advice to students to "trust the writing process." Also, I lacked confidence in my writing ability. My dark angel shouted, *Give it up. You can't do this.* Then one day, while preparing for class, I came across Vivian Gornick's observation on craft and reflection: "What happened to the writer is not what matters; what matters is the larger sense that the writer is able to make of what happened."

I managed to quiet down my inner critic, dug out the manuscript, dove into revising, and entered that first chapter in West Virginia Writers' annual competition. A second-place win in the nonfiction category boosted my confidence. Even though my inner critic still hovered (in fact, she never completely disappears), I pushed past her with lots of self-talk and plunged ahead.

Mary Karr writes, "If events you're writing about are less than seven or eight years past, you might find it harder than you think. Distance frees us from our former ego's vanities and lets us see deeper into events." Although I kept a journal during my marriage and after my husband's suicide, I didn't begin to work on my memoir until a few years after his death. My emotions were too raw and my judgment tainted. It took approximately ten years from writing that first chapter to completing the entire manuscript. Full-time teaching, family problems, and inertia intruded. I'm a slow and picky writer. I revise and revise.

Then there's the subject matter. Writing about a marriage shaped by alcoholism presented a minefield of challenges: how to chronicle the gradual changes within and between each of us over twenty years, and how to avoid blaming and self-pity. And then there's suicide. Heartbreak and trauma. Would I expose myself too much? Could I overcome my fear and shame? And what about the reaction of family members and friends? Kerry Cohen writes that a memoir is not just a shocking story. "It's a story of how those shocking events mattered to you. It's how you make sense of that story. Ultimately, it's how that understanding of your story shows your reader something they need to know about themselves, about the human beings in general, or about the world."

I had to face my vulnerability, expose myself, and reveal family secrets. I had to show both sides of my husband and myself, what Karr refers to as "some parcels of radical suffering and joy" (hence my memoir's subtitle: *My Husband of a Thousand Joys and Sorrows*). And I had to reveal who I once was and who I am now. Lots of writing balls to juggle, not to mention discovering, shaping, researching, and revising. Lots of revising.

What kept me going during those ten years of drafting and revising? First, my passion for the narrative truth of memoir. Second, the challenge of fashioning an honest and compelling story. And third, the encouragement and assistance of writing angels, including my friend Rosanna, who read and reread drafts, provided valuable feedback, and prodded me to continue when I faltered. "Fran, when are you going to get your butt in a chair and complete another draft? No excuses." Her faith helped modulate my inner critic and kept me going.

Natalie Goldberg notes, "Writing is a communal act." It's also lonely. That's why writers often benefit from participating in a writing group. Mine critiqued drafts and offered unstinting support. We established parameters (praise first, feedback second, questions last and "I" statements always) and held one another accountable. This chorus of writing angels provided inspiration, motivation, and deadlines.

Participating in writers' conferences also helped propel momentum. Although my Iowa experience was negative, I attended several others, including a pivotal one at the University of Nebraska. Workshop leader Megan Daum reviewed the entire manuscript and offered two significant suggestions. "You need to take the reins from Terry and make it your story—the story of a marriage and the story of a woman who found herself in a particularly difficult and complicated (though often joyous, too) situation." She also noted, "The big question, of course, was whether to reveal the suicide up front, as you did in this draft, or surprise us with it at the end." In yet another revision, I placed the suicide toward the manuscript's end, which resulted in the book's chronological structure and shifted the focus from my husband's story to mine.

At this point, the manuscript had undergone many revisions, based on feedback from Rosanna, my writing group, and workshop/conference leaders and participants. It was in good shape but lacked a "thread," an image woven throughout to pull the story together. That thread eluded me. I needed a "fresh" pair of eyes to help me make a good book better. Enter another angel, Laurie, a writer who had recently published a book on introversion. Our work together was seamless—both on the same page throughout the process. How marvelous is that?

One day during a coffee break, we discussed our childhoods. I shared memories of summers spent at my grandmother's cottage near Lake Ronkonkoma on Long Island, New York. "I took swimming lessons from the Red Cross in the Long Island Sound. Miss the ocean so much. Still swim regularly. Laps at the Y." Laurie said, "Fran, every time you talk about water, your face lights up. Why not try to come up with chapter headings with water imagery?" Eureka. We put our heads together, and new chapter titles rushed forward: "Setting Sail," "Sea of Desire," "Troubled Waters," "Empty Vessel." During this revision, I crafted a new first sentence, "I live in currents," which established the voice. And the last one, "So I reverse course and point my compass toward the sun and navigate toward serenity," which describes my recovery, where I was heading from the very first draft. And, finally, the title: *Dark Wine Waters: My Husband of a Thousand Joys and Sorrows.*

The book was complete. No more revisions (well, at least for now). What's next? Try to find an agent to represent me. Laurie helped me compose a query letter, lent me a copy of *Jeff Herman's Guide to Book Publishers, Editors, and Literary Agents* and a form she created for keeping track of outreach attempts. Using Herman's book and online resources, I researched agents who represent memoirs or creative nonfiction, as well as university presses and a few small publishing houses that handled memoir. I sent approximately sixty e-mails—maybe more—and a few print letters.

Most recipients did not respond. A few sent "I am not accepting manuscripts at this time" messages, or a simple "no thanks." Two asked to see the first three chapters. That was encouraging. However, both took forever to get back with "no thanks." During this tedious process, my dark angel surfaced. Sometimes she'd shout, *Your query letter really sucks.* Lots of self-talk to calm her down.

Perhaps I went about this the wrong way. I knew nothing of the business side of writing. What I do know is that I wasted a lot of time and psychic energy trying to find an agent. I've been told that face-to-face contact at writers' workshops and conferences is a better strategy. That publishing excerpts from your manuscript and winning contests establishes credibility. And that knowing someone who knows someone, like an old college roommate's sister-in-law who knows an agent, might help. With no bites in sight, I had to decide whether to self-publish or to box up my beloved manuscript and shove it in the back of a closet. Laurie and Rosanna insisted that boxing it up was not an option. Still.

Then the miracle. Each week I visit my local library and check its nonfiction new-releases display. One day I came across a book titled *It's Not About You, Except When It Is: A Field Manual for Parents of Addicted Children*, published by Central Recovery Press (CRP). I went online, read the submission guidelines (which included memoir), and sent off my query letter. In about a month, I was invited to submit a proposal. I knew little about a book proposal, but I'd written many grant proposals during my academic career, so I had a leg up. I checked out a few "how to write a book proposal" books from the library and spent the better part of two months conducting research on marketing and publicity and completing a final draft. (If you think that finishing your memoir is challenging, wait until you dive into the publicity-and-marketing side of publishing.) Rosanna edited and proofread (not my strong suit) my proposal. Off it went.

Soon I received a request for sample chapters, followed by a request for the entire, 250-page manuscript. I hired someone to proofread it before I sent it off. Several months later, CRP offered to publish my book. A lawyer friend reviewed the contract, which, she informed me, was standard. I signed in July 2013, and my book was published in June 2014. In the interim, I worked with CRP's editor, Helen, another angel, who offered more helpful insights and suggestions. This time, the revisions weren't extensive.

As a bonus, CRP invited me to sign copies at the prestigious Book Expo America (BEA), which took place at the Javits Convention Center in Manhattan. Rosanna joined me. The convention center is enormous. Hundreds of book publishers participated. One, from Italy, served wine and cheese. Famous authors like Neil Gaiman and Lois Lowry spoke and signed. We made the rounds and selected many free books. I remember a huge room lined with cardboard boxes in which we packed our books, before a young man carried them to be weighed. Then we paid postage. The books arrived at my home several weeks later.

Since I was invited to the expo, I believed that CRP had

high hopes for my book. The marketing campaign was to include a national radio tour, plus advertising in publications like *Library Journal* and those dealing with addiction. Not much came of this. *Library Journal* gave my book a so-so review, and the radio interviews never materialized. I've since learned from other authors that publishers (including large ones) generally give authors a six- to eight-week window and then move on to the latest releases. I'm grateful that CRP took a chance on an unknown writer.

Locally, I've had better luck with newspaper and TV interviews; a well-attended launch and signing at an independent bookstore; and talks and readings at churches, civic organizations, and professional conferences dealing with addiction and writing. A friend helped create my website, which provides information on both memoir and addiction (www.darkwinewaters.com) and which I update regularly.

It takes lots of time and energy to market your book. Be prepared for that. How does a writer toggle between writing and marketing? Some have shared that after their memoirs were published, they tried to devote half of their time to writing and the other half to publicity and marketing. That ratio might work for you.

Things have quieted down since those heady days when the book first came out. While I'm disappointed that my memoir didn't take off, I recognize that the competition is fierce. A *HuffPost* article, "The Ten Awful Truths—and the Ten Wonderful Truths—About Book Publishing," reported that more than three million books were published in the United States in 2010. The odds of emerging near the top of that colossal pile are slim. So why keep at it? Annie Dillard writes, "What impels the writer is a deep love for and respect for language, for literary forms, for books. It's a privilege to muck about in sentences all morning. It's a challenge to bring forth a powerful effect or to tell the truth about something." In telling our truths, we can touch and make a difference in people's lives.

I've received e-mails, letters, and phone calls from readers who have thanked me for sharing a story similar to theirs and offered a message of hope. Shortly after my book was published, I received a letter from a former student. Debbie wrote, "As one who also has had the experience of loving an alcoholic, your descriptions of the highs and lows reminds me of how wonderful and terrible it is to live life with someone who suffers from the disease of addiction. Your detail, your emotion, your story carries me away. This book will be a help to anyone who lives (or has lived) life with an addict. I hope it gets a lot of exposure."

Our stories can do more than entertain. They can guide and inspire us. In memoir, we look back and share lessons learned. Often these lessons involve overcoming hardship. The writer struggles and eventually discovers hidden abilities to triumph over adversity.

My memoir has become my platform to write about addiction from a loved one's perspective. I've been invited to write for magazines and blogs (I blog for *Psychology Today*). I've told my truth about alcoholism and suicide. The truth is, you can't fix an addict or an alcoholic, no matter how much you love them or how hard you try. You will enable, you will make mistakes, you will indulge in self-pity, blame, and shame. But with help, you can also learn the skills of self-care and ways to help your loved one change. None of this will be easy. Some, like my husband, will give up hope and die. You will grieve. Eventually you will recover and offer hope and support to those whose loved ones are caught in the clutches of substance abuse.

And for me, that has been a very big deal.

* * * * *

FRAN SIMONE is a Professor Emeritus from Marshall University, West Virginia, where she directed the West Virginia Writing Project, a statewide affiliate of the National Writing Project (University of California at Berkeley). Her essays have appeared in the *Charleston Gazette*, *The Forum* (a twelve-step fellowship magazine), and *The Sober World*. She blogs for a number of websites on addiction and recovery, including *Psychology Today*. Fran is a member of The National Memoir Association, Story Circle Network, and West Virginia Writers. Her website is www.darkwinewaters.com.

ON BECOMING A MEMOIRIST

Rosalyn Kaplus

I fancy it is 1954 and I am six years old, dining with my all-dolled-up family at the supper club the Holiday House, in Monroeville, Pennsylvania, a suburb of industrial Pittsburgh. Mom's red-bowed lipstick is indelible on her highball glass. Over the clatter of waiters' serving dishes, Daddy's cigarette smoke rings disappear into razzle-dazzle stage lights. Doves flutter from the magician's top hat. His hocus-pocus astounds. With glee, my older brothers and I sip maraschino-cherry Shirley Temple mocktails, effervescent with faux sophistication.

As the orchestra, comedian, and star-studded performers appear and disappear, ice melts on pink shrimp curlicues. Juicy steaks sizzle, partnered with foil-wrapped baked potatoes drenched in butter. For the finale, an ice-cream cake topped with a single pyrotechnic stick that explodes in sparkles; a pseudosurprise birthday song. Eyes twinkle, still amazed even after the fireworks fizzle. Mom fawns over us. Daddy circles the table and plants a wet smooch directly on our lips. The thrills sustain the sweetness of being six, when everything seems meringue perfect.

Growing up in the 1950s era of *The Adventures of Ozzie and Harriet* idealism, I am an eternal optimist. The dilemma of the day might be how to clear the bird's nest from clogging the rain gutter. My parents' roles: Daddy, breadwinner; Mom, Betty Crocker homemaker. My story used to be about delight.

At age seven, I start memory keeping in a pink diary, complete with heart-shaped lock and key, silver-edged pages, and grosgrain-ribbon placeholder, hidden in my bottom desk drawer. When I am ten, my fourth-grade workshop teacher, Miss Bartlett, asks the eager class to write about our summer vacation. Everyone's eyes glow, arms up, yipping, *Me, me, please*, each eager to share our incandescent tales. For me, a glorious day on the shores of Lake Erie shimmers. I caught a slippery, wiggly eel on the pier. I will never forget the reek of low tide or the intractable pull of saltwater taffy on my back teeth. What was my favorite flavor? Green apple, banana, cherry? Now I wonder, who caught the eel? My brothers and I have differing witness accounts.

In high school, memoir is a cherished keepsake rose pressed between pages, the sentimental fragrance dehydrated. In college, love letters collected in a shoebox, tied tight with a cord, preserve first enchantment and longing, lust, promises of love everlasting. I will leave those letters aside for future reference to make sense of lost feelings. In a corrugated box, deep in my closet, are newspaper clippings of wedding announcements and death notices, minutiae of a bygone era, from which to derive meaning later. When my middle brother moved, Mom's treasure chest of family photos was to be discarded. I insisted my oldest brother preserve them. He scanned the images, of unknown origin, featuring unknowable people, onto a thumb drive. I have yet to download the digital storehouse. I am not ready to embed my psyche with stale stories. I do not know why I am avoiding them.

My gold-edged journals wait to be explored, tethered to events and feelings of yesteryear. My imagination will play tricks and deceive. I want to believe there is no conflict. Having lived in Miami since college in the late '60s—the white-go-go-boots, *Laugh-In*, psychedelic-magic-carpet-ride times—I have adapted my lifestyle. I stroll the mirrored marina, immerse in nature, Thoreau's way, observe. My cell phone alarm chirps middream. I annotate at bedside in predawn light, the artist's way, appreciate. Then I return to another cycle of reverie.

✳

If life is lived longer than an instant, everyone has something to remember. It may be a disappointment, a betrayal, a lie, a crisis. Where does it reside: in a scar, in the attic, in the cellar, in a shell, in the tide? Why is it concealed? Whose memory is it?

I want to write of my stroke at age twenty-five in 1974. I do not, but I remember the indelible details. In 1978, I retire from teaching art in the inner city and give birth to my only child, a daughter. When she goes to nursery school, I volunteer there and return to studio painting. I delve into perfecting perspective, color theory, and figures. That is my therapy for life transition from art teacher to mother to artist again. Before my daughter's thirteenth birthday, before she goes off to Maine summer-camp bliss, my husband leaves us. I want to write of my prolonged divorce in 1995. I take a workshop in writing as a healing art, then divert to pick up a 35 mm camera and learn photography, and volunteer in the inner city for abused and neglected children in dependency court. I write, documenting court reports of others' dilemmas, and take photos of pretty images, possessing secrets of their own, to keep my mind and spirit engaged. I appreciate the fortunate life I have, instead of devolving into depression. Again, the optimist in me prevails.

In 2008, I explore a new relationship with a new boyfriend, found online. We survey real estate deals in a time of economic uncertainty. I go off-course in the relationship, mixing risky business and pleasure. And, like Icarus, I fly too close to the sun and the crucible of septic shock, a deadly illness with a mortality rate of 50 percent if you deteriorate to the shock state. I do not die. I survive the ER, ICU, stepdown, rehab, return home, and continuing care, then independence. The old woman and the sea, I fish for meaning, to live each day as lucky. I ask, *Why me?* I conclude: to tell my story so others learn of this highly prevalent but little-understood condition. I write to make sense of the what, the why, and the how of sepsis. Once you become a memoirist, you are more attuned to identity—yours, theirs, ours.

In 2009, clarity of mind and strength restored, I return to my computer. I research sepsis, its toll, its origin and statistics. Finally, I record my events, spurred to morph memory into memoir. I fashion a story of introspection, detailing my illness, survival, and recovery, searching for meaning in the unidentifiable, the known and unknown. I write, possessed, oblivious to time. I time-travel back through my stunted memory, write straight through a weekend, forgetting that I have tickets to a Broadway show, *Wicked*. I am tenacious, voracious. Scorpio strength is investigation and creativity.

✳

Rosalyn Kaplus ✳ 293

Then I stop writing. I question my purpose for writing this story of mine.

I'm finished. Then I question why I resist. Then insist upon delving deeply into my ego-id self. I tire of self-absorbed selfie surveying. My inner critic scolds me, asks, *Who is interested in your life anyway?*

I move for affirmation to my outer critic, my circle of friends. I consult with an avid reader friend because she has an étagère of biography and autobiography in her cushy, yellow chinoiserie family room. After I read her, aloud and with gusto, my enthralling survival story, she evaluates. "You don't have any dialogue, and you're not a celebrity," she says. "You write beautifully, but no one will care."

I am disappointed but not defeated. Her comments prompt me to attend local writing conferences, take classes, and have manuscript consults. Again I hear, "No one wants to read about illness, and you're not famous." Others say, "Interesting writing—lyrical." I pitch my story. Again, "You're not known. You don't have a platform." I lay down my memoir for a long nap after the second draft in 2013.

I switch. I research. Read model memoirs. *Darkness Visible*, by William Styron, provides me with an understanding of the phenomenon of unyielding depression, the disappearance of Mom's strong persona from exhaustion. I know why she surrendered. *My Stroke of Insight*, by Jill Bolte Taylor, neuroanatomist, mirrors, symptom by symptom, my left hemispheric hemorrhage and interrupted neural circuit failure. I attach to her plight. In *The Glass Castle*, Jeannette Walls writes off-the-grid, hardscrabble truths that contrast with her current, cosmopolitan life. I become aware of catharsis. What we see in others is a reflection of self.

I remember my first memoir mentor, a nonagenarian, trailblazer from the Bronx, a girl reporter and photographer in Panama, author of *Gringa*. She died in 2015. I still meet with two other novice writers from her class. We honor her every Wednesday, when we put our red-ink edit pens to paper. We maintain our passion. Boost our shared efforts. Question, "How does that feel?" Go deeper, wider.

I remember a workshop with Connie Mae Fowler and follow the forgotten suggestion "Keep at it; don't stop. Keep exploring." Not a sprint, but a marathon. Finish no matter what. Tenacity. Immerse yourself. Focus. Balance with calendared breaks from cabin fever or writing beyond midnight when inspired, or jotting down notes when awakened between REM cycles in the middle of the night. During the day, when seated at my computer, I set a timer. After twenty minutes, I get up to avoid dormant-butt syndrome, a writer's occupational hazard. Stretch. Walk. Chew some cinnamon gum, evoking memories of mulled spiked cider or dental rinse. Muse on my balcony. Telescope to the horizon of the Atlantic.

I am eager to learn and develop more sorcery, plot craft. I audit local university courses. I study nonfiction, braided essay. I reinvigorate investigative skills, jotting down overheard conversations on paper napkins, the same as when I recorded phrases, sentences, about my separation, divorce, and illnesses. On rainbow Post-it notes, words of doubts and self-revelation kaleidoscope, catchphrases as I pass again beyond legal proceedings and extended hospitalizations for medical crises to and through the eye of the needle.

I move from writer to author in 2015. I have a fiction short story, based on an obituary, published in an anthology. Friends attend the author talk. They believe my made-up story is theirs.

I attend a writing critique group at the university. In

2016, the Friday Night Writers evaluate a memoir, part of the boom of introspection. A retired, frail pediatrician parallels his wife's cancer battle with his relatives' and patients' comparative cancer crusade. He still writes with vigor, though in senior years we may lose our way in our mind's maze. Before dementia micro-shreds our map to the way back, record the richness.

The doctor's inquiry sparks fellow fiction writers to record their own stories before the plotlines and their meaning vanish. One writer, who hails from western Pennsylvania, re-creates her great-grandfather's arrival in America from Eastern Europe. Another, a world traveler, writes of his father's peccadillos and pet monkey in São Paulo, Brazil. A former Northern California landscape columnist wants to relate her centuries-old story of her ancestor onboard the *Mayflower* when a fire ignited below deck. Another participant, from Bogotá, glows as she shares her inspiration, spurred by her Boston University thirtieth reunion, to write about her roots in New England. My fiftieth high school reunion, in Pittsburgh, will be a prime opportunity to reminisce and memorialize long-forgotten yarns.

Excitement arises like fourth-grade enthusiasm over our personal accounts. We empathize, applaud, laugh, cry, praise. Ironically, the through thread is isolation. All are exiles of one sort or another. Our universal truth is feeling alien, different. We share the outsider experience, bonding yet alone. The same tapes race forward or back in our heads. We all look for belonging. Support is in the community audience.

In early 2016, I resuscitate my memoir, revive my draft from the needed nap, to mind-map, summarize chapters, and rebuild the scaffolding. At an author talk in an amber-lit church knave, Helen Macdonald, with predator-black hair and stark ivory skin, describes *H Is for Hawk*. She warbles briar-pecked grief from her father's death.

As she autographs her title page for me, I comment, "Some say I'm too lyrical."

Her avian blue eyes dart back. "That's the very direction you should follow."

Memoirists practice the destruction of something held firm—a belief, a possession or way of life, a relationship—to clear the path for self-discovery to share. I wanted everything to be perfect.

I realize how skillfully Mom hid her depression for so many years. I shift. I explore deeper. I find. I imagine. Isolated, she shrouded her happy self in the cellar laundry room when no one was home. No more Julie Andrews singing about the wash. No one speaks of it, but I reckon Dad found her on the floor, next to the wringer, a machine to squeeze water from wet clothes. In a photo in 1971, an ivory chiffon scarf conceals a neck abrasion. The delicate fabric surrounds her fresh, angry scar, her clothesline solution to her continuing struggle. Looking good is always a disguise.

In my family history, left unsaid, I believe when I got married in 1969 and moved to the tropics of Miami, that transition for me became Mom's life reversal forevermore. Mom bumped into that destructive mine underwater. It exploded. She dove deep into melancholy to escape her empty nest. She could not cope. I chose to keep my feelings about that incident sealed like a locket, a secret the family shared, hidden for her sake. Am I to blame? I never broached the subject with my brothers. They most likely have their own interpretations that fit their own witness explanation.

For me, the memory always begins pretty—who, where, how—then devolves into what is the camouflage. When I was a child in the '50s, Mom bedecked herself for special events. For the final touch, like women of that era, she secured her velvet pillbox hat, with an exotic feather poking up, to her coiffed brunette hair. Her short, netting veil, like Greta Garbo's, hid her insecurities from her 1920s Depression upbringing. She imitated wanting to be alone, fashionable, above reproach. I examine my memory through a gossamer gaze, a rerun on black-and-white television, the optimism of the 1950s. Perfection is protection.

✳

I write. Now I seek meaning. Mining for meaning. Meaning is magic, sleight of hand. Now, after a night of sleeping on it or a lifetime of slumber, in the morning, I find that revelation occurs—realism's Technicolor truth highlighted, the why awakened. In the *mine*, everyone sees their own story.

The return to me, to discover us, is we—the collective, the possessive ours, the universal, the raison d'être for memoir. Optimism is a foil for the pessimism, pain, and heartache everyone eventually has. Excavate. Dig deep. Move from light to chiaroscuro. Start with a spark, a desire, a fire in a grotto cave. Begin. Write what you know best, until you discover your portal to imagination, a path to the end.

Like Baked Alaska, the flambé dessert served at banquets' end, memoir is assembled, layered, nuanced, frozen, fierce and on fire, delicious, delightful, to be savored and remembered.

✳ ✳ ✳ ✳ ✳

ROSALYN KAPLUS, approaching her septuagenarian decade, has recently transformed from a night owl to an early bird. A former art teacher in Miami's inner city, then volunteer guardian ad litem advocate in dependency court, she has always been a keen observer and copious note-taker. Now, her creativity has turned to crafting compelling stories, memoir and fiction, long and short, painting with words. Her short story, "'37-It Was Heaven," appears in the anthology, *Everything Is Broken Too*. She's currently working on her memoir, *Seven Lives Life: A Memoir of Surviving Sepsis*.

✳ JESSICA VALENTI ✳

Author of *Sex Object*

BROOKE WARNER: Prior to writing *Sex Object*, you'd written four other issue-driven nonfiction books, often, if not always, with your personal story as a driving force. But *Sex Object* seems to me to be the first true memoir you've written, in terms of its form and with you at the center in a way you haven't been in previous books. Do you agree with this, and what made you decide it was time to write your memoir?

JESSICA VALENTI: Yes, absolutely. As you said, my past books have been very goal oriented. I had really specific hopes in mind with a lot of them. With *Full Frontal Feminism*, I hoped that young women who didn't identify as feminist would begin to. With *The Purity Myth*, I wanted to shed a light on abstinence education and the virginity movement. So it was definitely a change to write something that didn't have a tangible goal in mind. I actually didn't set out, consciously, anyway, to write a memoir. I had started writing a food column at *The Toast*, and so much of my experience with food and what I have to say about it is based on memories. So what I was writing for them felt very different than stuff I had written in the past. I didn't have necessarily a book in mind when I started writing the essays that appear in *Sex Object*, but then I was about halfway done and I realized, *This is a book; this is a memoir.*

✳

BROOKE WARNER: Your writing is so clear-eyed. I think this is one of the signature traits of your writing, actually, that you are able to extract deep and profound takeaways and messages from your stories. You're accessible and real, and honest to the point of discomfort. How and why do you write this way—pushing the envelope and exposing the truth in ways that I can only imagine must be difficult and uncomfortable for you at times?

JESSICA VALENTI: When it comes to writing about our lives, we don't mind when women tell or write about difficult truths so long as there's some sort of happy ending or silver lining. When I was writing about this particular issue, the issue of sexual objectification and the cumulative impact that sexism has on who we turn into and who we are, there didn't feel like a happy ending to that, and that was sort of okay with me. I wanted it to feel uncomfortable. After I finished one of the first essays for the book, I showed it to Andrew, my husband, and asked him, "What'd you think of it?" and he said he thought it was really punishing. And apparently, though I don't remember saying this to him, he told me I said, "Good, it's supposed to be."

BROOKE WARNER: In *Sex Object* you ponder what it would be like to live in a world that didn't hate women. It's such a bold question, and, I'm sure, startling to some people. How old do you think you were when you discovered we live in a world that hates women? And how do you deal with people's negative reactions (which have gone so far as to be threats on your life) to your work?

JESSICA VALENTI: In terms of the first question, I was on the receiving end of disdain for women from the time that I was a little girl, like a lot of people. At a pretty young age, I knew something was amiss, but I didn't have the language to put to it until I was in college, taking women's and gender studies courses and learning more about feminism. To be able to articulate what was going on was a revelatory experience. I'm still sorting out how to deal with the disdain today. That was part of why I wanted to write the book, to highlight a lot of the harassment that I get online. I think for a long time I put on a brave face about it—I would make fun of harassers and act as if it rolled off my back. But the truth is that it's extraordinarily overwhelming and it changes the way I interact with the world. The best approach I've come up with so far is not to be nervous about talking about how vulnerable and how terrible it can make me feel, not to feel obligated to put on a brave face for the sake of the cause. I have a supportive community around me, but that goes only so far. We need to be asking, "How can we stop this?" rather than, "How do we deal with this?"

✳

BROOKE WARNER: In the book, you write about a legacy of sexual abuse and harassment in your maternal line and suggest that you've gotten off easy, in a sense, because you've only had to experience men exposing themselves to you, or rubbing up against you, or writing publicly about your breasts. When I read this, I thought about how many women simply put up with all the harassment and abuse and discrimination we face, and that many women will dismiss your memoir as reactionary or somehow hysterical. Do you feel like you had to brace yourself for that as you wrote this book, and do you feel like things have gotten any better for women since you founded Feministing.com?

JESSICA VALENTI: I think the conversation has changed a lot, because I *was* bracing myself for that kind of reaction. I get a little bit of that from men, but for the most part, the response has been, "Ugh, me too." Honestly, I've heard from more men on this book than I've heard from on any other book—men writing and saying, "Jesus, I knew we lived in a sexist world, but I didn't realize how unrelenting it was." I do think, because of social media and the way women have been talking about their stories over the last ten years or so, people understand that what I'm discussing in the book is not hysteria, that these things do happen all the time, and that they become an everyday part of life. But just because something is an everyday part of life doesn't mean that it's not absurd and ridiculous or that it doesn't need to change.

✳

BROOKE WARNER: It sounds like, from your perspective, people are acknowledging, "Yeah, it *is* this bad."

JESSICA VALENTI: Absolutely. I definitely felt there were some antifeminists who were like, "Oh, I don't believe that." That was fascinating, because the book was so vastly different from their worldview that they just couldn't believe it. They were just like, "Oh, she lived in New York." I heard from a lot of people from a lot of different places, though. Yes, perhaps they didn't experience the same number of affronts on the subway, but what they went through was pretty close.

✳

BROOKE WARNER: What is the magic of memoir for you?

JESSICA VALENTI: I've always dabbled in using personal stories to make broader political points, and that's always been a big tool of feminism—making the personal political. What I like about writing memoir is that there's no room to hold back. When you're writing a nonfiction book or a political book, you're carefully choosing your words to make a particular point, or because you have a campaign or a goal in mind. But with *Sex Object*, my only job was to lay things as bare as I could. Telling the truth for truth's sake felt very different and very good. It also did the job I'd worked so hard to do with my other books. You strive to make a point or tell a story in a compelling way, and you cite facts and figures and laws and policies, but at the end of the day, what resonates with people are stories, because stories are the way we recognize ourselves. Through writing things in the most candid way possible, I was able to make the points I wanted to make.

✳   ✳   ✳   ✳   ✳

JESSICA VALENTI is a columnist for the *Guardian* (US) and the author of several books on feminism, politics, and culture. Her third book, *The Purity Myth: How America's Obsession with Virginity is Hurting Young Women*, won the 2010 Independent Publisher Book Award and was made into a documentary by the Media Education Foundation. She is also co-editor of the anthology *Yes Means Yes: Visions of Female Sexual Power and a World Without Rape*. She founded Feministing.com in 2004, and her writing has appeared in the *New York Times*, the *Washington Post*, the *Nation*, the *Guardian* (UK), the *American Prospect*, *Ms.* magazine, *Salon*, and *Bitch* magazine. She has won an IBIS Reproductive Health Evidence in Activism Award, a Choice USA Generation award and the 2011 Hillman Journalism Prize for her work with Feministing. Jessica lives in Brooklyn with her husband and daughter.

DOING IT WRONG TILL YOU GET IT RIGHT (EVENTUALLY)

Rosie Sorenson

Writing a memoir is like detasseling corn. You have to be strong and determined to work in a cornfield all day when the plants wave high above your head, and the sun burns your back and leaves a scar long after the blisters recede, and the stalks scrape your arms and legs until they bleed.

Writing a memoir is akin to that, except the Hulting Hybrid seed company in Geneseo, Illinois, hired you at sixteen because they needed you to pull off those tassels, and they paid you well.

No one needs your memoir.

No one asked you to write it. In fact, your mom, your sister, your aunt might all agree you're "wasting your time." You understand, of course, that this is code for *You'd by God better not write about the time Uncle Grayson got drunk on Christmas Eve, fired up the corn picker and got his hand chewed off, the fool.* No siree—you'd better not write about that.

✳

The ghost of my father, long since dead, often barked at me during the five years I was writing my book. "Who do you think you are? Some kind of big shot?" A dark, simmering storm, he often hurled that invective, his default setting, throughout my childhood, but most especially when he learned I intended to go to college. That was his line in the sand, and he threatened to divorce my mother if I didn't quit after the first semester. I didn't and he didn't. But still.

How could he possibly object to *Stray Love: Rescued by the Homeless Cats of Buster Hollow*, a memoir of the first seventeen years of my daily engagement with the colony of homeless cats who helped me recover after a car accident?

Well, see, here's the thing. The book I began to write was not the book I finished. The book I started had scant mention of him. The book I completed—well, let's just say his footprints were all over it.

I had intended to write a sequel to my collection of stories and photos: *They Had Me at Meow: Tails of Love from the Homeless Cats of Buster Hollow.* After the release of *Meow*, I received impassioned e-mails from readers begging for more. They wanted to know what happened to Buster, to Turtleman, to Green Eyes and the others.

Well. There's nothing like publishing success to keep a writer motivated. I thought I could easily bang out more cat stories, some of which I had already drafted. I could weave in material about the auto accident, along with my insane attempts to date during my rehabilitation—oh, those funny, awful dating stories! I could mash it all up into the overarching theme of how the cats facilitated my recovery and set the stage for me to meet my soul mate, Steve.

Killer story arc, right? Cats, men, sex, and renewal—what was not to like?

The first rain on my deluded parade showered upon me from an editor who offered an online query-letter contest. Though I didn't win, she wrote to say how much she liked my voice and my humor, but that she wasn't sure what the book was about. *What an idiot*, I thought. She encouraged me to write a few sentences addressing this topic. Certain that I had nailed the premise, I sent it, along with the first twenty-five pages. She liked the material but said that the beginning of my book did not match the premise as I'd stated it. *Big, fat idiot*, I thought.

(Note to reader: It's useful to get mad, to pout, to take umbrage at anyone who doesn't think your work is *très fabuloso*. Maybe even ponder your Second Amendment rights.)

I dismissed her criticisms and plowed blindly forward in the same vein for the next three and a half years. I sent that completed manuscript to a couple of writer friends, one of whom had just inked a traditional-publishing deal. Even though she didn't like cats, she loved the book. The other friend, whom I'd known for over twenty years to be a kind, caring healer, shocked me with her vitriol, which felt more like a personal attack on me than an honest critique of my memoir.

During our phone conversation, Julie told me, "I read your opening two pages to a friend, and she said, 'That author must have ADD.'"

I eked out a laugh. "Nope, never had that diagnosis," I said, feeling like Alice tumbling down the rabbit hole.

I wanted Julie to stop, but in my weakened flu state, I white-knuckled it as she napalmed her way through my manuscript. I eventually doused the conflagration by informing her that my recovery from the flu was slower than I had antici-pated, and *please, I have to go lie down now, bye-bye.*

That's when I quit writing—again. Who did I think I was? I had already quit the book twice, for several months each: once, after my best female friend of thirty years died; the second time, two years later, when my best male friend and champion of my work died. Nothing mattered after that.

Even though I stopped writing, I never stopped read-ing. I read thirty-one memoirs and twelve how-to books and attended many webinars offered by Brooke Warner and Linda Joy Myers and others. I had a burr under my saddle for the story, and it spurred me on to figure out what the heck I needed to say and how to begin and what to include. You'd think that would have been easy, and perhaps for others it is. But I worried on that opening chapter until I wanted to puke.

If it hadn't been for my profound love and gratitude for the homeless cats and my desire to change hearts and minds about them, to stop the killing, I never would have finished the book. I wanted—no, needed—to tell the story about the friendship, love, and fun the cats supplied me, giving me a reason to get out of bed, even when I had so much pain I didn't think I could move. Even in the rain.

By accepting unconditional love from Turtleman, Girly Girl, Buster, Smokey, Sweetie Pie, Green Eyes, Tuxedo, Jef-frey, and others, and by learning lessons that only the cats could teach me, I had begun to heal, not only from physical injuries but also from old psychic wounds. And, surprise—the portal they pawed open into my heart invited the slip-ping-in of a human soul mate: Steve.

Those cats deserved to be honored in a book, and I knew I was the only one to write it.

Up until I tackled the crafting of a 60,000-word mem-oir, I had scribbled mostly 750-word humor pieces for my column in the *Foolish Times*. You might say I am not a long-haul trucker.

After I indulged in months of wound licking, I fired up the computer, snuck up on the document, and with squinted eyes read an inelegantly written first chapter into which I'd crammed backstory upon backstory. Where was Cheryl Strayed when I needed her? No wonder Julie's friend thought I had ADD.

Time for a major rethink and rewrite. What was this story about? What were the themes? Where should I begin?

Out of desperation, I scrolled lickety-split through a copy of the manuscript, the DELETE button smoking as I sped down the pages and tossed one-third of them into the recycle bin.

It felt good, as though I were back in that Illinois corn-field, yanking and pulling and tossing those wicked tassels. Without their removal, there would have been no hybrid corn that year.

The dating stories? Gone. Mostly. Other tangents? Gone. Now what? I stared at the screen, asking aloud, again and again, *What is this about? What is the point? What does it mean?*

Finally, in a damascene moment, two themes lit up: grief and loss, and finding love in unexpected places—touchstones that would guide the organization of my book.

Grief and loss had shadowed me since age ten, when my father kidnapped and murdered my beloved black kitten, leaving a wound in my heart the size of Kentucky.

Giving the blade of pain its due, I crafted a new prologue, with grief and loss as the central anguish and finding love in unexpected places with the cats and Steve, the balm.

That's when my dead dad piped up. Just who did I think I was to rat him out like that? I shuttered the windows when I wrote so no one could hear me crying and yelling, "You're dead and I'm not, dammit, so leave me the hell alone!"

I had learned as a child to marshal all my resources to keep Dad from killing my spirit, and now I employed every one of them. There are less exhausting ways to be strong, I'm sure, but, as Molly Ivins once said, "You got to dance with them what brung you."

In editing the book, I realized that the homeless cats of Buster Hollow had become stand-ins for my little black kitten. I couldn't save him then, but I could save the homeless cats now. They, in return, saved me. One in particular, a handsome black cat, Turtleman, became our soul kitty.

It's not enough, however, to nail the story arc. I knew I hadn't yet mastered the techniques of reflective voice and takeaway. My understanding remained a bit dim even after I listened to Brooke and Linda Joy stress their importance. But one day when I read Brooke's blog, in which she recounted examples of reflective voice and takeaway from *Wild*, there it was—my "aha" moment. I typed Cheryl's words over and over and over until they melted into my brain. To elevate my book, I'd have to claw through my stoic midwestern upbringing and violate the sacred commandment: "Thou shalt not step out of the herd with your fancy-pants writing." *Who do you think you are?*

I had to set aside those voices and to acknowledge that I did indeed have plenty to say on those topics. My story demanded it, especially if I wanted readers to keep turning the page, instead of shutting the book with a sigh, a shrug, and a big "So what?" Newly invigorated, I scoured my manuscript to uncover places that cried out for reflection and/or takeaway. I made it a game. How could I use those techniques without sounding tippy-toe-precious, gimmicky, or, worse, preachy?

Another profound moment arrived when I read Mary Karr's *The Art of Memoir*. In it she shared a "before and after" passage from her best-selling memoir, *The Liars' Club*.

Anyone could have written the plain old vanilla "before." But the "after"? Genius. Topped with hot fudge.

I'd been let in on The Big Secret: sometimes not even Mary Karr can write like Mary Karr without revision. With those few paragraphs, she delivered a shot of hope. Just maybe . . .

Five years and 3,900 hours later—after three complete drafts and countless edits—I crossed the finish line, greeted by the checkered flag. I could finally exhale.

Takeaway? Never, ever ever ever (do you hear me?) never give up. Buy chocolate in bulk, ditto Kleenex.

I will always be proud of my resourceful self, the one who did a very big, very hard thing, fighting every impulse to quit, to give in, to knuckle under to all those questioning voices.

I owe whatever success my memoir might achieve to rewriting and rewriting and rewriting. To pulling those shiftless verbs, yanking the no-account adverbs, and flinging away the dishwater descriptions, replacing them with arresting images. And to following Cheryl Strayed's dictum "write like a motherfucker!"

My rational, linear self knows that outlining a memoir beforehand is a sensible idea, but for this particular book, my heart and soul just wouldn't have it. Despite the detours, the somersaults, the foolhardy mistakes, all of which kicked my ass to write a better book, I couldn't have done it any other way. Nothing was wasted as long as I kept my butt in the chair to finish it.

As Woody Allen once said, 80 percent of success is showing up. I say the remaining 20 percent comes from paying attention to any and all who have something to teach you, even when it hurts.

* * * * *

ROSIE SORENSON is a recovering psychotherapist and award-winning writer whose work has been published in the *Los Angeles Times*, the *Chicago Tribune*, the *Progressive Populist*, the *San Francisco Chronicle*, the *San Jose Mercury News*, the *Pittsburgh Tribune-Review*, and in popular anthologies. She won Honorable Mention in the Erma Bombeck Writing Competition, and is a regular contributor to the Erma Bombeck Writer's Competition website. She also writes a monthly humor column for the *Foolish Times*. Rosie's essays have been broadcast on KQED-FM, the popular San Francisco NPR affiliate, in its "Perspectives" series, one of which won the Listener Favorite Award. Her book, *They Had Me at Meow*, won the Muse Medallion from the Cat Writers' Association. Rosie lives with her sweetheart Steve and their four cats in Northern California. She can be found at www.theyhadmeatmeow.com and on LinkedIn and Facebook.

THE MYTHIC JOURNEY
OF MEMOIR

Paula Wagner

hecking my thesaurus, I find no fewer than a dozen synonyms associated with *magic* and *memoir*. *Magic*: *thrilling, powerful, supernatural, exquisite, enchanted, mystery, conjuring, fairy-tale, charmed, dreamlike,* and *mystic*. *Memoir*: *account, essay, biography, history, chronicle, description, record, diary, journal, dossier,* and *log*.

But beyond any single term, to write a memoir is to take a mythic journey. And, as with the Greek legend of Odysseus, getting to the heart of one's story may demand years of commitment, courage, pain, and patience; imagination, tenacity, humor, and humility; time, energy, money, and more (although I'm fortunate to be able to write on a computer, instead of papyrus, like Homer).

My first inkling of this magic came while composing my mother's obituary in 2010. As long as I kept writing, my words seemed to breathe her back to life. As I began writing a memoir, I again noticed how scene and dialogue could animate place and character. But this spell isn't always easy to cast. I cannot enter the magical realm of memoir without paying homage to its two strong female guardians—my mother, who gave me my first words and love of language, and the Muse, without whose inspiration I am mute. Beyond prose, poetry can sometimes take me to a deeper place, as in this piece:

Plying the seas of memory
Like Odysseus on his quest
I too encounter thrills and threats
Whirlpools, insights, and fascination
Anger, doldrums, and frustration
Jagged facts and waves of feeling
Sirens of elusive meaning
Shoals of pain and sensual pleasure
Myth and truth in slanted measure
Fear on my left and hope on my right
Intuition through darkness, searching for light
Stars as my guides, my heart at the helm
Compassion my compass when I feel overwhelmed.

Like Odysseus, I too must tackle the monsters of metaphor, character, dialogue, theme, and scene that live in the Jungle of Craft. But personifying my demons helps me conquer them. Although Odysseus could navigate by GPS today, he would still have to battle the Master of Distraction, the Sleepy Sloth, the Worry Dogs, and the Sirens of the Inner Critic singing, *Are you sure you can write? That word isn't right! What if my best isn't good enough?*

Humor is another great weapon against these foes. To

my Inner Critic, I offer an all-expenses-paid vacation to Hawaii, where everything is, uh, perfect. As long as she's sipping mai tais and surfing the waves, I'm free to write in peace. To quell the yipping Worry Dogs, I pack them off to a guide-dog school where they can channel their anxieties into productive service, instead of nipping at my heels. When Sloth and Distraction tire of long hours at my desk, I take breaks for yoga, biking, and swimming. Finally, if Despair threatens, I put on some blues or jazz to remind myself that writing a memoir shouldn't feel like forced labor.

In a more professional vein, envisioning myself as the "CEO" of my memoir helps create a sense of ownership, accountability, confidence, and control. As executive director, I can set timelines, deadlines, and expectations of success while encouraging my creative spirit and inner editor to believe their efforts matter.

When I'm finally ready to put my fingers to the keyboard, I meditate to clear my mind and climb into my time machine. Then, *whoosh*! Piloting through space and time, I visualize the people, places, conflicts, and takeaways I want to write about. Soon the landscape of memory rushes up to greet me as if I've just landed back in 1963, when my memoir begins.

When a girlish figure with bright red curls materializes on the tarmac, I recognize her as my adventurous, adolescent spirit, who first led me to Israel and France, fueled (or fooled?) by a mix of idealism, bravado, and naiveté. As I step onto the rocky soil, a blast of hot air hits me and I squint into the sun that blazes over the hills of Galilee. From a ramshackle shed nearby comes the sound of doves cooing. Suddenly, something pricks me through my sandal. *Ouch!* My entire body quivers. A scorpion? No, it's only a pesky thorn. Once more, the beauty and danger of this place envelop me, body and soul.

Feeling hungry, I follow the tantalizing scent of sizzling falafel to an outdoor stand where a cute young vendor deftly juggles balls of chickpea paste high in the air, catching them in a pocket of pita bread like a baseball mitt, to the delight of his customers. I savor the guttural sounds of Hebrew like the saucy condiments I stuff into my sandwich: *pilpelim* (peppers), *chamutzim* (pickles), and *chatzilim* (eggplant).

Writing with all five senses, plus a sixth for intuition, is definitely exhilarating. Still suspended between past and present, I hurry back to my time capsule and grab my laptop. I can't wait to share the adventures of my adoptive land with my readers!

But now that my first draft is almost done, I face new challenges. After writing for my own pleasure for over seven years, I have learned that the thought of publishing is daunting to my carefree younger self, who seems to have vanished like a sylph into the mists of time. Fifty years ago, her only nod to the future was that I should live an interesting life so I'd have something to write about when I got old. Now I want to tell her, *In case you haven't noticed, that time has come!* Should I simply mothball my story for posterity?

Clearly, if I want to publish, I'll need to challenge old assumptions, such as these messages from my parents: *writing is its own reward; creativity can flourish only when shielded from market forces.* As performing artists, they may have found that these mantras served them well. For them, the magic was all in the moment and the applause after a play or concert was enough. "Time to strike the stage," my mother would say at the end of a run, returning the exquisite costumes and props to the warehouse while I puzzled at her lack of sentimentality. *All that work—gone without a trace!* I'd think. Is it any wonder I internalized this model?

Yet the rapid changes in today's world of writing and

publishing have made these messages largely obsolete. Today I find invaluable guidance and support through workshops, conferences, and online classes with the National Association of Memoir Writers. Tectonic shifts in technology, and small press–, hybrid-, and online-publishing options, also offer alternatives to a traditionally male-dominated industry—another boon for women writers who value community over individual competition. As a feminist, maybe I'm finally in the right place at the right time!

But, like Greek legends, some of my parents' messages have endured. If my love affair with words comes from my mother, it was my father's reading of *A First Book of Jewish Bible Stories* that taught me their power. "Then God said the *word*, and the world was filled with light!" If God could create an entire universe with a few monosyllables, then *words* must be very powerful indeed, I reasoned, with five-year-old logic.

At the risk of extending a mixed metaphor, I find parallels between the narratives of Eden and the Greek myth of Odysseus. Both are parables of long and arduous journeys whose protagonists must leave home on a quest for truth and find the strength to face their demons, while experiencing great loss but also joy along the way. So too can memoir help us interpret and reclaim our reality from the ruins of the past, even if this means grappling with serpents or eating forbidden apples from our family trees.

Yet even the most fearless exploration of myth versus magic, facts versus feelings, or memory versus fantasy may not reveal a clear line between them. Still, on a bright day when the fog lifts on my memoir journey, my heart fills with a visceral sensation that I can describe only as thrilling, powerful, supernatural, exquisite, enchanted, mysterious, conjuring, fairy-tale, charmed, dreamlike, mystical, and, yes, even spiritual.

And that is the magic of memoir!

* * * * *

PAULA WAGNER (www.paula-wagner.com) is a memoir writer, poet, and career counselor living in the San Francisco Bay Area. Born in London to a Jewish American father and an English mother, she and her identical twin sister spent their first decade moving across America. But their taste for adventure didn't stop when the family finally settled in Northern California. *Chameleon Season* chronicles the lessons of language and love Paula learned when, at age eighteen, she set out to find a home and identity of her own and spent the next decade building a life in Israel and France.

Paula earned an MA in career development from John F. Kennedy University and a BA in women's studies from San Francisco State University, and studied Hebrew, French, and English at the Hebrew University of Jerusalem. As principal of LifeWork Careers, she coaches others to articulate their talents and find fulfillment in work and life.

LIFE INTO STORIES: THREE HABITS, THREE RULES, AND THREE STAGES

Jerry Waxler

I entered college in 1965, striding confidently toward my goal of becoming a doctor. Then Vietnam War protests shocked me out of my original plan and replaced it with an even more tantalizing one: I could band together with my peers and fix the world. All I needed to do was to reject everything that was hateful and corrupt. By the time I finished college, I had rejected so much, there was nothing left.

Vulnerable and confused, I fell into an abyss, with no plan and no hope. The only option was to change direction, again. My new goal was to reclaim my sanity.

To climb out, I wrote in a journal, meditated, and talked to a therapist. I joined groups, turned to God, and even accepted that I would have to find a job. I kept moving forward, and gradually I got the hang of adulthood. But when I looked back, all I could remember were disturbing snips.

In 2004, I noticed memoirs of ordinary people appearing on best-seller lists. To learn why they were so popular, I read a few and found that I wasn't the only one who had struggled to grow up. If they could turn their messy memories into good stories, maybe I could, too.

The possibility of writing a memoir seemed far-fetched at first. Despite having journaled for years, I had never written stories. And even if I could learn, how would I ever tease apart and portray my intricate thoughts, feelings, and events?

IN STAGE ONE, I FOLLOWED THREE HABITS

Despite all the obstacles, my desire burned. I longed to make sense of one of the most important periods in my life. The first step was a memoir class, where I learned that in order to start this journey, I would have to develop three simple habits.

Habit one: write

My memoir project gave me a new focus for my daily writing sessions. When I remembered even a vague incident, I wrote a few sentences. Each snip helped me tease out the details of vague or disturbing memories. I filed it away and went on to the next. Incident by incident, I transformed the images in my mind into pieces I could reread and edit.

Habit two: share

My snips at first seemed too private to reveal. But in memoir classes, when other writers read their awkward moments, I joined the group's hearty laughter. When others shared pain and humiliation, my heart went out to them. Once I felt safe enough, I shared my vulnerable moments and discovered that even my most embarrassing memories evoked positive responses. When I shone a light into the dark corners of my mind, shame evaporated. In its place flourished a new sense of mutual and self-acceptance.

Habit three: read

To learn all I could about the genre, I read memoirs. After enjoying each uplifting story, I examined the book to figure out how the author had transformed the kaleidoscope of memories into an interesting form. By repeating this habit dozens and eventually hundreds of times, I got the sound of memoirs in my ear. I learned about their structures and figured out what I liked. In my favorite ones, the author had worked hard to earn the wisdom at the end.

The three habits led me to a higher vantage point, from which I could look back across at and understand my past better than I did when I was in it. But to turn my fragments into a story as compelling as the ones I enjoyed reading, I would need to aim higher.

IN STAGE TWO, I FOLLOWED THREE RULES

I wanted to offer my experiences in the form of a story, not a collection of anecdotes. So I took more classes and reflected on the many memoirs I read. From the lessons and examples, I extracted three rules.

Rule one: readers enter stories through scenes

To offer readers a vicarious experience of my life, I needed to show them the world through my eyes. For example, instead of saying, "I was in a riot," I needed to write what I saw, heard, and felt. "Hundreds of us jammed into the hallway, defiantly blocking the passageway. The sound of breaking glass shattered our confidence. Screams filled the air as the police poured through the shattered picture windows. Students fell under the blows of billy clubs. I turned and ran." By building evocative scenes, I began to see myself from a slightly removed point of view.

Rule two: chronological sequence reveals the bones of the story

In memory, bits of the past tumbled over each other, with no particular meaning. When I lined them up in chronological order, I could see how one thing led to another. This was the first time I had ever reviewed my glimpses in the order in which they occurred. In this sequence, they stopped tumbling and started to lead forward through time.

Rule three: a story follows a hero's purpose

Readers since the beginning of time have jumped into the mind of the protagonist and attempted to achieve some noble mission. That observation about ancient myths made by Joseph Campbell in *The Hero with a Thousand Faces* also seemed to apply to modern stories. For example, in murder stories, the detective must unmask the villain and restore order to the world. To follow this universal model, I would need to figure out my own heroic mission.

At first, my motives seemed bewildering. How could I have made so many impractical and ultimately self-destructive choices? The longer I tried to figure out what made my character tick, the more I understood myself. Viewing my past through the lens of the story shed light on my fears, my confusion, and my interactions with other characters.

Before I started writing, my long journey to hell and back was hidden in a chaotic repository of memories. After years of applying these three rules, I untangled the jumble of anecdotes and knitted them together into a compelling narrative with a hopeful end. I celebrated the completed manuscript and the achievement of stage two.

IN STAGE THREE, I AIMED FOR THE TOP

Many brave memoir authors shared their lives with me. Now, I wanted to pay the favor forward and share my story with the public. However, publishing it seemed like another impossible challenge. I didn't feel capable of producing a book as polished as the ones I had enjoyed reading.

My fellow writers had provided suggestions and support, but for this next step, I needed a professional editor. I was nervous about handing my labor of love, essentially my own life, to someone who might be more interested in telling a good story than in capturing the essence of my inner journey. How would I find the right person?

Through networking, I found candidates and paid them to edit samples of my work. I finally found someone I trusted, who believed in the shape of a good story while also understanding the need to stay true to the facts.

She offered feedback at every level of detail, all the way from word choice to story flow. Using her recommendations, I revised the entire book. Then I sent it to readers. Some of them said they read it straight through. A few even said they couldn't put it down. Some flagged missing scenes. Others highlighted spots that dragged. Through their eyes, I recognized unresolved and irrelevant details. I revised again and sent it to other readers. When I felt I had done enough, I returned it to my editor for a final round of suggestions.

This should have been the end, and yet I knew that book readers abhor typos. Before I could publish it, I had to hire a proofreader to weed out such flaws. Finally, the book was ready, but was I?

I had reached the top of the mountain and could not think of any other ways to improve my writing. The next step was to publish it, but I wasn't sure if I had the courage. I had been willing to share my insecurities and flaws in the safe space of critique groups. But the public? What if readers didn't like my best work? The only way to find out was to throw myself off the edge.

Eventually, I ran out of excuses. I faced my fear of exposure and published it anyway, concluding my long journey from a private past to a shared one.

Connect with people by sharing stories

Cynics warned me that writing a memoir would make me self-involved or, worse, prove I was a narcissist. My experience suggested the opposite. By studying memoirs, I became more sensitive to the thoughts and feelings of other people. And by crafting my own memoir, I saw how my decisions contributed to my downfall. The entire process nurtured empathy and cultivated a wiser understanding of my responsibility toward others.

In the 1960s, when I and my peers went on a rampage to find truth, I thought I could contribute to a better society by tearing everything apart. I did a great job of destroying my beliefs, but in the process, I destroyed myself. Fifty years later, the Memoir Revolution offered a new way to search for truth. This time, instead of tearing everything apart, this cultural zeitgeist showed me how to fit the pieces together.

Every culture on Earth has embraced the ancient system called story. Some scientists even theorize that the top of the brain, the neocortex, evolved as a storytelling machine. Now, finally, we have collectively found a way to turn this fundamental craft of storytelling into a modern tool for self-development and mutual understanding.

Try it yourself

To take advantage of this cultural trend, consider parts of your life you have never shared, revisited, or knitted together into a coherent whole. The Memoir Revolution provides an opportunity to find your voice.

Start by collecting anecdotes. As the story takes shape, cast yourself as the hero of your own journey. If you choose to go all the way and publish your memoir, you will offer a gift that storytellers have been giving since the beginning of time.

By crafting the story of your life, you can show the rest of us how you went about your journey. Your example will encourage and support others to seek their own truths.

This mission to write your story may be scary at first. Perhaps, like I did, you'll even think it's far-fetched. But there's no harm in starting. Like any hero, once you enter the land of the adventure, you will face the unknown. With courage, persistence, and effort, you will take one of the most interesting creative journeys of your life.

JERRY WAXLER, teacher and therapist, wrote *Memoir Revolution* to champion the cultural trend to read and write the stories of our lives. His blog contains hundreds of essays on the same subject.

His own memoir, *Thinking My Way to the End of the World*, describes his struggle to come of age during the chaotic '60s. His book *How to Become a Heroic Writer* offers tools to help you develop the courage and habits to write your own.

BY THE GRACE OF GOD, I WRITE MEMOIR

Ruthie Stender

A s a memoirist, I sometimes question myself about why I feel called to write about my life. It's like I need a reason, a justification, in order to keep at it, not so much for others as for myself.

About two years ago, while poking around online for some inspiration, I landed on a sermon by Reverend Ed Bacon, who said, "The reason God gave you your story is so you could tell it." A sense of freedom came over me. I knew that God was talking directly to me, saying, *Ruthie, you don't need a reason. Just write*. Getting the go-ahead from God was the permission I needed, and the quality and quantity of my writing improved.

Through the process of writing my memoir, I've come to understand that our stories are what show us just how much alike we all are and how interconnected we are as humans. This type of heart connection is what true love feels like—natural and easy, yet at the same time magical because there's no explaining it.

In sharing our stories, we automatically—or, as I like to say, *auto-magically*—find greater compassion, understanding, and love for each other.

My original memoir wasn't really my story; it was my little sister Grace's. Grace died just a month shy of her fourteenth birthday. If I hadn't been so consumed with my own trauma and drama, fifteen years old and nine months pregnant, I might have taken the time to grieve her death when it happened. But I didn't. That would come more than fifteen years later, the winter of 1996, when I began volunteering as a ski instructor for people with disabilities. This work awakened tenderness in my heart and triggered a need to write for my sister, to give her a voice. What I know now is that my urge to write Grace's story was the beginning of my grieving process, and what ultimately turned out to be a spiritual awakening of sorts.

In the spring of 1997, when I was thirty-two, I went on my first personal writing retreat, to a lodge in the Olympic National Forest, where I sat down to write Grace's story. I opened with a scene of my little sister dying in my oldest brother's arms. I'm not sure if she was already dead when my mom placed her in my brother's arms or if she died while my brother held her. All I know is that as I wrote, Grace came alive inside me. I was channeling my sister. Her spirit gave me visions and sensations of being in her crippled body and mind as she passed away. Problem was, I couldn't get through a page or two without being left curled up in a ball on the floor for hours, sobbing. After less than a year, I put the writing away.

Five years later, I pulled out my writing, cleaned some stuff up, and signed up for a writers' workshop. After the first class, I decided I couldn't do it, but my husband urged me on, so I stuck it out. In the end, a writing teacher convinced me to change the story to my point of view. It didn't help, and I put the work away again for a few more years.

It's a bit shocking to realize that I've now been working at this memoir for twenty years, but I've been all over the place with what and how to tell it. Finally, in 2012, I decided it was time to write *my* story once and for all. That fall, my mom suffered a massive stroke and died. It was then, because of how her dying happened, that I got serious about writing my memoir.

I sat awake all night in the ICU with my sister Kay, waiting for my mom to come to and to be okay—or to die. Kay stayed with me, she said, so that I wouldn't be alone in case Mom passed. But then she stepped out with my brother Clay for a cup of coffee, and, for the first time since I had arrived from Seattle, there I was—alone with my mom.

I'd been fiddling with the *mala* beads on my wrist and around my neck throughout the night. I read poems to my mom. I talked to her. I chanted *om*, silently and sometimes in a whisper, as I visualized the essence of peace running through and around her body. I told her she'd been good and that we all loved her like crazy. I forgave her for all of us. For not looking after us and pretending that she did. For making up fantasies about how she cooked all those Sunday dinners—pot roast and potatoes smothered in gravy—and gathering all nine of her kids around a table we didn't have. It was a weekly feast she worked hard to prepare. I told her that we all knew the stories were her way of surviving and that, though we made fun of her, even to her face, for making shit up, we loved her more than anything on Earth.

Thinking about why my mom fabricated fantasies broke my heart wide open as I imagined her suffering with nine kids, living in poverty with a man who tried to beat the beauty from her face. I wept as I felt her suffering leave this world and her godlike essence fill the room. It was just after six in the morning when my mom decided finally to let go. She'd been holding on for just the right moment.

Standing at her bedside, I laid my hands on my mom's heart and kept them there until it stopped. I stood there for half an hour with her and then watched her take her last breath. I watched her eyes open for the first time since I'd arrived at the hospital from Seattle. Green eyes, like mine. Blank. Fixed. Dead. Although I'd come to understand death as part of life's cycle at an early age from watching Grace die over the years, as well as through near-death and out-of-body experiences of my own, I'd never been with it directly in the moment it happens.

Being in this divine space with my mom shifted something in me I can describe only as grace. I've come to call this state of being my Amazing Grace. This experience allowed me to feel more human while at the same time more connected to higher consciousness, to God. I was on both sides of living and dying at the same time. I felt like Mom gave me a part of her just then so that it would last me forever. It was my heart's strong desire to stay connected to this essence, this tenderness that overwhelmed all of me.

Following my mom's death, I spent several weeks in West Virginia with my brothers and sisters, all older than I am, asking questions I wished I could still ask my mom. I felt the slipping away of information and details I'd never be able to recover. Filled with an insatiable need to know, I listened to stories and remembered things I'd tucked away. I took notes and captured stuff on my voice recorder because

I just couldn't keep up with it all. In those weeks after losing my mom, I entered a new state of understanding and acceptance that we all have our own way of being human, our own version of living or dying, and our own stories. And that was when I started writing with more determination and when I set an intention to finish my memoir.

Aware that my connection to this sacred space could fade once I returned to Seattle, where I'd need to ease back into day-to-day living, I put on hold my yoga and meditation classes and limited my interaction with people. I was afraid these things would pull me away from my mom, from the grace that we'd shared and that now consumed me. But then something happened that assured me it was here to stay.

I was walking along the lake near my house about a week after getting home, when I called out to my mom, asking her how to hold on to what she'd given me. "How do I keep your wisdom alive inside me?" I pleaded. "How do I know you are with me? How do I keep you with me, always?"

As I approached a nearby bench, I noticed a small piece of paper on the ground. I picked it up, then sat down. When I unfolded it, warmth filled my heart. The words brought a salty sting that blurred my eyes. My mom's essence embraced me as I read, "I still call out for you sometimes."

Before my mom died, this God space that I call my Amazing Grace was familiar, just not as easily accessible. But now, it's always a breath away. It's solid. Always there. And I call to it. Often. Especially when I write.

Through the early inspiration of my sister's story, I was able to find my own voice and tell a tale from my point of view. My outline went through so many iterations I've lost track, but if I hadn't gone through so many versions I wouldn't have figured out where to start the story or where to end it. What I have now is a full manuscript and extra material for my next memoir.

My writing coach talked to me about theme throughout these revisions. I didn't quite understand what she meant by theme at first, and it wasn't until I wrote a lot of material that I saw my story's theme: resilience.

Although my main theme is resilience—about bouncing back from adverse circumstances—the biggest circumstance has been (and continues to be) overcoming a chronic case of ignorance I inherited from being raised in a holler by neglectful parents while stumbling my way through life. Profound ignorance is like having a disability, because it limits your ability to thrive. Ignorance makes thriving harder, but it makes success sweeter. This understanding keeps me writing.

Even though I developed some level of resilience to hard stuff as a kid—like going hungry, dirty, and cold, even having worms—none of that compares to having your ignorance exposed when you're trying to come off as smart in the world.

It wasn't until the later chapters that I allowed myself to feel this truth and let it be part of my writing without censoring it. I'd spent my whole life covering up what a dumb-ass I was, how seriously ignorant I was, and now this secret was trying to show up in my memoir. When I saw this truth punching its way out, I felt my chest tighten. My mind cringed and my breathing went shallow. I was embarrassed of myself. My cheeks turned hot while I sat all alone at my desk. I guess I thought I could write a memoir and skip over a main part of who I am. It's a little funny to me now, but it was painful and hard to move through. However, I came to know that I'd have to expose my secret life as a dumb-ass if I really wanted to finish my memoir. And I decided that I'd rather have the temporary pain of shame and humiliation than have a festering secret eat a hole in my gut.

I've read that to be a good and honest writer, you're supposed to write about what makes you uncomfortable. By tapping into my Amazing Grace, I've done my best to write honestly and openly while moving through my discomfort.

* * * * *

RUTHIE STENDER is an award-winning author in both memoir and spiritually based self-help. Her memoir, *Glowing Houses*, took second place in the nonfiction/memoir category in the 2015 Pacific Northwest Writers Association literary contest. As a past columnist for *New Spirit Journal*, Ruthie offered readers self-healing strategies based on the principles of yoga, meditation, and energy medicine. These articles served as inspiration for her book, *The Eight Aspects of God, A Pathway to Bliss* (HenOli Press, 2012), a finalist in the 2013 National Indie Excellence Awards. Ruthie also writes for *Contemplative Journal* about building resilience through the practice of meditation and contemplation. In addition to being a fulltime writer, Ruthie is an inventor, certified meditation teacher, and registered yoga instructor. Learn more about Ruthie at www.ruthstender.com.

ABOUT THE EDITORS

LINDA JOY MYERS, PHD, is president and founder of the National Association of Memoir Writers. Her memoir *Don't Call Me Mother: A Daughter's Journey from Abandonment to Forgiveness* was a finalist for the Foreword Book of the Year Award and a finalist in the Indie Excellence Awards and won the BAIPA Gold Medal award. She's the author of three books on memoir writing: *The Power of Memoir: How to Write Your Healing Story*; *Journey of Memoir*; and *Becoming Whole*. Her new memoir, *Song of the Plains*, will be released by She Writes Press in 2017. Myers writes for the *Huffington Post*, and her passion is to help people capture their stories through coaching, editing, and nationwide online workshops.

BROOKE WARNER is publisher of She Writes Press and president of Warner Coaching Inc., where she coaches writers to publication. Brooke is passionate about helping writers finish their books and get published. Brooke has been in the publishing industry for fourteen years, including eight years as the executive editor of Seal Press. She's guided hundreds of authors from idea to publication with her blend of upbeat encouragement and firm direction. Her publishing background gives her an understanding of the inner workings of a complicated industry, which she uses to steer her authors toward their publishing goals. She's full of insider tips that demystify the publishing process, and writes regularly for the *Huffington Post*. She's the author of *Green-Light Your Book*, *What's Your Book?*, and *How to Sell Your Memoir*.

* * * * *

Together, Linda Joy and Brooke teach the six-month memoir course, Write Your Memoir in Six Months (www.Write YourMemoirInSixMonths.com) and are coeditors of *The Magic of Memoir* and coauthors of *Breaking Ground on Your Memoir*.

Author photos © Reenie Raschke

GRATITUDE

LINDA JOY AND BROOKE would like to thank the 150-plus students who have gone through our Write Your Memoir in Six Months program, and the many other writers who've joined us for our free webinars, best-selling memoir series, and other classes and events. All of you inspire us to keep pushing the edge of our own understanding about memoir, and you're proof that memoir is far from dead, as seems to be regularly forecasted by naysayers in the media. In fact, it's a thriving, exciting, and inspiring genre that's still emerging and growing—and we're proud to be in the heart of it all.

Thank you to the memoirists whose books we've taught so far in our best-selling memoir series for all we've learned from reading and teaching their work: Cheryl Strayed, Elizabeth Gilbert, Jeanette Walls, Frank McCourt, Mary Karr, Helen MacDonald, Caroline Knapp, Koren Zailckas, and Susannah Cahalan.

We want to acknowledge the nearly two hundred writers who submitted to be a part of this anthology. Choosing whom to include was one of the most difficult tasks we've faced in our work together. And we offer our heartfelt thanks and congratulations to those contributors whose essays grace this inspiring collection.

Finally, huge gratitude to our interviewees: Mary, Liz, Professor Jefferson, Dani, Hope, Dr. Nafisi, Daisy, Mark, Sue, Raquel, and Jess. You've been sources of inspiration in different ways to both of us and we appreciate your time and the gift of your words. Thank you for writing your memoirs, for the work you do in the world, and for allowing us to interview you for *The Magic of Memoir*.